Joann,

Best enjoyed with
2 beer,

Cheers,

PUNISHING THE PRINCE

A THEORY OF
INTERSTATE RELATIONS,
POLITICAL INSTITUTIONS,
AND LEADER CHANGE

Fiona McGillivray

and

Alastair Smith

PRINCETON UNIVERSITY PRESS   PRINCETON AND OXFORD

Published by Princeton University Press, 41 William Street, Princeton,
New Jersey, 08540

In the United Kingdom: Princeton University Press, 6 Oxford Street,
Woodstock,
Oxfordshire OX20 1TW

Library of Congress Cataloging-in-Publication Data

McGillivray, Fiona, 1967–
Punishing the prince : a theory of interstate relations, political
institutions, and leader change / Fiona McGillivray, Alastair Smith.
p. cm.
Includes bibliographical references and index.
ISBN 978-0-691-13606-6 (hardcover : alk. paper)—
ISBN 978-0-691-13607-3 (pbk. : alk. paper) 1. Heads of state—
Term of office. 2. Political leadership. 3. Debts, Public.
4. Political corruption. I. Smith, Alastair, 1967– II. Title
JF285.M34 2008
327.1′17—dc22   2007046326

British Library Cataloging-in-Publication Data is available

This book has been composed in Galliard
Printed on acid-free paper. ∞
press.princeton.edu

Printed in the United States of America

1 3 5 7 9 10 8 6 4 2

To our children:
Angus, Duncan, and Molly

Contents

Illustrations

Tables

WHAT IS THE MECHANISM that allows democrats, but not autocrats, to make credible commitments? This is the challenging question that Helen Milner posed to us over lunch nearly a decade ago. Our answer was leader specific punishments in repeated play prisoners' dilemma, the game we explore in chapter 1. Thus was born the basis of this book.

While the basic mechanism is straightforward, the implications of targeting punishments against individual leaders rather than the nations they represent are both subtle and profound. We sought to explain how democrats could commit to deeper, more robust levels of cooperation than could other leaders. Yet, by developing these ideas we ended up examining the dynamics of cooperation and leadership change, a previously uninvestigated topic. Our emphasis throughout has been on deriving novel implications of the theory and finding new empirical puzzles. We believe scientific inquiry is best enhanced by enlarging the number of dimensions on which our explanations can be tested. To this end we derive hypotheses relating leadership change and cooperation. Chapter 5 examines these relationships with respect to dyadic trade flows, while chapter 6 examines sovereign debt and how the institutional context affects whether leader turnover alters the willingness of people to hold sovereign debt. We thank Leslie Johns for her assistance in preparing these data.

In the process of developing the theory we have produced a series of articles, which have appeared in *International Organizations, Journal of Conflict Resolution*, and *Journal of Politics*. This book focuses primarily on problems of cooperation. In an article with Alexandra Guisinger in the *Journal of Conflict Resolutions* we develop the implications of leader specific punishments in conflictual situations. We are very grateful to her for allowing us to use this material in chapter 7 and for enhancing our understanding of the implications of leader specific punishments.

Although our models are internally consistent and our statistical tests find empirical relationships consistent with the theoretical predictions, one of the responses to our work (which we had not anticipated) was that some people found it inherently unbelievable that punishments are targeted against leaders. To alleviate these concerns we embarked on a series of human subject experiments in which team leaders play the prisoners' dilemma game on behalf of their team. These experiments show that leader change provides opportunities to restart cooperative relations between teams—the dynamic at the heart of leader specific punishments. We are grateful to Andrew Schotter for the use of the New York University experimental economics lab and to Severin Webber for his programming help. Our colleagues in the politics department also deserve thanks for serving as guinea pigs while we ironed out our program and procedures.

We both received our training in political science at the University of Rochester in the early 1990s. It was here that the importance of the scientific method was instilled in us. We could not have asked for better training, and we are deeply grateful to our advisers, David Austen-Smith, Jeff Banks, Ted Bird, Bruce Bueno de Mesquita, Bing Powell, and Larry Rothenberg.

Parts of this project have been presented at the 1998 Peace Science Society annual meeting and at the Center for International Studies' Conference on Compliance and International Law, University of Southern California, 2004. This work has also been presented in seminars at Yale University, University of Rochester, Washington University, and New York University. We are grateful for the feedback and comments we received at these venues. Bruce Bueno de Mesquita, David Cameron, Bill Clark, George Downs, Matt Gabel, Geoffrey Garrett, Mike Gilligan, Alexandra Guisinger, Leslie Johns, Pauline Jones Luong, John Oneal, David Rocke, Peter Rosendorff, Bruce Russett, Shanker Satyanath, Andy Sobel, Alan Stam, David Stasavage, Andrew Stigler, Mike Toms, Jim Vreeland, and numerous editors, readers, and anonymous reviewers have provided comments, suggestions, and invaluable support. We gratefully acknowledge the financial support of the National Science Foundation, SES-0226926.

CHAPTER 1

We Have No Quarrel with the People

The United States has no quarrel with the Iraqi people.
—*U.S. President George W. Bush,*
September 12, 2002

DESPITE THIS AND OTHER declarations of friendship, President Bush ordered U.S. troops to invade Iraq on March 20, 2003. Dropping bombs is an unusual way to express felicitations. Yet, as Bush stated, U.S. anger was directed toward the political leadership of the Iraqi government, not the people themselves. British Prime Minister Tony Blair in a November 2, 2002, speech was even more explicit: "[W]e have absolutely no quarrel with the Iraqi people. We want you to be our friends and partners in welcoming Iraq back into the international community." The targets of foreign policies are often political leaders rather than the nations they represent. This book explores the implications of, what we shall call *leader specific punishments.*

We assigned the initial quotation to U.S. President George W. Bush. However, by simply substituting nationalities we might equally well have assigned the quotation to many recent presidents, be it Ronald Reagan discussing Libya, George H. W. Bush discussing Iraq, or Bill Clinton discussing Yugoslavia. Robert Fisk (2002), in an article for the *Independent* newspaper, describes the statement "we have no quarrel with the people of . . ." as "the mantra that means this time it's serious."[1]

One might argue that Bush's targeting of leaders is nothing more than rhetoric that makes his action more palatable to domestic and international audiences alike. After all, whether U.S. policies were targeted against Saddam Hussein or Iraq more generally, it was still the Iraqi people who suffered the loss of loved ones, their homes, and their livelihoods. Yet, we shall argue that leader specific punishments have a profound and, at times, surprising impact on the dynamics of interstate relations.

---

[1] More flippantly, in their list of categorized quotations, the Web site www.righteouswarrior temple.org describes this phrase as "a well known presidential code-phrase, used many times in the past, which roughly translates as 'We're about to bomb your monkey asses into the Stone Age.'"

From the perspective of the nation issuing the threat, leader specific punishments have two important (and related) properties. First, by targeting a specific leader, rather than the nation as a whole, leader specific punishments identify an end to sour relations and an opportunity to rejuvenate good relations. Commitments, to impose sanctions for example, are not open ended. They last only as long as the recidivist leader remains in power. Targeting leaders provides a mechanism to restore good relations. In comments to the BBC World Service, July 20, 1999, on the eve of the Kosovo conflict, NATO's Supreme Allied Commander in Europe, General Wesley Clark, stated, "[I]t is a real political problem for the people of Yugoslavia because I think world leaders have made very clear that they don't see Yugoslavia really being readmitted into the European Community of nations or receiving the kinds of reconstruction that it really needs while he's [Milosevic] still in place as the President." General Clark was correct in his assessment. Following the deposition of the Serbian president Milosevic, economic assistance flooded into Yugoslavia.[2] When punishments are leader specific, leader turnover ends the punishments.

Acrimonious relations often end with leader change. This provides nations with an opportunity to start afresh. After years of failed attempts to negotiate a settlement with the Palestinians, Prime Minister Ariel Sharon explained in a speech before the Israeli Knesset on April 8, 2002, that the Palestinian people were not the problem. Rather, he argued, the obstacle to peace was the Palestinian leadership, which consistently showed itself unwilling or unable to maintain agreements. "We have no quarrel with the Palestinian people and we want to see the Palestinians, like us, live in peace, security and dignity. . . . But peace can only be attained if, once we evacuate the territories, we find a responsible Palestinian leadership, willing to accept the primary responsibility of every regime—to prevent the use of its territory for the purpose of killing and murdering its neighbors. Peace negotiations can commence and move forward only after terrorism has ceased." New Palestinian leadership is needed if the Israelis and Palestinians are to move beyond past recriminations and start constructive negotiations.

Second, leader specific punishments create internal political cleavages within the targeted state. Threats against a nation often create internal cohesion, a phenomenon often referred to as the "in-group, out-group" effect (Coser 1956). In contrast, leader specific punishments partly mitigate the risk of interstate relationships descending into a feud, by creating internal divisions. Since leader turnover normalizes relations, the citizens in the targeted state can end the punishment by deposing their

---

[2] See for example, "Aid Talks after Milosevic Drama," CNN.com, June 29, 2001.

leader.[3] Whether or not leader specific punishments lead to the removal of the targeted leader depends, in part, on how difficult it is to overthrow the leader. We study how the costs of leader removal affect the effectiveness of leader specific punishments. The *New York Times* argued in its discussion "Were Sanctions Right?" (February 28, 2003) that "[b]y making life uncomfortable for the Iraqi people, [sanctions] would eventually encourage them to remove President Saddam Hussein from power." Leader specific punishments encourage citizens to depose their leader, as it triggers a restoration of cooperative relations. British Prime Minister Neville Chamberlain, in his September 3, 1939, speech before Parliament declaring war on Germany at the start of World War II expresses amicable relations with the German people and the view that regime change within Germany would remove all need to resort to war: "We have no quarrel with the German people, except that they allow themselves to be governed by a Nazi Government. As long as that Government exists and pursues the methods it has so persistently followed during the last two years, there will be no peace in Europe."[4]

LEADER SPECIFIC PUNISHMENTS AND INTERSTATE RELATIONS

Although in motivating the topic above, we discussed largely conflictual events, such as war, the impact of leader specific punishment is just as relevant in explaining the everyday economic, financial, and diplomatic interactions between nations. Indeed, for most of the book, we focus on cooperative interactions betwveen states. The theory we develop examines the interplay between individual leaders, political institutions, and interstate relations. We articulate some of the main insights and derive a simple exposition of the theory in the context of the prisoners' dilemma.

Consider a simple example of nations wanting to establish norms of cooperation and trust between themselves in order to provide mutual benefits for both sides. Although both nations are better off if they cooperate,

---

[3] In a related argument with respect to interethnic cooperation, Fearon and Laitin (1996) describe how a combination of between-group and within-group punishments best maintains intergroup cooperation. While the majority group might easily threaten to punish the minority group (an intergroup punishment), the same threat has much less bite for the minority group. Instead, Fearon and Laitin argue that the minority group should internally punish those members of its group that cheat members of the majority in order to maintain good relations with the majority.

[4] Russett (1993) quotes U.S. President Woodrow Wilson, who also expressed that the United States had no quarrel with the German people on April 2, 1917 during the First World War.

each side could make itself even better off if it allowed the other nation to make the greater contribution to the common good. The incentive for each nation to renege on its contribution makes cooperation difficult. The standard Liberal approach, a literature we shall discuss in detail later in this chapter, explains the evolution of cooperation via the use of reciprocal punishment strategies (see for example Keohane 1984 and 1986). For instance, if nation A threatens to withdraw all future cooperation if nation B cheats, then provided that nation B values long-term cooperation more than the myopic gains from cheating, such a threat is sufficient to sustain cooperation. Following Liberal arguments we shall develop these ideas within the context of an infinitely repeated prisoners' dilemma game.

Cooperation evolves when nations choose reciprocal punishment strategies. Yet while treating nations as unitary actors is a convenient device, it is political leaders and not some personified nation that choose foreign policies. Suppose, therefore, that instead of directing reciprocal punishment strategies against a foreign nation, leaders implement strategies against the opposing leader that cheated them. That is to say that once the leader in nation B cheats, the leader of nation A refuses to cooperate with this leader ever again. However, since the punishment is directed against a specific leader, once that leader leaves office, nation A will restore cooperation with the new leadership in nation B (who after all has never cheated nation A). The replacement of a leader who previously cheated rejuvenates interstate relations.

Leader specific punishments enable the citizens of a nation to avoid punishment by simply replacing their leader if she cheats. Whether the citizens choose to do so, however, depends upon domestic political institutions and in particular how these institutions shape the cost of replacing a leader. If the value of restored cooperation exceeds the cost of leader replacement, then the citizens depose their leader if she cheats. Under institutional arrangements that make it difficult to replace leaders, however, the benefits of restored cooperation are too small to justify the high cost of leader replacement.

The Prisoners' Dilemma

We now formalize these arguments using the standard metaphor for international relations, the prisoners' dilemma. This game, shown in figure 1.1, captures the inherent difficulties of international cooperation. In each period, nations A and B choose between cooperate (C) and defect (D) and the payoffs are such that $T > R > P > S$. Nations have a dominant strategy to play defect, since whether nation B plays C or D, nation A's payoff is improved by playing D. This results in the noncooperative outcome of

| | | Nation B | |
		Cooperate, C	Defect, D
Nation A	Cooperate, C	R, R	S, T
	Defect, D	T, S	P, P

Figure 1.1. The prisoners' dilemma. $T > R > P > S$ and $R \geq (T+S)/2$.

(D,D). Yet both nations improve their payoff if they mutually cooperate. Unfortunately, once one nation cooperates, the other has the incentive to exploit their cooperation by defecting to obtain the temptation payoff, T. It is this mix of mutual gains from cooperation and incentives to cheat that has made the prisoners' dilemma such a powerful metaphor for international interactions.

In the single-shot game the prospects for cooperation are dismal. Yet, through the use of reciprocal punishments, in which nations condition their willingness to cooperate on past behavior, cooperation is possible provided nations are sufficiently patient. Patience is measured using the discount factor δ ($1 > \delta > 0$), which states the proportionate value of having to wait until the next period to receive a payoff. When δ is high, nations are patient and discount future payoffs relatively little. In contrast, δ is low for impatient nations who strongly discount the value of future payoffs.

We start our exposition of how mutual cooperation can be maintained between unitary actor nations through reciprocal punishments by considering the Grim Trigger (GT) strategy. Afterward we will adapt this strategy to explain the logic of leader specific punishments. In the GT strategy each nation starts cooperating and continues to do so in every future period unless either nation ever defects. Once either nation plays D, nations refuse to cooperate in all future periods. The GT has several advantages for illustrating how cooperation can be fostered through reciprocal punishment strategies. First, it provides the simplest illustratation of how the threat to withdraw future cooperation induces cooperative behavior. Second, this strategy is a limiting case. Since the threat to withdraw cooperation permanently is the harshest threat that a nation can make, if this threat is insufficient to support cooperation, then cooperation is impossible. Third, it is straightforward to mathematically show how the strategy shapes incentives to cooperate and to derive the limits of cooperation, as we shall now show.

If both nations play the Grim Trigger strategy then they cooperate in every period and so receive the payoff R in every period of the game. The net present value of this stream of payoffs is

$$R + \delta R + \delta^2 R + \cdots = \sum_{t=0}^{\infty} \delta^t R.$$

An extremely convenient mathematical result is that the value of this infinite sum of payoff equals $R/(1 - \delta)$. In the immediate period nation A could improve its payoff by defecting (D). However, if nation B is playing GT, then this ends all future cooperation. Therefore the net present value of playing defect is

$$T + \delta P + \delta^2 P + \cdots = T + \sum_{t=1}^{\infty} \delta^t R = T + \frac{\delta P}{1 - \delta}.$$

Nations can only commit to cooperate if the value of future cooperation relative to immediate rewards is sufficiently high. Consistent with standard approaches we can express this by finding the minimum discount factor such that maintaining cooperation is each nation's preferred option, that is,

$$\frac{R}{1 - \delta} \geq T + \frac{\delta P}{1 - \delta}.$$

If this condition holds, the GT strategy is a subgame perfect Nash equilibrium. This result implies that cooperation is possible if nations are sufficiently patient,

$$\delta \geq \frac{T - R}{T - P}.$$

Modeling Leader Specific Punishments

Although it is convenient to personify nations, it is national leaders, and not nations, who set foreign policy. We consider a simple principal-agent structure within each nation. Nation A is composed of leader α and citizens (a). Leader α sets policy that, in the context of the prisoners' dilemma exposition of international cooperation, means choosing between C and D. Nation B is led by leader β, who chooses whether to cooperate or defect on behalf of nation B. Having observed the outcome of the prisoners' dilemma interaction, the citizens can replace their leaders at cost K_A and K_B, respectively. The game is shown in figure 1.2.

In addition to receiving the payoffs associated with the outcome of the prisoners' dilemma (that is T, R, P, or S), leaders receive a payoff of Ψ for each period they are a leader and citizens pay the costs K_A or K_B if they decide to replace their leader. To reflect our belief that leaders are primarily office seeking, we assume the reward for office, Ψ, is large relative to payoffs from the prisoners' dilemma. After deposition, leaders become ordinary

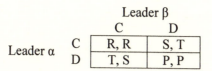

Figure 1.2. The prisoners' dilemma game between representative leaders. Step (1) Leaders α and β choose Cooperate (C) or Defect (D) in the prisoners' dilemma game. Step (2) The citizens in nations A and B decide whether to replace their leaders at costs K_A and K_B, respectively.

citizens and receive the payoffs from PD only.[5] For technical convenience we assume there is an infinite pool of alternative leaders.

Domestic political institutions shape the ease of leader replacement. In democratic systems, deposing a political leader is relatively costless; citizens need only vote for the challenger rather than the incumbent. In autocratic regimes, deposing leaders is much more costly. In chapter 3 we use Bueno de Mesquita and his colleagues' (2003) selectorate model of domestic competition to examine how domestic political institutions shape the policy incentives of leaders and how this in turn affects the ease of political survival. For the time being, we distinguish between political regimes only in terms of the cost of replacing a leader, K_A and K_B, and, for ease of language, refer to low replacement cost regimes as democracies.

The Leader Specific Grim Trigger strategy (LSGT) utilizes the reciprocal punishment strategies of GT, but conditions punishments at the level of leaders. If leader α plays the LSGT strategy, then initially she plays "cooperates" in the PD. Indeed she will continue to play cooperate provided that neither she nor the current leader of state B (β) has ever cheated. If, however, leader β ever cheats, then leader α will never cooperate with her again and plays D in all subsequent periods. Leader α conditions her punishment strategy against the specific leader that cheated her and not the nation she represents. If incumbent leader β is replaced, then leader α returns to cooperating with β's successor.

The key conceptual distinction between LSGT and the unitary actor GT strategy described above is that the LSGT conditions punishment—that is, the refusal to cooperate in the future—against the specific leader who cheated and not against the nation she represented. Below, we specify the LSGT for leader α. Leader β's strategy is analogous. In this description we

[5] Goemans (2000a, b) argues that many deposed leaders are killed or punished following deposition. He further argues the probability of punishment differs by regime type with democratic leaders least likely to be punished and autocratic leaders most likely to be punished. The prospects of postdeposition punishment further enhance leaders' officeholding motivations.

use the term leader i "cheats" to mean that leader i plays D while leader j plays C.

The Leader Specific Grim Trigger (for leader α)

1. If β, the current leader in state B, has ever cheated, then α plays D.
2. If leader α has ever cheated, then α plays D.
3. Under all other contingencies, α plays C.

Part (1) of this definition indicates that α uses the reciprocal punishment strategy of refusing to cooperate if the current leader β has cheated. Whether prior leaders in nation B have ever cheated is immaterial with respect to α's punishment decision. It is important to note that under the LSGT leader β need not have actually cheated against the current leader in nation A, but just have cheated some leader of nation A. For instance, although Cuba's Fidel Castro "cheated" during the Eisenhower administration by nationalizing U.S. interests in Cuba, all subsequent U.S. administrations recognize Castro's regime as having previously cheated.

We now turn to examining the impact of leader specific punishment strategies on the relations between nations and how the introduction of a leader specific component to the strategy affects the possibility of interstate cooperation. The analysis separates into two distinct cases depending upon the cost of leader replacement. When the cost of leader replacement is high, in particular K_A, $K_B \geq (R - P)\delta/(1 - \delta)$, then the citizens never replace their leader whatever the state of relations between the nations. Under these conditions, behavior is equivalent to the unitary actor GT case. Therefore, as in the GT case, cooperation is possible only if nations are sufficiently patient that the value of maintaining cooperation outweighs the short term gains from defection:

$$\delta \geq \frac{T - R}{T - P} \ .$$

If leaders play the LSGT strategy and the cost of leader replacement is low, specifically K_A, $K_B \leq (R - P)\delta/(1 - \delta)$, then the citizens replace any leader who cheats. Remember that under the LSGT, leader α only refuses to cooperate with the specific leader who cheated her nation; she will cooperate with this leader's successors. If leader β cheats, then the citizens in nation B can end the punishment phase (that is, noncooperation) by replacing leader β. This desire to replace cheaters in order to restore cooperation helps prevent cheating in the first place, since leaders do not want to be removed from office. We formally state the conditions under which LSGT is an SPE (subgamee perfect equilibrium) with low leader replacement cost. We explain the logic of the argument via the process of proving the following claim.

Proposition 1.1: *In the infinitely repeated PD between representative leaders, if $K_A \leq (R - P) \delta/(1 - \delta))$ and $K_B \leq (R - P) \delta/(1 - \delta))$ and $\delta \geq (T - R)/(T - R + \Psi)$, then leaders α and β playing the LSGT and citizens deposing any leader who cheats or has cheated in the past is an SPE.*

To prove that the above constitutes an SPE requires showing that under every possible contingency, for every player, playing these strategies is a best response given the strategies of all other players and play in future periods. In particular, if this strategy profile is an SPE, then there cannot be any profitable single period deviation from this equilibrium path for any player.

First we consider the contingency that leader α has either cheated in the current period or cheated in some previous period. Given this instance of cheating, leader β refuses all opportunity to cooperate in the future as long as leader α remains in power. Leader β does not hold a grudge against nation A per se, however, and will resume cooperation with α's successor. The leader specific component of LSGT offers the citizens in A an opportunity to restore cooperation if they remove α.

If the citizens of nation A replace their leader, then they must pay cost K_A to do so. In the PD between representative leaders, the only dimension on which the citizens evaluate their leader is the outcome of the PD game. If their leader's integrity is intact, meaning their leader has never cheated in the past, then future international cooperation occurs whether they replace their leader or not. Replacing their leader under this circumstance only imposes additional costs with no benefits.

Now consider the case where leader α has tarnished her integrity by cheating. If the citizens in nation A retain her, then leader β will refuse to cooperate in the next period, and the outcome of the PD game will be (D,D), giving the citizens a reward of P. If the citizens retained leader α indefinitely, then cooperation ceases indefinitely, the net present value of which is $\delta P + \delta^2 P + \ldots = \delta P/(1 - \delta)$. If instead the citizens replace their leader, at a cost of K_A, then in the next period leader β cooperates, and under LSGT the cooperation continues in every future period. The net present value of deposing leader α is $-K_A + \delta R + \delta^2 R + \ldots = K_A + \delta R/(1 - \delta)$. Provided that $K_A \leq (R - P) \delta/(1 - \delta)$, then the citizens in A prefer to depose α immediately. The leader specific component of β's punishment strategy means that on average the value of the challenger is $(R - P) \delta/(1 - \delta)$ greater than the value of retaining an incumbent who has cheated.

The condition $K_A \leq (R - P) \delta/(1 - \delta)$ was derived by considering whether the citizens remove α or retain her indefinitely. Technically, the proof that proposition 1.1 is an SPE requires consideration of single period defections from the equilibrium path. In this context a one period deviation from the path means retaining leader α after she has deviated for one period before removing her. The payoff from doing so is $\delta P - \delta K_A + \delta^2 R/(1 - \delta)$. Comparing this with the payoff from removing α immediately, $- K_A + \delta R/(1 - \delta)$ also yields the same condition $K_A \leq (R - P) \, \delta/(1 - \delta)$. When the cost of removing leaders is low, then the citizens replace leaders who cheat. With the effects of cheating on domestic political survival established, how do leaders play PD?

Suppose neither leader has previously cheated. Under this contingency LSGT dictates that leader β plays C. If leader α plays C, then her payoff is $R + \Psi$ in the current period, plus $R + \Psi$ in every future period. The net present value of cooperation is thus $(R + \Psi)/(1 - \delta)$. However, leader α can improve her payoff in the immediate period by playing D. This yields the temptation payoff and officeholding rewards in the current period, but α is removed by the citizens and so does not receive the officeholding benefits in future periods. However, since α's replacement will restore cooperation, α receives the reward payoff R in all future periods. The net present value of cheating is therefore $T + \Psi + \delta R/(1 - \delta)$. Provided that $\delta \geq (T - R)/(T - R + \Psi)$, the value of cooperation exceeds that of cheating and so α cooperates in every period.[6]

When the cost of leader replacement is low ($K_A, K_B \leq (R - P) \, \delta/(1 + \delta)$), citizens replace leaders who cheat or who have cheated in the past. Given this replacement strategy, leaders who cheat lose office. We believe leaders are primarily driven by officeholding motives; that is, Ψ is large relative to $T - R$. Therefore, the condition $\delta \geq (T - R)/(T - R + \Psi)$ ensures that except under all but the smallest discount factors, full cooperation can be sustained.

Figure 1.3 graphs the minimum discount factor required to support full cooperation in the PD between representative leaders for high and low costs of leader replacement. When the cost of leader replacement is high, leaders who cheat retain office but forgo future cooperation. When the cost of leader replacement is low, leaders that cheat are removed from office. If, as we believe, leaders are primarily motivated by officeholding motives, then the punishment threatened for noncooperation in the latter case is much larger than in the former case. The greater the threatened punishment becomes, the easier it is for leaders to commit to cooperate.

Figure 1.3 is plotted assuming $T = 4$, $R = 3$, $P = 2$, and $S = 1$. It shows, once leaders value officeholding at least as much as the difference between the temptation and reward payoffs ($\Psi > T - R = 1$), then cooperation can

---

[6] We also need to check the optimality of LSGT under the remaining contingencies. If β has cheated in a previous period, then under LSGT, β will play D. Leader α's best response is also to play D. If leader a has previously cheated, then leader β will play D. Leader α's best response is to also play D.

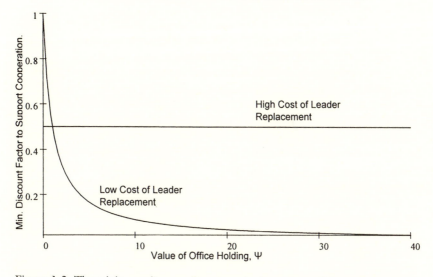

Figure 1.3. The minimum discount factor required to support full cooperation in the PD between representative leaders for high and low costs of leader replacement.

be maintained in the PD game under a wider range of conditions when leader removal is easier. If, for example, leaders care about office holding ten times more than the value of cooperation, then leaders require a discount factor of only 1/11 to maintain cooperation. In contrast, when leader removal is hard, the maintenance of cooperation requires a discount factor greater than ½. It is interesting to note that the leader, as agent of the citizens, can commit to cooperate under conditions that the principals themselves could not commit to cooperate under. If the citizens themselves choose the nation's foreign policy directly, then they would only cooperate if $\delta \geq 1/2$. Furthermore, when the cost of leader replacement is sufficiently low ($K_A < T - R$), the citizens want their leader to cheat. By doing so, the citizens gain the temptation payoff and can then replace their leader at cost K_A and so avoid the punishment phase. Of course, the leader does not want to cheat despite the public popularity of such a policy. Although by cheating the leader is carrying out the citizens' wishes, such a popular course of action will still lead to her dismissal.

By simultaneously examining interactions at the level of interstate relations, domestic political institutions, and individual leaders, leader specific punishments theory provides predictions about (1) how domestic political institutions shape the level of international cooperation, (2) how foreign policy outcomes affect the survival of leaders, and (3) the dynamics of interstate relations and how they depend upon domestic institutions. Since the theory combines different levels of analysis, it is appropriate to pause and examine the units of the international system.

PROPER NOUNS IN INTERNATIONAL RELATIONS

Who are the actors in international politics and what are the organizing principles in the study of international relations? The most common answer to these questions would be nations. Certainly the concept of nations provides a useful organizing principle. However, the extent to which nations are the "true" actors of international politics is questionable. While it is convenient to say the United States decided to invade Iraq on March 20, 2003, or to say France opposed the United States' actions in the United Nations, neither of these statements is strictly true. The United States never decided to invade Iraq. The decision was made by U.S. President George W. Bush's administration, having gained congressional approval for the use of force on October 11, 2002, with a 296–133 vote in the House of Representatives and a 77–23 vote in the Senate.[7] On March 10, 2003, Jacque Chirac, president of France, announced that he would direct the French ambassador to the United Nations, Jean-Marc de La Sabliere, to veto U.S. calls for the UN to authorize the use of force to remove and destroy Saddam Hussein's alleged weapons of mass destruction.[8]

One might argue that these distinctions are pedantic. After all, leaders enact policies that best fulfill national goals! Of course social choice theorists show us that there is no such thing as a "national will." National will is a construct of the institutional rules used to aggregate preferences. Had butterfly ballots in Palm Beach County Florida not confused so many voters, Al Gore, the Democratic candidate in the 2000 U.S. presidential election, would in all likelihood have been elected instead of Bush and perhaps the 2003 war with Iraq might never have taken place. Despite these social choice niceties, it is often useful to simplify a problem by classifying some outcomes as preferred to others by a massive majority in a nation. We are as guilty as anyone else of using this assumption. Throughout this book we assume that, all else equal, a nation unambiguously prefers to win a war rather than lose. However, whether the United States decides to launch a war against Iraq depends upon whose preferences get represented.

The 2003 U.S.-Iraq war is poorly conceived as a war between the United States and Iraq. At least according the Bush administration's foreign policy statements, the *causi belli* was Iraqi President Saddam Hussein. President Bush was explicit: "The U.S. is the friend of the Iraqi people." If Bush's foreign policy statements are to be believed, the Iraqi people were

---

[7] "Congress Backs Bush War Powers," BBC News, October 11, 2002. http://news.bbc.co.uk/1/hi/world/americas/2318785.stm.

[8] "Timeline: Steps to War,"BBC News, March 20, 2003, http://news.bbc.co.uk/1/hi/world/middle_east/2773213.stm.

not the target of the bombing. The target was Saddam Hussein and his regime. The targets of U.S. foreign policy are often not nations, but specific leaders, administrations, or political regimes in foreign nations.

In historical terms, treating nations as the actors of international relations makes even less sense. When the English King John (1199–1216) rowed with the French, classifying the conflict as a war between England and France would badly misconstrue the dispute. The feudal system in place at that time was a series of hierarchical structures, in which people lower down the structure paid homage to those above. In England, King John ruled through the support of the barons, each of whom was obligated to do him homage and provide military resources at times of war. In return these barons held lands. As authors of histories are always quick to remind us, our modern concept of nations presumes distinctions that people of the medieval times would not recognize (Warren 1997). The politics of the time were between kings, barons, knights, and ecclesiastical actors and not between states. For example, the foundations for what we regard as wars between England and France were over feudal rights. Although John was king of England, he was also duke of Normandy and via his mother, Eleanor of Acquintane, he also held great swaths of land in southwestern France.

The feudal system was arcane. In one regard John as king of England was an equal of Philip Augustus, king of France. Yet on another level he was subservient to the French king, as he held his French lands as a vassal of the French king. To provide further complications, the pope would like to have claimed supremacy of over all secular authorities. Rather than war between England and France, John and Phillip fought for control of lands that are in modern-day France, such as Normandy, which John held as part of his feudal rights that were independent of his role as king of England.

At the same time, of course, John faced rebellion in England from his barons. These barons had no interest in John's confrontations with the French king over rights to lands in France in which they had no stake. Their feudal obligations made them duty bound to provide the king resources for his wars in France, but it was his fight, not theirs. It is perhaps small wonder then that the barons rebelled, forcing John to make concessions in his famed signing of the Magna Carta in 1215. While the Magna Carta is often thought of as having enormous historical significance in establishing the rights of commoners and nobility vis-à-vis the king, as a contemporary document its importance was minimal. Pope Innocent III quickly annulled the document; he liked John's policies of Crusading and war with France.

While from a twenty-first-century perspective we refer to the wars of King John's reign as Anglo-French wars, few if any people at the time would have identified themselves as English or French. King John himself did not even speak English; Edward I (1272–1307) was the first (post-1066) English king to speak English (Gunaratne 2003). During the medieval period international politics rarely had much to do with nations.

According to many international relations textbooks (for example, Russett, Starr, and Kinsella 2005) the nation-state came into existence in the Treaty of Westphalia of 1648, a series of treaties that concluded the Thirty Years War. The Treaty of Westphalia contains provisions that allowed princes to freely choose the religion of lands they controlled (although the people themselves still had little choice in their religion). The Thirty Years War is often seen as a battle over religious rights between Catholic and Protestant rulers. While contemporary international relations scholars focus predominantly on these aspects of the Treaty of Westphalia, a greater percentage of the treaty dealt with which individuals get what in terms of lands, rents, and other booty.[9]

In the post-Westphalian era many wars can indeed be portrayed as conflicts fought between nations for national interests. One does not have to dig deeply to see that many of these wars are not based around national competition, however, but rather are driven by domestic political interests. For instance, the Prussians started the Wars of the French Revolution by invading France to restore the monarchy of Louis XVI.

Although our modern conception of the international system is organized around nations, the policies nations pursue depend upon who is national leader and which domestic interests this leader represents. Who gets to be leader of a nation and which interests the leader represents depend upon the nation's domestic political institutions. Foreign policies are drawn up with goals and targets. While in some case these targets might be a nation (the national unit as a whole), in other cases foreign policies are either implicitly or explicitly targeted against a specific feature of a nation's polity, such as the leader. This book treats international politics not as competition between amorphous national groups, but as foreign policies composed by political elites in one nation with regard to elites in another nation. Domestic political institutions and the preferences of leaders interact to shape the types of policies that elites choose. Domestic institutions in a foreign nation determine how its political elites respond to these foreign policies.

This book builds a theory of international politics based on the actions of individual leaders constrained by domestic political institutions. The

---

[9] Bueno de Mesquita et al. (2003, pp. 432–34) categorized the clauses of a number of treaties according to whether they concerned public policy, private benefits (such as the allocation of lands and rents to individuals) or implementation and procedural issues. Of the treaties 128 clauses, they code only 36 (28 percent) as being involved with issue of public concern. In contrast, 55 (43 percent) clauses concern the allocation of private benefits. The remaining 37 clauses mainly concern implementation and procedural issues.

interactions between nations depend upon the goals of these individual leaders and political institutions. The theoretical basis of our arguments is individual choice and the aggregation of preferences. However, we do not generate our results by considering wide varieties of preferences and arguing in favor of different sets of preferences to explain different events. Instead we consider a simple set of goals for each actor. For instance, we assume political leaders primarily want to retain their jobs and that all the citizens of a nation have a common objective function with respect to international outcomes.[10] From this sparse framework we examine how the strategies of leaders interact to produce international outcomes and how domestic institutions modify these interactions.

INTERNATIONAL COOPERATION

Cooperation and coordination represent fundamental problems in international relations. Although later, in chapter 7, we consider to more conflictual relationships, the bulk of our study investigates cooperation. In a domestic setting if two groups wish to work together for some common goal, they can sign a contract. If one party subsequently shirks its obligations, the other group can sue it in a court of law and receive compensation. The threat of being sued is sufficient to ensure that both parties contribute to the joint goal in accordance with their agreement. Unfortunately, the anarchy of international relations makes international cooperation much more difficult. Without courts and police to enforce contracts, nations have little incentive to honor their obligations.

The problems involved with international cooperation are well known to political scientists. Following Keohane (1984, p. 12), we take international cooperation to mean "mutual adjustment." Keohane (1984, chap. 4) is careful to distinguish between harmony—a situation where nations' interests are already sufficiently aligned that by default they want to take actions that are mutually beneficial—and cooperation, where there is some discord between the objectives of each nation such that adjusting their policies for mutual gains requires changing policies from those the nations would adopt absent attempts to mutually improve welfare.

Whether the topic under consideration is trade and tariff arrangements, coordination of monetary policy, arms control agreements, sharing of

---

[10] There is a substantial literature that argues individual characteristics of leaders, such as their gender, age, marital status, and even birth order, affect national policy. Others argue a leader's psychological and behavioral makeup plays an important part (Goldstein 2001; Horowitz, McDermott, and Stam 2005; Hermann, Tetlock, and Diascro 2001; Post 2003; Rosen 2005). Although we do not want to dismiss these factors, here we show that the effects of leader turnover can be explained even when all leaders are assumed to be homogenous.

common pool resources, environmental agreements (or other external-ity problems), contributions to a common defense commitment (Olson and Zeckhauser 1966), or shared technology and research, the difficulty of cooperation can be explained in terms of a collective action problem. Of course not all the interactions between states can be thought of as opportunities to cooperate: however, such cases present a wide range of interesting problems from which to start (Simmons and Martin 1998).[11] Later we discuss more conflictual and less cooperative interactions.

Although they can be divided into a number of different categories, such as the provision of public goods, externalities, or common pool resources problems (Olson 1965), collective action problems share some basic fea-tures. If all parties agree to undertake some socially preferred set of policies, then each party is better off than if all parties acted myopically. Depending upon the topic under consideration, there are numerous examples. For instance, in the context of international trade between two nations, free trade is mutually beneficial relative to each nation being autarkic. In an-other example, international liquidity aids international trade, investment, and capitalism. If all nations contribute to a fund to ensure liquidity for distressed banks and other financial institutions overseas, all nations ben-efit from avoiding international financial shocks. International liquidity is a public good that benefits all members of the international community. No member of the international community can be excluded from the benefits of a robust international economy; neither does any nation's enjoyment of a robust international economy diminish another state's enjoyment. Once the public good of international liquidity is provided, all parties benefit, whether or not they provided any of the resources required to produce the good. Given they benefit whether or not they contributed to the public good, each party wants to minimize its contribution. The net result is an underprovision of the public good. Of course in the domestic setting, legal and contractual arrangements can be used to overcome the collective action problem. For instance, governments collect compulsory taxes from their citizens to provide for such public goods as national defense and public health. Theories of public goods provision have been well developed, and we need not go over the details here (Olson 1965). As with other collec-tive action problems, the key features are that even though all parties could make themselves better off by coordinating their actions, each party could make itself even better off by free riding on the efforts of others.

As we saw earlier, the prisoners' dilemma is a convenient model that encapsulates the inherent problems of international collective action (Axelrod 1984; Axelrod and Keohane 1986; Bendor 1987; Downs and

---

[11] Morrow (1994) provides a useful framework from which to consider coordination problems.

Roche 1990; Gourevitch 1996; Milner 1992; and Pahre 1994). In the classic explication of the game, two criminals have been caught. The district attorney separately offers each a deal if he agrees to testify against his partner in crime. The payoffs *T, R, P,* and *S* reflect the length of sentences the criminals can expect to receive depending upon who rats on whom or who remains silent.

To see why the prisoners' dilemma serves so well as a model for international cooperation, we need only change the actions of each party. Returning to the example of international financial liquidity for instance, cooperation (*C*) means contributing resources to the provision of the public good, while defecting (*D*) means shirking. Both parties are better off if each contributes its share ($R > P$), but each party is even better off if it keeps its resources while benefiting from the partial provision of the public good by the other nation ($T > R > P$).

Whether we think of the prisoners' dilemma as a game between prisoners negotiating with the DA, nations contributing to a public good, or any other collective action problem, each party wants to defect. Cooperation is difficult in PD because whatever the strategy of the other side, each party has a dominant strategy to defect. That is to say, if player *A* chooses *C*, then player *B* obtains the maximal payoff *T* by defecting. If player *A* defects, then player *B* chooses between cooperating, which produces *S*, the worst payoff, or defecting and obtaining the payoff *P*. In either case, player *B* is better off playing *D* to *C*. In the context of PD, the prospects for international cooperation appear bleak. Yet, international cooperation frequently occurs: therefore, at least one of the assumptions in the prisoners' dilemma model of international cooperation must be wrong.

Hegemonic Theory

Hegemonic stability theorists argue that hegemons—that is, nations that predominate over all other states—promote international cooperation (De Cecco 1975; Feis 1930; Ford 1962; Kindleberger 1981; Lindert 1969; Wallerstein 1980). In the context of economic issues, such as trade and financial liquidity, they argue that a hegemon controls such a large proportion of the world economy, and its share of the gains from the provision of public goods is so large that this outweighs the cost of providing the public good. In the context of the prisoners' dilemma, this would be to say that the hegemon's preferences are $T > R > S > P$. Given that the hegemon would prefer to unilaterally provide the public good rather than see it not provided, the hegemon's optimal strategy is to unilaterally provide the public good by playing *C*. The smaller state has no incentive to provide the public good, since the hegemon is already doing all the work.

One convenient way to think of the hegemonic argument is a division of a pie. By providing a public good, nations can increase the size of the overall pie. However, when a large number of nations each has a small share of the pie, no nation individually gains from investing in the public good, since it receives only a small share of the increased size of the pie. In contrast, a hegemon receives such a large share of the pie that it pays for the hegemon to increase the size of the pie since such a large proportion of the increased pie goes to the hegemon.

Hegemonic arguments have been used to explain the expansion of trading and international banking under the hegemony of the British prior to 1914, Pax Britannica. Despite explaining cooperation as the presence of a hegemon in these cases, Carr (1962) argues that the collapse of the world economy during the 1930s was largely due to the United States' unwillingness to provide public goods despite its hegemonic position. Although hegemonic arguments explain cooperation in the presence of a hegemon, they fail to explain cooperation in the absence of a hegemon. Indeed, one might argue that increasingly high levels of cooperation achieved through such organizations as the World Trade Organization in the latter part of the twentieth century, coupled with declining U.S. hegemony, falsifies hegemonic arguments. Liberal theory offers an explanation for cooperation in the absence of a hegemon.

Liberal Theory

In his classic book, *After Hegemony*, Robert Keohane (1984) explains that even in the absence of a hegemon, international cooperation can arise if nations use reciprocal strategies. That is to say, nations condition their current and future play on the outcome of past interactions. As Liberal theorists argue, provided that nations are sufficiently patient, such strategies make cooperation possible, and collective action problems can be solved (Axelrod and Keohane 1986; Axelrod 1984, 1986; Baldwin 1993; Busch and Reinhardt 1993; Goldstein 1991; Gowa 1986; Keohane and Nye1977; Krasner 1983; Milgrom, North, and Weingast 1990; Milner 1992; Oye 1986; Ruggie 1993).

Earlier we formalized these arguments within the context of the prisoners' dilemma using the Grim Trigger. Of course, GT is just one strategy through which cooperation can be obtained. When nations are sufficiently patient, there are infinitely many SPEs that exhibit many patterns of behavior—a result known as the Folk theorem (Fudenberg and Maskin 1986). To prove the existence of these other patterns of equilibrium behavior, Folk theorem type results find a punishment schedule that nations want to implement if a nation deviates from a prescribed pattern of play. The GT strategy is a limiting case because it utilizes the harshest punishment schedule—the permanent removal of cooperation. In short, if GT does not work, there is no other way of securing cooperation in equilibrium.

Although GT defines the theoretical limits of cooperation in infinitely repeated PD, from a practical perspective, cooperation is much harder to achieve. In reality, once cooperation fails, nations want to try to restore it. Unfortunately, the desire to try to renegotiate cooperation once the punishment phase starts undermines the threat of the punishment in the first place. Formally, equilibria that are immune from attempts to renegotiate an end to the punishment phase are referred to as *renegotiation proof* (Farrell and Maskin 1989). GT is not renegotiation proof. Given the prospects of indefinite punishment, both parties prefer to negotiate a return to cooperation. Unfortunately, this undermines the strength of the punishment threat in the first place.

The GT strategy assumes a noiseless world of perfect information and no errors. Unfortunately, the real world is a noisy place where nations are liable to misinterpret each other's actions. Further, in practical terms nations do not choose between C or D. In reality, nations' choices are much more complex. For example, nations might choose how high to set tariffs or whether to impose non-tariff barriers. These actions can be thought of as shades of gray rather than the black-and-white choices of C and D. In our formal analysis of international cooperation in chapter 2, we allow for the integration of both continuous choice action spaces and noise.

Despite these limitations, the Liberal interpretation of international cooperation as an infinitely repeated PD with cooperation made possible via reciprocal strategies has been a powerful idea in political science. The importance given to this result is well founded. These ideas explain how cooperation is possible when collective action problems suggest the prospects for cooperation are poor. Unfortunately, whatever the value of the infinitely repeated PD analysis, it inherently remains a possibility result. Above we showed that GT is an SPE. However, both nations always playing D in every period is also an SPE. The analysis tells us that the former cooperative equilibrium is possible when the temptations to cheat are not too great, when the rewards from cooperation are large, and when nations are patient: specifically, $\delta \leq (T-R)/(T-P)$. Beyond these limits, however, the result tells us nothing about when cooperation is most likely. The SPE analysis provides us no comparative static results with regard as to whether cooperation is more likely between nations A and B or between nations X and Y.

Empirical analyses suggest some pairs of states are more likely to cooperate with each other than are other pairings. Scholars such as Russett and Oneal (2001), Leeds (1999), and many others show that democratic dyads cooperate at far higher levels than do other dyadic pairings of states.[12] The basic Liberal analysis cannot explain these differences without resorting to arguments that PD payoffs for democratic states differ from the PD payoffs for other states, or that democracies are inherently more patient.

We believe the failure of Liberal theory to predict which nations are most likely to cooperate is a major limitation of the approach. Liberal scholars have also done little to show the dynamics of reciprocal strategies in the pattern of cooperation (Goldstein 1991). The GT strategy predicts that once defection occurs, cooperation permanently ends. As the brief anecdotes at the start of this chapter indicated, the end of cooperation is rarely permanent. After several years of harsh economic sanctions and international isolation, Yugoslavia (Serbia) is again an active member of the international community that receives economic assistance and investment from Western states. Obviously, GT cannot account for the restoration of interstate relations. While other strategies, such as Tit-for-Tat (Axelrod 1984), allow for the restoration of cooperation on the equilibrium path, Liberal theorists have done little to provide empirical evidence that reciprocal strategies explain the restoration and termination of international cooperation.

Liberal theory treats nations as unitary actor states. As we argued above, nations are not the only proper nouns of international relations. Although Liberal theory has made an appropriately huge impact on the study of international relations, it cannot explain how institutional differences between states shape the level of cooperation. Neither can it explain the dynamics of cooperation. We believe a theory of leader specific punishments addresses these deficiencies.

Leader Specific Punishments and International Cooperation

Nations are not unitary actors interested in maximizing social welfare. Leader specific punishment (LSP) theory dispenses with the unitary actor assumption and replaces it with a principal-agent framework in which representative leaders are the agents and the citizens are the principals. Although leaders are assumed to care somewhat about international outcomes, they

---

[12] The literature emphasizing the ability of democracies to cooperate more than autocracies is wide and varied: Bliss and Russett 1998; Busch and Reinhardt 1993; Gaubatz 1996; Gowa 1994; Leeds 1999; Mansfield, Milner, and Rosendorff 2000; Mansfield and Pevehouse 2000; Mansfield and Pollins 2001; Martin 1993; McGillivray 1997, 1998; Milner 1997; Milner and Rosendorff 1997; Morrow, Siverson, and Taberes 1998; Oneal and Russett 1997, 1999a, b, 2000, 2001; Oneal, Russett, and Berbaum 2003; Polachek 1997; Pollins 1989; Remmer 1998; Reuveny and Kang 1996, 1998; Reuveny 2000, 2001; Russett and Oneal 1999, 2001; Verdier 1998.

primarily want to keep their jobs. Domestic political institutions affect the ease with which citizens can replace their leader. When the cost of leader replacement is high, a leader's political survival is relatively detached from her ability to produce successful foreign policy outcomes. In contrast, when a leader is easily replaced, her political fate depends upon being able to deliver good international outcomes.

LSP examines how targeting punishments against individual leaders, rather than the nation they represent, affects the level of cooperation between states, the survival of political leaders, and the dynamics of interstate cooperation.

LEVEL OF COOPERATION

Democratic dyads—that is, pairs of democratic states—cooperate at higher levels than do other dyadic pairings of states. This empirical result has been established in numerous settings. We dwell on these extant results for a moment. Although leader specific punishment theory predicts these results, our empirical tests do not focus on the level of cooperation between states. As we are about to summarize, the impact of domestic political institutions on the level of cooperation has been well established in the empirical literature. To repeat similar tests would be largely redundant, as it would provide little new information. Instead, our empirical tests will focus on the novel and relatively underinvestigated results regarding the dynamics of cooperation and leader change.

That pairs of democracies behave differently from other dyadic pairings of nations has been a common theme of the international relations literature over the past decade. The impetus for this research stems from the democratic peace, an observation that democracies do not fight each other (Maoz and Abdolali 1989; Ray 1995; Bremmer 1992). Although numerous cases, from ancient Greece to the United States imperialist wars against Native American tribes, have been proposed as potential examples and counterexamples (see Russett 1993 and Weart 1998 for discussion of many of these cases), the result appears to have been generally accepted by much of the discipline. Indeed, Jack Levy (1988) has gone so far as to call it a *law*. The principal democratic peace result is that democracies do not go to war with each other. However, democracies do become involved in wars with nondemocratic states (Maoz and Abdolali 1989). Democracies also become involved in violent conflict with other democracies: it is just that these conflicts do not escalate to war (Oneal and Russett 1997; Senese 1997). The literature appears conflicted as to whether democracies are more or less aggressive, in terms of overall war participation, than other regime types (Benoit 1996; Ray 1995). The conflict behavior of democratic states has also been shown to differ greatly from that of other states in a variety of ways. Democracies generally win the wars they fight (Lake 1992; Reiter and Stam 1998a, 2002). Further, they typically win quickly and with relatively few casualties (Reiter and Stam 1998a, b; Siverson 1995; Bueno de Mesquita et al. 2004). Democracies also tend to fight for policy change or regime change, while nondemocratic states are more likely to fight for land (Bueno de Mesquita et al. 2003). Democracies are also more likely to use conflict management techniques (Brecher and Wilkenfeld 1997; Dixon 1994; Mousseau 1998; Raymond 1994). Democracies often initiate conflict against nondemocracies (Reiter and Stam 1998b). Transitional status and size also appear to affect the conflict involvement of democracies (Mansfield and Snyder 1995; Ward and Gleditsch 1998; Morgan and Campbell 1991).

Many of the theoretical efforts to explain these regularities have focused on either normative arguments or institutional constraints (Maoz and Russett 1993). Unfortunately, few of these theoretical arguments have satisfied the criteria of explaining all the known empirical regularities and predicting novel hypotheses (Rosato 2003); although we believe that Bueno de Mesquita and his colleagures' selectorate politics explanation of the democratic peace has made substantial progress in this direction (Bueno de Mesquita et al. 1999, 2004).

Motivated in part by a desire to explain the democratic peace result, scholars have sought to find other regularities associated with democracy outside of conflict behavior. For example, numerous studies have found that regime type influences trade (Bliss and Russett 1998; Gowa 1994; Mansfield and Pevehouse 2000; Mansfield and Pollins 2001; Milner and Rosendorff 1997; Morrow, Siverson, and Taberes 1998; Oneal 2003; Oneal and Russett 1997, 1999a, 1999b, 2000, and 2001; Polachek 1997; Pollins 1989; Reuveny 2000 and 2001; Reuveny and Kang 1996 and 1998; Verdier 1998). Even controlling for their typically large economies and regional concentration, democratic dyads appear to trade with each other to a greater extent than do other pairs of nations. Scholars such as Russett and Oneal (2001) argue this affinity between democratic states extends beyond simple trade and affects their propensity to invest in each other, join international organizations together, and generally cooperate at a high level. (For evidence on the greater propensity of democratic states to join international organizations see Jacobson, Reisinger, and Mathers 1986; Shanks, Jacobson, and Kaplan 1996; Russett and Oneal 2001; Russett, Oneal, and Davis 1998; Mansfield, Milner, and Rosendorff 2002; Mansfield and Pevehouse 2006).

Leeds (1999) finds further evidence of greater cooperation between pairs of democratic states using COPDAB data (Azar 1982). These data are compiled through the reporting of news events. She finds that pairs of democratic states have systematically more cooperative relations than do other pairs of states.

The empirical evidence portrays a clear picture. Relations between states with democratically accountable leaders are more cooperative than relations between other pairs of states. Although we shall show further evidence of this in our subsequent analyses, we do not focus on this result. It is already well established, and repeated analysis does not help us understand why. Many of the works cited above propose theoretical explanation for this result. For example, Leeds (1999) argues democracies cooperate because their leaders face audience costs from breaking their commitments. Russett and Oneal (2001) compare a wide range of structural and normative approaches to explain democratic behavior. Unfortunately, based only on evidence relating to the level of cooperation, it is impossible to distinguish between rival theoretical explanations, all of which predict elevated levels of cooperation between democracies. Only by extending the analyses to consider dimensions on which the theories have differing predictions can we separate them. In this book most of our empirical tests have this goal in mind. We are less interested in describing behavior that is broadly predicted by many theories than we are in testing the hypotheses generated by LSP theory that distinguish it from other approaches.

IMPACT OF FOREIGN POLICY ON LEADER SURVIVAL

Democratic dyads cooperate more than other dyads. According to the theory of leader specific punishments, democratic leaders cooperate because a failure to do so costs them their jobs. The theory predicts a relationship between policy choice and leader removal. Democratic leaders who cheat on their agreements or otherwise violate norms of international behavior and so incur the ire of other states are removed from power. In contrast, the high cost of leader removal in authoritarian states means autocrats can incur the wrath of the international community and trading partners with impunity, at least with respect to domestic political removal. Unfortunately, directly testing this hypothesis is extremely difficult as leaders do not make policy choices that jeopardize their own political survival. There is a selection effect. If cheating on an international agreement would cost a leader her tenure in office, she does not cheat. Therefore, instances where we observe a leader being removed for cheating are extremely rare.

The term *audience costs* is commonly used to describe any costs leaders face as a result of their foreign policy decisions (Fearon 1994). Fearon argued that leaders involved in crises face domestic political repercussions from escalating crises and then subsequently backing down. He argued that democratic leaders, being more accountable, face higher audience costs than autocratic leaders. These higher costs enable democrats to more effectively commit themselves and help them prevail in crises and maintain cooperative agreements (Bueno de Mesquita and Lalman 1992; Eyerman and Hart 1996; Guisinger and Smith 2002; Leeds 1999; Mansfield, Milner, and Rosendorff 2002; Martin 1993; Partell and Palmer 1999; Schultz 1998, 1999, 2001, 2002; Smith 1998).

The basis articulation of audience cost theories simply asserts the existence of audience costs without deriving their origin within the political system. Unfortunately, this creates something of a time inconsistency problem in the credibility of the audience costs. Audience costs allow a leader to tie her own hands, thus enabling her to commit to a course of action that she would not otherwise take (Fearon 1997). Audience costs turn bluffs into credible commitments. However, should the commitment fail to get the opposing leader to concede, the citizens do not want the leader to carry out her stated policies. Yet it is the threat that the citizens will punish their leader that causes her to stay the course and enact the policies that she and the citizens do not want. For the citizens, enforcing audience costs is against their interests once a leader's bluff has failed. Leader specific punishment theory resolves this inconsistency because it simultaneously derives the origins of audience costs and their effect on bargaining and other relations between states.

Audience costs affect interstate relations by making it possible for leaders to commit to carry out threats or commit to cooperate (depending upon the context). Unfortunately, it is difficult to directly test the audience cost mechanism. The basic argument is that leaders face costs for taking particular actions. Unfortunately, we cannot effectively measure whether leaders are indeed punished for these actions. If audience cost theories are correct, democratic leaders who escalate crises and back down or who break agreements are likely to be punished domestically. However, the larger the audience cost is likely to be, the smaller the chance becomes that we actually observe the audience cost being imposed. This creates sample selection problems in that we can only assess audience costs when they are modest. Schultz (2001) demonstrates why this makes the direct observation of audience costs impossible (Gelpi and Grieco 2000) and why it creates biases in many other empirical tests.

One immediate criticism of leader specific punishment is the lack of direct evidence for it. Leaders who are easily deposed and who violate international agreements should be removed. Analyses of public opinion, such as Hermann and colleagues (2001), suggest it is indeed costly for leaders to violate agreements. Unfortunately, direct evidence of democratic leaders being removed for cheating should be (and is) rare. Such leaders are unlikely to cheat if it costs them their jobs. Throughout this book we offer examples of nondemocratic leaders cheating and the restorative effects of their subsequent replacement. We can offer far fewer examples of democrats cheating. This is precisely what the theory predicts. We cannot assess the impact of cheating on the domestic political tenure of democrats because democrats typically don't cheat.

DYNAMICS OF COOPERATION

The most novel and interesting hypotheses derived from leader specific theory concern the dynamics of leader change and interstate cooperation. To our knowledge, outside of our work, these dynamics have not been systematically explored before. Leader specific punishments endogenously provide opportunities to restore cooperative relations. It is individual leaders, rather than the nations they represent, who choose to cheat. It is, therefore, perhaps natural to expect that punishments are targeted against leaders.

If the leader of nation A adopts leader specific punishments against nation B and the leader of nation B cheats, then nation A withdraws cooperation, or otherwise imposes sanctions, until the leader in nation B changes. Leadership change refreshes sour relations as the following example illustrates. During the 1991 Gulf War, Jordan's King Hussein sided with Iraq. Although Jordan did not become involved militarily, it kept its border with Iraq open, making the enforcement of multilateral sanctions much more difficult. Jordan is relatively devoid of natural resources and has traditionally received substantial financial support from other, wealthier, Arab states. Most Arab states joined the U.S.-led coalition to remove the Iraqi forces that had occupied Kuwait. In retaliation for Jordan's support of Iraq, most Arab states cut off their traditional economic support for Jordan. The February 7, 1999, death of King Hussein provided the impetus to renew relations. Once Hussein's son ascended the throne, Arab states renewed their economic assistance despite few signals of policy change (*New York Times*, February 19, 1999. p. A3).

Leadership change brings about shifts in policy and reshapes external relations. These dynamics are not constant across all political systems, however. Domestic political institutions play an important role in determining the extent to which the citizens hold political leaders accountable for international outcomes. As we already argued, the greater ease of leader replacement in democratic nations encourages the citizens of these nations to replace their leader if she is caught cheating. The desire to avoid such a removal from office enables democratic leaders to commit to not cheat. This allows for greater levels of cooperation between democratic states than is possible between other pairs of nations. It also means that instances of sour relations between democratic nations are unlikely.

Further, leadership turnover in democratic states has little impact on the restoration of sour relations because it is unlikely that the relations were sour as a result of the democrat's actions in the first place.

DOMESTIC POLITICAL INSTITUTIONS

Thus far we have derived the effects of leader specific punishments on interstate relations in terms of the ease of domestic leader replacement. For convenience of language, we have substituted the term *democracy* for systems with *low cost of leader removal*. However, equating these terms is not strictly accurate. To our knowledge, political institutions are never classified as democracies on the basis of the ease of leader removal. To operationalize leader specific punishment theory we require a metric for the cost of leader removal. Bueno de Mesquita and his colleagues' (2003; hereafter BdM2S2) theory of selectorate politics, classifies institutions according to the size of the winning coalition (W)—the number of loyal supporters whom the leader needs to retain power—and the selectorate (S), the size of the group from which these supporters are drawn.

BdM2S2 argue that small winning coalitions systems, especially in the presence of a large selectorate, induce a strong loyalty norm toward the incumbent, which makes it relatively easier for such leaders to survive relative to leaders in large coalition systems. A leader's policies provide rewards for individual supporters (private goods) as well as public goods that benefit all members of society. The number of supporter whose loyalty a leader must maintain to survive in office shapes the balance of her policies between private rewards for her supporters and the provision of public goods. When a leader requires the support of only a small coalition to survive in office, she can effectively enrich this small group by providing them with private benefits and the particularistic policies they desire. However, as coalition size increases it becomes increasingly expensive for leaders to buy support with private goods, and leaders must rely increasingly on public goods to reward supports.

In large coalition systems most of a leader's resources and energy goes toward the provision of public goods. Although large coalition leaders provide their supporters with some of their particularistic wants, the focus of government policy is on good public policy. In a large coalition system members of an incumbent's coalition jeopardize relatively little if they defect to a political challenger. Although once in power the challenger is likely to reorganize his coalition of supporters and potentially replace the defector, the supporter has little to fear from being excluded from the coalition. In a large coalition system most of the rewards are provided in the form of public goods. All members of society benefit from these goods whether they are coalition members or not. Indeed, since private goods make up only a small proportion of the rewards in a large coalition system, those outside the coalition are only slightly worse off than those inside the coalition. Potential defectors have relatively little to fear from being excluded from the coalition and thus have little loyalty to the incumbent. If the challenger can better provide public goods (such as international cooperation), coalition members readily defect.

Small coalition systems engender a strong norm of loyalty toward the incumbent. The leaders of such systems predominantly rely upon private goods to reward their supporters. The welfare difference between those inside and those outside the winning coalition is therefore large. Supporters of the incumbent are reluctant to risk losing the highly valuable private goods the incumbent supplies. Although the challenger might offer a supporter huge rewards to defect, supporters are aware that once ensconced in power, the new leader is liable to reorganize a coalition. When the coalition size is small, so the leader needs only a limited number of supporters, and the selectorate is large, so the leader can choose the supporters from a large pool, then supporters recognize that there is a substantial chance of their being excluded from the coalition (and therefore from access to the valuable private goods) if they defect. When coalition size is small, such that access to private goods is very valuable and the risk of exclusion from the challenger's coalition is high, the incumbent's supporters are extremely loyal.

Selectorate politics, in the process of deriving the types of policies pursued under different political institutions, generates a metric for the ease of leader replacement. The selectorate model also suggests that leadership change in small coalitions produces much large variability in policies than occurs when leaders change in large coalitions. In large coalition systems leader survival is predicated on the effective provision of public goods. Leader change does not change this policy goal. The incoming leader, like his predecessor, enacts those policies that best further the interests of the nation at large. In contrast, small coalition leaders survive by pandering to interests of their small number of supporters. Providing rich rewards for these supporters is more important to a leader's survival than effective governance. However, since leader change often leads to a change in coalition membership, wild shifts in policy can occur as the incoming leader drops the particularistic interests of his predecessor's coalition and panders instead to the wants of his supporters.

The essential public goods focus of large coalition systems remains unchanged by leader change. Leader change therefore has relatively little impact on the relations between states. However, leader change in small coalitions creates great policy variability. This volatility potentially disrupts relations between states. For instance, trade can be severely disrupted as the government switches from favoring one sector of the economy to another.

The selectorate model of politics provides a metric for the cost of leader replacement that is an essential component of LSP theory. In chapter 2 we develop our leader specific punishment theory through a careful examination of the underlying assumptions of the theory and two formal models. These models relax the simplistic assumptions of the prisoners' dilemma game between representative leaders developed in this chapter. As noted above, the prisoners' dilemma makes the unrealistic assumptions of perfect observation of a binary action choice. The first model introduces randomness into the payoffs of the prisoners' dilemma and assumes that leaders face mortality risks. The second model is a continuous choice prisoners' dilemma model with noise. This is to say, a leader chooses an action on a continuum and the other leader cannot perfectly observe the leader's action. Instead each leader receives a noisy signal from the other leader's actions. The models formally derive the properties and dynamics of leader specific punishments to which we have informally alluded in this chapter. These models are developed in terms of the cost of leader replacement.

In chapter 3 we examine the selectorate model of politics and use it to link the cost of leader replacement, a vital component of LSP theory, with political institutions. The selectorate theory also generates an additional series of hypotheses concerning how political institutions affect the variability of policy change associated with leader change and its implications for international cooperation.

Broadly the theory predicts the following relationships between political institutions, leadership change, and interstate relations:

1. Nations with large winning coalitions maintain higher levels of cooperation than other nations.
2. Nations with small winning coalitions experience greater volatility in their external relations with other states than do nations with large coalition governments.
3. Leader change in a small coalition nation is more likely to alter interstate relations than is leader change in a large coalition system.
4. Leaders from small coalition systems are more likely to cheat on international agreements or otherwise incur the ire of the international community than are leaders from large coalition systems.
5. Leader turnover helps reinvigorate tarnished relations between states, although due to the selection effect that large coalition leaders are unlikely to take actions that lead to the breakdown of cooperation, this effect is only generally observed for small coalition leaders.

Chapters 4, 5, and 6 turn to testing the implication of the theory. Chapter 4 describes a series of human subject experiments designed to closely mirror the prisoners' dilemma game between representative leaders discussed in this chapter. The evidence from the experiments supports the intuitive plausibility of leader specific punishments. In particular we show that a change in leader reduces the dependence between the past history of play and a leader's choice, which aids in the restoration of cooperation. At least in the experimental setting, it appears that leader turnover helps rejuvenate previously sour relations.

Chapter 5 examines how institutions and leader change affect trade relations between nations. Our analyses of dyadic trade flows support theoretical predictions. Pairs of nations with large coalition systems experience greater trade than do other pairs of nations. The effects of leader change on trade flows depend strongly on political institutions. In large coalition systems, leader change has no appreciable affect on trade flows. However, as implied by the high policy volatility in small coalition systems, leader change in such systems substantially reduces trade. We code instances of sour relations between states by identifying collapses in the value of trade between nations. These collapses occur more often between trading partners that include small coalition systems rather than large coalition systems. Consistent with LSP, we find that during periods of sour relations, leadership turnover in small coalition states provides a major boost to trade.

Chapter 6 examines sovereign debt. The terms of sovereign debt depend upon the lenders' beliefs that they will be repaid. We examine the impact of leader specific punishment in the context of sovereign debt borrowing by developing a simple formal model of borrowing and repayment. Consistent with the themes developed throughout this book, LSP allows large coalition leaders to credibly commit to repay loans. We test the dynamic predictions of the theory using sovereign debt bond indices. These indices reflect changes in the willingness of investors to hold regularly traded U.S. dollar denominated sovereign debt bonds. In particular, we examine how institutions moderate how these indices respond to leader change. In large coalition systems leader change has no appreciable effect on the value of sovereign debt bonds. In contrast, in small coalition systems leadership change generally lowers the price of the index, reflecting a decreased willingness of investors to hold these bonds. After examining instances of sovereign default, we examine the effect of leadership change on the bond price. Consistent with LSP ideas, leadership change following default helps increase the value of sovereign debt bonds.

In chapter 7, we examine leader specific punishments in conflictual situations of crisis bargaining and economic sanctions. Through a discussion of a number of historical events we examine the impact of LSP within crises. We use McGillivray and Stam's (2004) analysis of leadership change and the termination of economic sanctions to motivate a discussion of LSP in economic warfare. Consistent with the anecdotal evidence offered in this chapter, leader turnover has a major impact in the termination of sanctions.

In chapter 8 we conclude by considering the broader policy implications of LSP theory. In particular, we address how leader specific punishments could improve the efficacy of a nation's foreign policy in crisis bargaining and lead to a deepening of cooperation and compliance within international agreements.

CHAPTER 2

A Theory of Leader Specific Punishments

LEADER CHANGE MATTERS. The dynamics of interstate relations are shaped by leadership turnover. However, the strength of the relationship between leader change and the pattern of interstate relations depends upon domestic political institutions. Changes in the U.S. president or the British prime minister have comparatively little impact on the United States' or Britain's external relations. However, in autocratic states, such as Cuba, leader turnover can drastically alter interstate relations. Fidel Castro's departure from office is likely to profoundly change U.S.-Cuban relations. In the introductory chapter we sketched leader specific punishment (LSP) theory. Here we formally develop our arguments, taking care to rigorously define our assumptions and explain the logic of our arguments.

Leader specific punishments result from the interaction of objects from different levels of analysis. Nations' foreign policies interact to determine international outcomes. Individual leaders pick foreign policies based upon how domestic political institutions shape political survival. Domestic political institutions determine the extent to which citizens hold leaders accountable for international outcomes. We develop our theory within the context of the following framework:

1. Leaders are office seeking. While leaders may care about other issues, their predominate concern is to retain office.
2. Political institutions affect the ease with which the citizens can replace their leader and the type of policies that leaders should use to best achieve their goal of survival in office.
3. Political leaders choose the foreign policy of their nation.
4. International outcomes depend upon the interaction of the foreign policy choices of leaders of each nation.
5. The citizens evaluate the policy performance of their political leader and, based upon the institutional context in which the leader serves, the citizens decide whether to retain or to replace their leader.

Our theory involves interactions from three levels of analysis. As a result, our arguments are necessarily involved. To ensure that we explain the working parts of our theory as clearly as possible, we started in the previous chapter with as sparse a model as possible. Spartan models help us understand the underlying features of a theory. Unfortunately, simplicity comes at the cost of reality.

The leader specific model in chapter 1 considered the simple interaction of PD between two nations. The model assumed a simple binary choice between two nations in an environment with perfect information, no variation, and no noise. The domestic setting assumed no policy divergence between members of each nation with everyone within a nation receiving the same payoff from the outcome of the prisoners' dilemma. Clearly these assumptions are massive simplifications of the real world. However, the simple model predicted cooperation over a greater range of conditions between democratic states than other pairing of states. Further, we informally extended the logic of the arguments to make predictions about patterns of leader survival and the dynamic of interstate cooperation. It is time to rigorously check the logic of these informal arguments by relaxing the assumptions in the basic model and check those intuitions in a more complex setting.

This chapter proceeds as follows. We reexamine the PD model by developing a stochastic prisoners' dilemma with leader mortality. In chapter 1 the simple PD model predicted that leader specific punishments allowed cooperation under a greater range of conditions between two states with accountable leaders than between other dyadic pairings of states. While the PD model provided intuitions about the dynamics of leader change and international cooperation, on the equilibrium path there is no change in behavior. Now, rather than consider an identical PD game in every period, we assume the payoffs of the PD vary period to period (Bendor 1987, 1993; Bendor, Kramer, and Stout 1991; Signorino 1996; Wu and Axelrod 1995). Additionally we subject leaders to an actuarial risk such that leadership turnover occurs within the model, although for reasons, such as mortality, that are exogenous to the outcomes of international interactions.

The prisoners' dilemma assumes the interactions of states are constrained to simple binary choices: to cooperate or not. Building on technology developed by Downs and Rocke (1995; see also Downs and Rocke 1990; Green and Porter 1984; Porter 1983), we develop a continuous choice prisoners' dilemma in which nations choose a level of cooperation. In this game we show that, using leader specific punishments, the extent to which nations can cooperate is strongly dependent upon domestic political institutions. While both these innovations to the PD model create more realistic models of international cooperation, both continue to assume that all the citizens of each state have identical preferences over policy outcomes. Indeed to this point, we have assumed no differences in domestic political institutions beyond their defining the cost of leader replacement. Chapter 3 uses the selectorate theory of politics (Bueno de Mesquita et al. 2003) to derive the relationship between institutions and the ease of leader removal.

| | | Leader β and Nation B | |
		Cooperate, C	Defect, D
Leader α	Cooperate, C	R, R	S, T$_B$
and	Defect, D	T$_A$, S	P, P
Nation A			

Figure 2.1. The stochastic prisoners' dilemma with leader mortality. ($T > R > P > S$ where $T_A = R + \varepsilon_A$ and $T_B = R + \varepsilon_B$ with $\varepsilon_A > 0$ and $\varepsilon_B > 0$ independently and identically distributed).

In addition to providing a metric for the cost of leader removal, the selectorate model predicts how institutions shape the types of policies leaders use to fulfill their goal of survival in office.

The selectorate model of domestic political survival and the models of international cooperation presented in this chapter provide predictions that we test in subsequent chapters.

A STOCHASTIC PRISONERS' DILEMMA WITH LEADER MORTALITY

In common with the PD model in chapter 1, we assume an infinitely repeated prisoners' dilemma interaction between nations A and B. In each period the current leaders in each of these states, labeled α and β, choose whether to cooperate (C) or defect (D). The relationship between foreign policy choices and actions are the same as in the standard PD game. As shown in figure 2.1, mutual cooperation (C,C) produces the payoff of R for each nation, and so forth. However, to reflect variation in incentives over time, the payoffs are not identical in every period. Specifically, we assume the temptation payoff (T) for each state varies over time. We index the temptation payoff for state A at time t as T_{At}.

The stage game proceeds as follows. First the leaders for each nation learn the temptation payoff for their nation in that period. We assume this information is private to each national leader, such that while leader α knows her temptation payoff she does not know leader β's temptation. However, both leaders (and the citizens) have common knowledge as to the distribution from which T is drawn. Specifically, we assume $T_{At} = R + \varepsilon_{At}$ where R is the reward for mutual cooperation and $\varepsilon_{At} > 0$ is identically and independently distributed according to the distribution function $F(x)$ (with associated density $f[x]$) in each period.[1] Having

---

[1] We assume that F(x) has the standard "nice" properties: continuity, differentiability, and full support.

learned their temptation payoff, leaders α and β play the PD game, choosing either C or D. The outcome of the game is revealed and all members of each nation receive the relevant PD payoff. In addition, each leader receives a payoff of Ψ to reflect the value of officeholding. The citizens in each state then independently decide whether to retain their leader or replace her at cost K_A or K_B, respectively. Following this endogenous retention decision, each leader faces an actuarial or mortality risk. This is to say, with probability ρ a leader survives to the next period. With probability $(1 - \rho)$ she dies. By the term *die*, we mean any kind of deposition that is exogenous to the leader being removed by the citizens as a result of her actions in the PD game. Once dead or removed from office, a leader receives a payoff of zero in each period. For the purposes of generating numerical examples, we assume that $R = 3$, $P = 2$, $S = 1$, and $F(x)$ is the exponential distribution, $F(x) = 1 - e^{-x}$. In the previous chapter and again later in this chapter when we develop the continuous choice model, we assume that once removed from office, a leader becomes a regular citizen and receives the payoffs from the prisoners' dilemma in future interactions. In the current case the leader could die, be removed for exogenous reasons, or be endogenously removed. Rather than deal with the technicalities of assigning different payoffs to each of these eventualities, we assume leaders receive no payoff once removed from office. However, the results of the model do not hinge on this assumption.

We analyze the game by considering analogous strategies to the Leader Specific Grim Trigger considered in chapter 1. There are two main differences in the equilibria between the stochastic game and simple PD game. First, the temptation payoff is random. Sometimes the temptation is sufficiently high that a leader takes the temptation even though it jeopardizes either future cooperation (if the cost of leader removal is high) or the leader's tenure in office (if the cost of leader replacement is low). The size of the temptation that is sufficient to cause a leader to defect rather than maintain cooperation depends upon the institutional context in which the leader serves. When the cost of leader removal is low, and hence citizens replace leaders who have cheated, the temptation required to induce a leader to defect is much higher than when the cost of leader removal is high.

Second, leaders face mortality in this more complex version of the PD. When nations play leader specific punishments, leadership change allows for the restoration of cooperation should nations be in the punishment phase. Unlike the simple version of PD, in the stochastic game, cheating and the restoration of cooperation occur on the equilibrium path. However, domestic political institutions shape the relative likelihood of these events.

Leader Specific Punishments in the Stochastic PD Game

We now characterize leader specific punishment strategies in the context of the stochastic PD game. Although we characterize equilibria under a variety of circumstances, all equilibria share several common features. First, the strategies we analyze are leader specific punishment strategies. That is to say, if leader β who represents nation B has ever cheated, then leader α refuses to cooperate with her and plays D. Leader α will however cooperate with β's successor who, after all, has not cheated. Leader α plays D once she has previously cheated since she knows that β will no longer cooperate. Given these leader specific punishments, once either leader has cheated, cooperation ends until the leader who cheated is removed, which can occur either because the citizens depose the leader or through the leader's death.

In the stochastic PD game the temptation to cheat varies. If the temptation payoff in some particular period is extremely high, then leader α might play D to obtain this temptation whatever the consequences are for future play. Remember that the temptation reward for nation A at time t is $T_{At} = R + \varepsilon_{At}$. The equilibria are characterized by a cut point threshold τ_A for leader α and τ_B for leader β. If in some particular period ε_{At} exceeds the threshold τ_A, leader α cheats and plays D. Similarly, if ε_{Bt} exceeds τ_B, β cheats.

The key substantively interesting feature is that the size of the temptation payoff required before leader α cheats—that is, τ_A—depends upon the ease with which the citizens in nation A can replace her. If the citizens face a high cost to deposing their leader, they do not remove her even if she has cheated. In this setting, once α cheats, she forgoes future cooperation. In contrast, when the cost of removing leader α is low, the citizens replace her to restore cooperation. Therefore, if leader α plays D to obtain the temptation reward, she is removed from office and loses all future access to officeholding benefits. Since the primary goal of leaders is to retain office, the threat of dismissal is a more powerful threat than the threat of the loss of future cooperation. Therefore, when a leader is easily removed, the temptation needed to cause the leader to cheat is much higher than when cheating does not jeopardize tenure in office.

Unfortunately, while these ideas appear straightforward to state in words, rigorously analyzing the stochastic PD game requires considerable technology. It is to the development of this formal technology that we now turn. The leader's choice to play C or D and the citizens' choice to depose their leader depends upon prior play of the game. Rather than condition these choices on the entire history of past play, we describe the relevant history as Markovian state variables and analyze Markovian strategies, that is, strategies conditioned only on these state variables that describe the relevant aspects of the prior play of leaders. We informally refer to the state variables, I^t_A and I^t_B, as the integrity of each nation at the start of period t. Initially both nations start with an honest integrity, $I^t_A = 0$ and $I^t_B = 0$, and retain their integrity provided they do not cheat the other nation. Once nation A loses its honest integrity, $I^t_A = 1$, it remains dishonest until leader α is replaced. Leader changeover restores a nation's integrity. In this context nation A's integrity can be thought of as belonging to the incumbent leader.

It should be noted that we use the terms *cheat, integrity,* and *honesty* as convenient ways to describe to play of the game. We imply no normative judgments by these terms. When we say that nation A has an honest integrity we mean simply that the incumbent leader has not cheated in the past. The fact that she might be an unscrupulous person who is prone to lying is irrelevant with respect to the current definition of integrity. As a precursor to what is to follow, however, our theory shows that whether a leader can be trusted depends more upon the institutions under which the leader serves than personal moral characteristics.

REPUTATION AND INTEGRITY

In formulating our model we consider a leader's integrity or reputation purely in terms of past behavior. Some care is needed here, however. In political science literature the term *reputation* is often associated with one player's attempting to shape the beliefs of another player about some underlying characteristic, such as how strong a nation is or its willingness to bear costs (Mercer 1996). For example, in Alt, Calvert, and Humes's (1988) model of hegemonic stability, a hegemon decides whether or not to punish a dissenting colony. Sometimes the hegemon can punish the colony very cheaply; at other times it can be more expensive. The hegemon, knowing its own strength, knows the likelihood that punishment will be cheap. In contrast, the colonies are uncertain whether the hegemon will frequently or infrequently be able to punish them at low cost.

When the hegemon decides whether or not to punish a dissenting colony, it does so knowing that other colonies are watching its decision and will base their future decisions to dissent on their beliefs about the relative likelihood that the hegemon can cheaply punish them. By punishing the first dissenting colony, the hegemon hopes to build a reputation for having a high chance of being able to punish cheaply in the future, as this will deter future dissent. Of course, in equilibrium, colonies discount the extent to which punishment signals a high probability that future punishment will be low cost because of this incentive for the hegemon to appear tough.

Alt, Calvert, and Humes's conception of reputation differs from the idea of integrity that we utilize here. Reputation building is an attempt to shift another player's beliefs about some underlying characteristic, the likelihood of low-cost punishment in Alt, Calvert, and Humes's case. Our concept of integrity does not rely upon beliefs about private information, but rather is simply a designation of whether a leader has previously lied or cheated. Milgrom, North, and Weingast's (1990) analysis of the role of law merchants in the revival of trade in medieval France utilizes integrity as a reputational mechanism. They use the prisoners' dilemma as the basis for a model of trade between relative strangers. The law merchant acts as a centralizing agent for collecting information on dishonest traders. For a fee the law merchant informs the potential traders if either of them is without integrity. Should either of the traders subsequently cheat, the other player can appeal to the law merchant, who can issue a fine against the cheater. If the cheater does not compensate the defrauded trader, the law merchant records his tarnished integrity, which effectively prevents him from being able to trade in the future. In the law merchant situation, a trader's reputation does not describe beliefs about his characteristics, but rather is simply a description of whether he has previously cheated.

The following exchange between Queen Victoria and her minister of foreign affairs, Lord Clarendon, over defining English obligations to support fellow European states during the tumultuous period of the late 1860s illustrates the distinction well. Victoria, fearing England was perceived as weak by both European rivals and allies, demanded greater intervention in European affairs. She wanted to shift other nations' beliefs about England's strength. She claimed that a lack of action on the part of England had encouraged its rivals in Europe to believe that "the aggressive Power may dismiss all fears of England across its path." In contrast, Clarendon's concerns were over integrity: "It would seem more honest and dignified on the part of England not to menace, if she is not sure of being able to strike, and not to promise more than she may be able to perform" (quoted in Baldelli 1998, p. 32).

The integrity variable at the start of period $t+1$ depends upon the integrity of the nations at time t and play during period t. L_A^t is a dummy variable to represent whether leader α is replaced either by the citizens or via mortality in period t: $L_A^t = 0$ indicates no leader change in state A, and $L_A^t = 1$ indicates leader turnover. Nation B has analogous notation. Formally we represent the evolution of the Markov state variable as follows:

$$I_A^{t+1} = \begin{cases} 0 & \text{if} & L_A^t = 1 \\ 1 & \text{if} & I_A^t = 1 \text{ and } L_A^t = 0 \\ 0 & \text{if} & I_A^t = 0 \text{ and } I_B^t = 1 \\ 0 & \text{if} & I_A^t = 0, I_B^t = 0 \text{ and } \alpha \text{ plays } C \\ 1 & \text{if} & I_A^t = 0, I_B^t = 0, L_A^t = 0 \text{ and } \alpha \text{ plays } D \end{cases}$$

This can be stated in words as follows. First, if leader replacement occurs in nation A, then A's integrity is restored. Second, if leader α has cheated in the past ($I_A^t = 1$), then nation A remains dishonest if leader α remains leader. Third, if nation A has an honest integrity but nation B has dishonest integrity, then whatever the play of the PD game, nation A retains its integrity. Fourth, if both nations have honest integrity and leader α plays C in the PD game, then nation A remains honest. However, fifth, under this later contingency if leader α plays D and remains as leader, then nation A loses its integrity.

We analyze Markovian strategies, meaning that a player's choice of action is conditioned only on Markovian state variables. In the stochastic PD game, when leader α decides whether to cooperate or defect, there are three relevant state variables: her integrity, leader β's integrity, and the temptation payoff, $T_{At} = R + \varepsilon_{At}$. We focus on the following Markovian leader specific punishment strategy (MLSP), which we describe for leader α.

(1) If $I_A^t = 0$, $I_B^t = 0$, and $\varepsilon_{At} \leq \tau_A$, then leader α plays C.

(2) If either $I_A^t = 1$, $I_B^t = 1$, or $\varepsilon_{At} > \tau_A$, then leader α plays D.

This means α cooperates provided neither leader has ever cheated before and the temptation is not too large. If either leader has ever cheated or the temptation is too large, leader α defects.

We now characterize Markov Perfect Equilibria (MPE) that utilize MLSP strategies and the conditions under which they exist. An MPE is a subgame perfect equilibrium in which strategies are contingent only on Markovian state variables. MPE are a proper subset of Subgame Perfect Equilibria. In the main text we characterize two such equilibria. In the first equilibrium, in neither nation do the citizens ever replace their leader. In this case the costs of leader replace are too high to justify renewing cooperation. The citizens prefer to forgo future cooperation. In the second equilibrium, the cost of replacing leaders is lower and the citizens in both nations replace those leaders who cheat. In the appendix we formally characterize a "mixed" case, where the citizens in nation A replace their leader for cheating but the citizens of nation B do not. We also consider a unitary actor equivalent of the stochastic PD game. We use comparable numerical examples of each of these four equilibria to discuss the impact of domestic political institutions on cooperation, the survival of political leaders, and the dynamics between leader turnover and the restoration of cooperation.

HIGH COST OF LEADER REPLACEMENT

When the cost of leader replacement is sufficiently high, citizens never replace their leader. The leaders use MLSP. Should leader α cheat and play D

with the intention of obtaining the temptation payoff, then future cooperation ceases. Since leaders value future cooperation, they are reluctant to cheat and do so only when the temptation payoff is sufficiently large. Once a leader cheats, cooperation ceases until that leader is replaced through mortality.

Proposition 2.1: *Leader Specific Punishments in the Stochastic PD with High Cost Leader Replacement (Equilibrium 2.1):*

If $K_A \geq \delta V_A^{00} - \delta \rho_A V_A^{10} - \delta(1 - \rho_A) V_A^{00}$ and $K_B \geq \delta V_B^{00} - \delta \rho_B V_B^{10} - \delta(1 - \rho_B) V_B^{00}$, then leader α plays C if $I_A^t = 0$, $I_B^t = 0$, and $\varepsilon_{At} \leq \tau_A$, and plays D if either $I_A^t = 1$, $I_B^t = 1$, or $\varepsilon_{At} > \tau_A$; leader β plays an analogous strategy and the citizens never replace their leaders is a Markov Perfect Equilibrium, where $\tau_A \geq 0$ is given by the solution to equation 2.1, where a solution exists and $\tau_A = 0$ otherwise:

$$
\begin{aligned}
\Psi + F(\tau_B)(R + \tau_A) &+ (1 - F(\tau_B))P + \delta \rho_A V_\alpha^{1\cdot} \\
&= F(\tau_B)(R + \Psi + \delta \rho_A V_\alpha^{00}) \\
&\quad + (1 - F(\tau_B))(S + \Psi + \delta \rho_A (\rho_B V_\alpha^{01} + (1 - \rho_B) V_\alpha^{00}))
\end{aligned}
\tag{EQ 2.1}
$$

where the continuation values of the citizens are

$$
V_A^{11} = P + \delta(\rho_A \rho_B V_A^{11} + \rho_A(1 - \rho_B)V_A^{10} + (1 - \rho_A)\rho_B V_A^{01} + (1 - \rho_A)(1 - \rho_B)V_A^{00}),
$$
$$
V_A^{01} = P + \delta(\rho_B V_A^{01} + (1 - \rho_B)V_A^{00}), \quad V_A^{10} = P + \delta(\rho_A V_A^{10} + (1 - \rho_A)V_A^{00}),
$$
$$
V_A^{01} = P + \delta(\rho_B V_A^{01} + (1 - \rho_B)V_A^{00}), \text{ and}
$$
$$
\begin{aligned}
V_A^{00} = {}& F(\tau_A)F(\tau_B)(R + \delta V_A^{00}) \\
&+ (1 - F(\tau_A))F(\tau_B)(R + \int_{\tau_A}^\infty \varepsilon f(\varepsilon)d\varepsilon + \delta \rho_A V_A^{10} + \delta(1 - \rho_A)V_A^{00}) \\
&+ (1 - F(\tau_B))F(\tau_A)(S + \delta \rho_B V_A^{01} + \delta(1 - \rho_B)V_A^{00}) \\
&+ (1 - F(\tau_A))(1 - F(\tau_B))(P + \delta \rho_A \rho_B V_A^{11} + \delta \rho_A(1 - \rho_B)V_A^{10} \\
&+ \delta(1 - \rho_A)\rho_B V_A^{01} + \delta(1 - \rho_A)(1 - \rho_B)V_A^{00}).
\end{aligned}
$$

The continuation values for leader α are

$$
V_\alpha^{10} = V_\alpha^{11} = V_\alpha^{1\cdot} = \frac{P + \Psi}{1 - \delta \rho_A}, \quad V_\alpha^{01} = P + \Psi + \delta \rho_A (\rho_B V_\alpha^{01} + (1 - \rho_B)V_\alpha^{00}), \text{ and}
$$
$$
\begin{aligned}
V_\alpha^{00} = {}& F(\tau_A)F(\tau_B)(R + \Psi + \delta \rho_A V_\alpha^{00}) \\
&+ F(\tau_A)(1 - F(\tau_B))(S + \Psi + \delta \rho_A (\rho_B V_\alpha^{01} + (1 - \rho_B)V_\alpha^{00})) \\
&+ (1 - F(\tau_A))F(\tau_B)(R + \Psi) + F(\tau_B)\int_{\tau_A}^\infty \varepsilon f(\varepsilon)d\varepsilon \\
&+ (1 - F(\tau_A))F(\tau_B)\delta \rho_A V_\alpha^{11} \\
&+ (1 - F(\tau_A))(1 - F(\tau_B))(P + \Psi) + (1 - F(\tau_A))(1 - F(\tau_B))\delta \rho_A V_\alpha^{11}.
\end{aligned}
$$

Proof: We now prove the claim, taking time as we do so to explain the logic of the argument. MPE requires that no player can improve her payoff through a one-period deviation from the equilibrium path in any (Markovian) state. In order to proceed, we calculate the value each player receives from playing the game on the equilibrium path starting from each state. Having calculated these continuation values, we show that no player profits from deviating from the equilibrium path.

We start by calculating the continuation values for leader α for playing the game starting at the beginning of each period for each state. We use the notation $V_\alpha^{I_A I_B}$ to represent the value of the game to leader α given states I_A and I_B. If leader α has previously cheated ($I_A = 1$), then no leader in nation B will ever cooperate with her; hence her continuation values are

$$V_\alpha^{10} = V_\alpha^{11} = P + \Psi + \delta\rho_A(P+\Psi) + \delta^2\rho_A^2(P+\Psi) + \ldots = \frac{P+\Psi}{1-\delta\rho_A}.$$

This reflects that in each future period that she survives, α receives the punishment payoff (P) and officeholding payoff Ψ; α survives with probability ρ_A; and payoffs are discounted with discount factor δ.

If leader β has previously cheated ($I_B = 1$) but α has not ($I_A = 0$), then α's continuation value is $V_\alpha^{01} = P + \Psi + \delta\rho_A(\rho_B V_\alpha^{01} + (1-\rho_B)V_\alpha^{00})$. Given β's past cheating, in the current period neither leader will cooperate, so α receives the punishment payoff P and the office reward Ψ. With probability ρ_A, α survives to the next period. The value of game starting in the next period depends upon whether leader β is replaced. Since the citizens in nation B do not replace β, leader replacement occurs in nation B only through exogenous means. With probability ρ_B leader β survives, in which case the value of the game in the next period to α is V_α^{01}. If, however, leader β dies, which occurs with probability $(1-\rho_B)$, then nation B's integrity is restored and cooperation restarts so the payoff for the game starting next period for leader α is V_α^{00}.

If neither leader has ever cheated then leader α's continuation payoff is

$$
\begin{aligned}
V_\alpha^{00} &= F(\tau_A)F(\tau_B)(R+\Psi+\delta\rho_A V_\alpha^{00}) \\
&\quad + F(\tau_A)(1-F(\tau_B))(S+\Psi+\delta\rho_A(\rho_B V_\alpha^{01} + (1-\rho_B)V_\alpha^{00})) \\
&\quad + (1-F(\tau_A))F(\tau_B)(R+\Psi) + F(\tau_B)\int_{\tau_A}^\infty \varepsilon f(\varepsilon)d\varepsilon \\
&\quad + (1-F(\tau_A))F(\tau_B)\delta\rho_A V_\alpha^{11} \\
&\quad + (1-F(\tau_A))(1-F(\tau_B))(P+\Psi) + (1-F(\tau_A))(1-F(\tau_B))\delta\rho_A V_\alpha^{11}.
\end{aligned}
$$

This continuation value deserves explanation. Given her honest integrity, unless the temptation reward is sufficiently large, $\varepsilon_{At} > \tau_A$, leader α

plays C. However, when the temptation reward is larger than τ_A, then α plays D. Therefore, prior to learning the value of ε_{At}, α plays C with probability $F(\tau_A) = \Pr(\varepsilon_{At} \leq \tau_A)$ and cheats with probability $(1 - F(\tau_B))$. Likewise β plays C with probability $F(\tau_B)$ and plays D with probability $(1 - F(\tau_B))$. The first term of the continuation value, $F(\tau_A)F(\tau_B)(R + \Psi + \delta\rho_A V_\alpha^{00})$, refers to the case where both leaders play C. In this case, α receives $R + \Psi$ in the immediate period and survives with probability ρ_A to receive the (discounted) continuation value V_α^{00} for the game starting next period.

The second term, $F(\tau_A)(1 - F(\tau_B))(S + \Psi + \delta\rho_A(\rho_B V_\alpha^{01} + (1 - \rho_B)V_\alpha^{00}))$, refers to the case where α plays C and β plays D. This occurs with probability $F(\tau_A)(1 - F(\tau_B))$. α's payoff for this eventuality is $S + \Psi$ in the immediate period plus either discounted V_α^{01} or V_α^{00} for the game starting in the next period, should she survive. Whether α receives V_α^{01} or V_α^{00} for the game starting next period depends upon whether leader β dies. Given that β cheats in the current period, if β survives (which occurs with probability $(1 - \rho_B)$), then the state in the next period is $I_A = 0$, $I_B = 1$. If, however, β dies, then cooperation is not interrupted. The third term, $(1 - F(\tau_A))F(\tau_B)(R + \Psi) + F(\tau_B)\int_{\tau_A}^\infty \varepsilon f(\varepsilon)d\varepsilon + (1 - F(\tau_A))F(\tau_B)\delta\rho_A V_\alpha^{11}$, relates to the case where α cheats and β does not. This occurs with probability $(1 - F(\tau_A))F(\tau_B)$. In this case leader α receives $T_{At} + \Psi$ in the immediate period. Given that α only cheats when $\varepsilon_{At} > \tau_A$, the expected value of T_{At} under this contingency is

$$R + \int_{\tau_A}^\infty \varepsilon \frac{f(\varepsilon)}{1 - F(\tau_A)} d\varepsilon.$$

Having cheated in the current period, leader α cannot cooperate, so the continuation value associated with surviving to the next period is V_α^{10}. The fourth term, $(1 - F(\tau_A))(1 - F(\tau_B))(P + \Psi) + (1 - F(\tau_A))(1 - F(\tau_B))\delta\rho_A V_\alpha^{11}$, represents the contingency that both α and β cheat. In the current period α receives $P + \Psi$ and the value of the game in the next period, should α survive, is V_α^{11}. Given the above derivation of the continuation value in each state, we can test the optimality of α's decisions. First, we consider the straightforward cases of α's best response given prior cheating. If either $I_A = 1$ or $I_B = 1$, then leader β plays D. Given that under either of these contingencies α integrity in future periods is unaffected by play today, α's best response is to play D.

If neither leader has cheated, $I_A = 0$ and $I_B = 0$, then α's payoff from playing C is

$$U_\alpha(C \mid I_A = 0, I_B = 0, \varepsilon_{At}) = F(\tau_B)(R + \Psi + \delta\rho_A V_\alpha^{00})$$
$$+ (1 - F(\tau_B))(S + \Psi + \delta\rho_A(\rho_B V_\alpha^{01} + (1 - \rho_B)V_\alpha^{00})).$$

This expression is composed of two terms. The first term refers to the contingency that leader β also chooses to cooperate, which occurs with probability $F(\tau_B)$: α's payoff is $R + \Psi$ in the immediate period, and the value of playing the game tomorrow (if α survives) is V_α^{00}. The second terms represents the contingency that β plays D, which occurs with probability $(1 - F(\tau_B))$. The payoff for this event is an immediate reward of $S + \Psi$, and the discounted continuation value associated with future play should α survive. Since β cheats under this contingency, the continuation value will be V_α^{01} unless β should die and be replaced (in which case the relevant continuation value is V_α^{00}). It is worth noting that α's expected payoff from playing cooperation is constant in ε_{At}.

If alternatively leader α plays D then α's payoff is

$$U_\alpha(D \,|\, I_A = 0, I_B = 0, \varepsilon_{At}) = F(\tau_B) T_{At} + (1 - F(\tau_B)) P + \Psi + \delta \rho_A V_\alpha^{1\cdot}$$
$$= \Psi + F(\tau_B)(R + \varepsilon_{At}) + (1 - F(\tau_B)) P + \delta \rho_A V_\alpha^{1\cdot}.$$

Again this expression depends upon two contingencies; one relates to β playing C and the other relates to β playing D. If β plays D, which occurs with probability $(1 - F(\tau_B))$, then α's immediate payoff is $P + \Psi$. With probability $F(\tau_B)$, β plays C and so α's immediate payoff associated with playing D is $T + \Psi$. Once β plays D, she loses her integrity, so the continuation value associated with future play is $V_\alpha^{1\cdot}$. Since if α cheats she obtains the payoff $T_{At} = R + \varepsilon_{At}$ with probability $F(\tau_B)$, α's payoff from playing D is linearly increasing in ε_{At}.

Since α's payoffs associated with playing both C and D are continuous but only the payoff associated with playing D is increasing, then either $U_\alpha(D \,|\, I_A = 0, I_B = 0, \varepsilon_{At}) > U_\alpha(C \,|\, I_A = 0, I_B = 0, \varepsilon_{At})$ for all $\varepsilon_{At} \geq 0$ or there exists a value of ε_{At} that equates these payoffs. Equation 2.1 defines τ_A for the latter contingency. Under the former contingency we define $\tau_A = 0$. When $\varepsilon_{At} > \tau_A$, then α plays D. When $\varepsilon_{At} \leq \tau_A$, then α plays C. The proposition specifies best responses for leader α for every state given the strategies of the other players. The case for leader β is symmetric.

Next we examine the citizens' decision to retain leader α. If without leadership turnover the state at the beginning of the next period will be $I_A^{t+1} = 0$, then deposing leader α only imposes the cost K_A on the citizens but does not change the prospects of future cooperation. Hence the citizens do not depose their leader under this contingency. Next we consider the contingency that without leadership turnover the state at the beginning of the period will be $I_A^{t+1} = 1$. This contingency arises if either $I_A^t = 1$ or ($I_B^t = 0$ and α plays D). We consider the case that $I_B^t = 0$ and leader β played C (i.e., the case where $I_B^{t+1} = 0$). If leader β has also lost her integrity, then replacing leader α is less attractive because cooperation does not necessarily resume. If the citizens replace α, then they pay the cost K_A and the continuation value associated with play next period is V_A^{00}: $U_A(deposition \mid I_A = 1)$ or (α plays D and $I_B = 0$)) $= -K_A + \delta V_A^{00}$. If alternatively the citizens retain α, then unless leader α dies, cooperation in the next period ceases. In particular, $U_A(retain \mid I_A = 1)$ or (α plays D $I_B = 0$)) $= \delta \rho_A V_A^{10} + \delta(1 - \rho_A)V_A^{00}$. We adopt analogous notation for the continuation values associated with the citizens as we did for the leaders. These continuation values are

$$V_A^{11} = P + \delta(\rho_A \rho_B V_A^{11} + \rho_A(1 - \rho_B)V_A^{10} + (1 - \rho_A)\rho_B V_A^{01} + (1 - \rho_A)(1 - \rho_B)V_A^{00}),$$

$$V_A^{10} = P + \delta(\rho_A V_A^{10} + (1 - \rho_A)V_A^{00}), \quad V_A^{01} = P + \delta(\rho_B V_A^{01} + (1 - \rho_B)V_A^{00}), \text{ and}$$

$$V_A^{00} = F(\tau_A)F(\tau_B)(R + \delta V_A^{00})$$

$$+ (1 - F(\tau_A))F(\tau_B)\left(R + \int_{\tau_A}^{\infty} \varepsilon f(\varepsilon)d\varepsilon + \delta \rho_A V_A^{10} + \delta(1 - \rho_A)V_A^{00}\right)$$

$$+ (1 - F(\tau_B))F(\tau_A)(S + \delta \rho_B V_A^{01} + \delta(1 - \rho_B)V_A^{00})$$

$$+ (1 - F(\tau_A))(1 - F(\tau_B))(P + \delta \rho_A \rho_B V_A^{11} + \delta \rho_A(1 - \rho_B)V_A^{10}$$

$$+ \delta(1 - \rho_A)\rho_B V_A^{01} + \delta(1 - \rho_A)(1 - \rho_B)V_A^{00})$$

where $\overline{\varepsilon_A} = \int_{\tau_A}^{\infty} \varepsilon f(\varepsilon)d\varepsilon$.

By the terms of the proposition, if $K_A \geq \delta V_A^{00} - \delta \rho_A V_A^{10} - \delta(1 - \rho_A)V_A^{00}$, then the citizens' best response is to retain α. Therefore, the citizens in nation A play optimal strategies in every state given the strategies of the other players. Parallel arguments apply for the citizens in state B. Since there are no utility improving deviations for any player in any state, the strategies stated in the propositions are MPE. QED.

LOW COST OF LEADER REPLACEMENT

We now turn immediately to the case of low leader replacement cost. Given this low cost of leader removal, the citizens replace any leader who cheats. If a leader cheats, she is removed from office. Since leaders predominately care about holding office, compared to the case above where leaders are not replaced, the threshold τ_A beyond which leaders cheat is much higher. Therefore leaders are less likely to cheat and so cooperation is less likely to break down.

Proposition 2.2: *Leader Specific Punishments in the Stochastic PD with Low Cost Leader Replacement (Equilibrium 2.2):*
    If

$$K_A \leq \frac{V_A^{00}\delta(1 - \delta) - P\delta\rho_A}{1 - \delta^2 \rho_A} \quad \text{and} \quad K_B \leq \frac{V_B^{00}\delta(1 - \delta) - P\delta\rho_B}{1 - \delta^2 \rho_B},$$

then the strategy that leader α plays C if $I_A^t = 0$, $I_B^t = 0$, and $\varepsilon_{At} \leq \tau_A$, and plays D if either $I_A^t = 1$, $I_B^t = 1$ or $\varepsilon_{At} > \tau_A$; and the citizens in nation A replace leader α if either $I_A^t = 1$ or ($I_B^t = 0$ and α plays D), (leader β and the citizens in B play analogous strategies) is a Markov Perfect Equilibrium, where $\tau_A \geq 0$ is given by the solution to the equation where a solution exists and $\tau_A = 0$ otherwise:

$$\delta \rho_A V_\alpha^{00} + F(\tau_B)R + (1 - F(\tau_B))S = F(\tau_B)(R + \tau_A) + (1 - F(\tau_B))P. \quad \text{(EQ 2.2)}$$

Where
$$\begin{aligned}
V_\alpha^{00} &= F(\tau_A)F(\tau_B)(R + \Psi + \delta \rho_A V_\alpha^{00}) \\
&\quad + F(\tau_A)(1 - F(\tau_B))(S + \Psi + \delta \rho_A V_\alpha^{00}) \\
&\quad + (1 - F(\tau_A))F(\tau_B)\left(R + \Psi + \int_{\tau_A}^\infty \frac{f(\varepsilon)}{1 - F(\tau_A)} \varepsilon d\varepsilon \right) \\
&\quad + (1 - F(\tau_A))(1 - F(\tau_B))(P + \Psi) \text{ and} \\
V_A^{00} &= F(\tau_A)F(\tau_B)(R + \delta V_A^{00}) + F(\tau_A)(1 - F(\tau_B))(S + \delta V_A^{00}) \\
&\quad + (1 - F(\tau_A))F(\tau_B)(R - K_A + \delta V_A^{00}) + F(\tau_B)\int_{\tau_A}^\infty f(\varepsilon)\varepsilon d\varepsilon \\
&\quad + (1 - F(\tau_A))(1 - F(\tau_B))(P - K_A + \delta V_A^{00}).
\end{aligned}$$

Proof: As with the previous proposition, we start by examining leader α's continuation values associated with playing the game given each state. If leader α has previously cheated $I_A^t = 1$, then β plays D and her citizens depose her. Therefore, the continuation value $V_\alpha^{11} = V_\alpha^{10} = P + \Psi$. If α has an honest integrity but β does not, then in the current period both α and β play D, the citizens in B remove β and so cooperation starts in the next period: $V_\alpha^{01} = P + \Psi + \delta \rho_A V_\alpha^{00}$. If neither leader has previously cheated, then

$$\begin{aligned}
V_\alpha^{00} &= F(\tau_A)F(\tau_B)(R + \Psi + \delta \rho_A V_\alpha^{00}) + F(\tau_A)(1 - F(\tau_B))(S + \Psi + \delta \rho_A V_a^{00}) \\
&\quad + (1 - F(\tau_A))F(\tau_B)\left(R + \Psi + \int_{\tau_A}^\infty \frac{f(\varepsilon)}{1 - F(\tau_A)} \varepsilon d\varepsilon \right) \\
&\quad + (1 - F(\tau_A))(1 - F(\tau_B))(P + \Psi).
\end{aligned}$$

The first term corresponds to both α and β playing C. In this case, which occurs with probability $F(\tau_A)F(\tau_B)$, α receives the immediate payoff of $R + \Psi$ and continuation value V_α^{00} if she survives. The second term corresponds to the case where α plays C but β cheats. In this case α receives the sucker's payoff in the current period, but cooperation resumes immediately because the citizens in nation B replace β immediately. The latter two terms correspond to the contingency that α cheats. In the immediate period she gains either $T_{At} + \Psi$ or $P + \Psi$ (depending on β's play), but receives no future rewards, as her citizens immediately depose her.

We now examine the optimality of α's strategy. If there has been any prior cheating (either $I_A^t = 1$ or $I_B^t = 1$), then β plays D. Therefore, α's best response is D. Suppose instead that no prior cheating ($I_A = 0$, $I_B = 0$) has occurred. If α cheats, she receives the immediate payoff of either $\Psi + R + \varepsilon_{At}$ if β plays C (which occurs with probability $F(\tau_B)$) or $P + \Psi$ if β plays D (which occurs with probability $1 - F(\tau_B)$). α receives no future payoffs, as she is immediately removed from office. Therefore, α's expected payoff from playing D is

$$U_\alpha(D \mid I_A = 0, I_B = 0, \varepsilon_{At}) = F(\tau_B)(\Psi + R + \varepsilon_{At}) + (1 - F(\tau_B))(\Psi + P).$$

This payoff is continuous and linearly increasing in ε_{At}.

If α plays C then she maintains her integrity, and so the continuation value for the next period is V_α^{00}, if she survives. Therefore,

$$U_\alpha(C \mid I_A = 0, I_B = 0, \varepsilon_{At}) = \Psi + \delta \rho_A V_a^{00} + F(\tau_B)R + (1 - F(\tau_B))S.$$

This payoff is constant in ε_{At}. Given that $U_\alpha(D \mid I_A = 0, I_B = 0)$ is linearly increasing in ε_{At}, either there exists a point τ_A that equates

$$U_\alpha(C \mid I_A = 0, I_B = 0, \varepsilon_{At}) \text{ and}$$

$$U_\alpha(D \mid I_A = 0, I_B = 0, \varepsilon_{At}) \text{ or}$$

$$U_\alpha(C \mid I_A = 0, I_B = 0, \varepsilon_{At}) < U_\alpha(D \mid I_A = 0, I_B = 0, \varepsilon_{At})$$

for all $\tau_A \geq 0$. Equation 2.2 defines τ_A in the former case and $\tau_A = 0$ in the latter case.

Next we examine the citizens' decision to retain leader α. If without leadership turnover the state at the beginning of the next period will be $I_A^{t+1} = 0$, then deposing leader α only imposes the cost K_A on the citizens but does not change the prospects of future cooperation. Hence the citizens do not depose their leader. However, if either $I_A^t = 1$ or ($I_B^t = 0$ and α plays D), then the state next period will be $I_A^{t+1} = 1$ unless α is deposed. For the citizens of A the expected value of deposing α is $U_A(depose \mid .) = -K_A + \delta V_A^{00}$. Remember that on the equilibrium path the citizens in B always depose their leader if she has cheated, so the citizens in A know that replacing α guarantees the ending of the punishment phase. If, however, the citizens retain α, then their payoff is $U_A(retain \mid .) = \delta \rho_A(P - \delta K_A + \delta V_A^{00}) + \delta(1 - \rho_A)\delta V_A^{00}$. The first term refers to the eventuality that leader α does not die. In this case there is no cooperation in the next period, and the citizens replace α in this next period.

The second term refers to the contingency that leader α dies, in which case cooperation is restored immediately. Provided that $U_A(\textit{depose}\,|.) \geq U_A(\textit{retain}\,|.)$, the citizens depose α if she has cheated. This condition implies deposition only if

$$K_A \leq \frac{V_A^{00}\delta(1-\delta) - P\delta\rho_A}{1-\delta^2\rho_A}.$$

The continuation value associated with state $I_A^t = 0, I_B^t = 0$ is

$$V_A^{00} = F(\tau_A)F(\tau_B)(R + \delta V_A^{00}) + F(\tau_A)(1 - F(\tau_B))(S + \delta V_A^{00})$$

$$+ (1 - F(\tau_A))F(\tau_B)(R - K_A + \delta V_A^{00}) + F(\tau_B)\int_{\tau_A}^{\infty} f(\varepsilon)\varepsilon\, d\varepsilon$$

$$+ (1 - F(\tau_A))(1 - F(\tau_B))(P - K_A + \delta V_A^{00}).$$

Analogous conditions apply to β and nation B. Since each player plays best responses in every state, the strategies described in the proposition are MPE. QED.

In the appendix we characterize a mixed case where nation A has a low cost for leader removal and nation B has a high cost for leader removal. Unlike the cases characterized here, the game is no longer symmetric such that the τ_A that characterizes leader α's strategy is larger than the τ_B that characterizes leader β's strategy.

The Influence of Domestic Political Institutions and Leader Turnover on Patterns of Cooperation

The formal analyses above characterize leader specific punishment strategies in the stochastic prisoners' dilemma game. It is time to consider the substantive importance of these results. In the stochastic PD game, the temptation payoffs vary with each interaction. Sometimes relatively little might be gained from cheating a partner; in other cases the potential rewards might be huge. The equilibria characterize a threshold level, τ_A. If the temptation, ε_{At}, in a particular period is greater than this threshold, then leader α plays D. Similarly if $\varepsilon_{Bt} > \tau_B$, then leader β cheats. Once a leader cheats, neither nation will cooperate until that leader is removed.

Table 2.1 shows a numerical example of the four equilibria calculated assuming $R = 3$, $P = 2$, $S = 1$, $\Psi = 5$, $\rho_A = 0.9$, $\rho_B = 0.9$ and $F(x) = 1 - e^{-x}$. In this table, the label Cut Point Thresholds gives the thresholds, τ_A and τ_B, associated with each equilibrium. Since in the absence of prior cheating by either leader, leaders cooperate providing $\varepsilon_{At} \leq \tau_A$ and ε_{At} is

TABLE 2.1

Numerical Examples of MPE for the Stochastic Prisoners' Dilemma with
Leader Mortality

Case	Equilibrium	Cut Point Thresholds	Cost of Leader Removal	Probability of Cooperation Breakdown
High Cost of Leader Removal	1	$\tau_A = \tau_B = 1.1794$	$K_A \geq 0.788$ $K_B \geq 0.788$	0.520 per period
Low Cost of Leader Removal	2	$\tau_A = \tau_B = 34.105$	$K_A \leq 3.985$ $K_B \leq 3.985$	3.086×10^{-15} per period
Mixed Case: Removal Cost is High in A and Low in B.	3	$\tau_A = 34.257$ $\tau_B = 4.320$	$K_A \geq 0.392$ $K_B \leq 4.320$	0.013 per period
Unitary Actor	4	$\tau_A = \tau_B = 1.284$	N/A	0.477 per period

Note: Examples constructed assuming $R = 3$, $P = 2$, $S = 1$, $\Psi = 5$, $\delta = 0.9$, $\rho_A = 0.9$, $\rho_B = 0.9$, $F(x) = 1 - \exp(-x)$, and $f(x) = \exp(-x)$.

distributed $F(x)$ then it is straightforward to calculate the probability of cooperation breakdown in each period. These probabilities are shown in the final column. The column labeled "Cost of Leader Removal" calculates the range of leader removal costs that are consistent with each case. We use these numerical examples to motivate our discussion of leader specific punishments.

Domestic political institutions affect the ease with which cooperation is maintained through leader specific punishments. When the cost of leader removal is low in both nations (equilibrium 2.2), cooperation hardly ever breaks down. In the example, leader α does not cheat unless the temptation is excess of $\varepsilon_{At} > 34.105$. The likelihood of this occurring is so low that the expected time until any breakdown of cooperation occurs is too large to calculate on a calculator. In contrast, when the cost of leader removal is high in both nations (equilibrium 2.1), then leader α cheats if $\varepsilon_{At} > 1.179$, which occurs with probability 0.308. Since leader β cheats with a similar likelihood, the probability of cooperation breakdown in any period is 0.520. These examples make stark the distinctions that domestic political institutions make to the maintenance of cooperation between states.

Cooperation is much easier to maintain when the cost of leader removal is low. Under leader specific punishments once leader α cheats, cooperation ends. To restore cooperation, the citizens in nation A depose leader α if she cheats. Cheating costs leader α all her future officeholding benefits. If, as we believe, these officeholding benefits are a political leader's primary motivation, then the temptation reward the leader needs to obtain from putting her tenure in office in jeopardy must be huge. In contrast, when removing leaders is difficult, as in equilibrium 2.1, cheating does not cost a leader her tenure in office. Under this contingency, once leader α cheats, cooperation ceases for the rest of her term in office. While leader α would prefer to be able to cooperate in the future, this opportunity is worth much less than her hold on power. As the example shows, maintaining an honest integrity is worth relatively little, since cooperation is so unreliable anyway. Indeed, even if neither leader has previously cheated, leader α can expect leader β to cheat about 30 percent of the time. Since cooperation is unlikely to be maintained in the long run anyway, it does not take much of a temptation before leader α chooses to defect.

In equilibrium 2.1 the citizens do not depose leaders who cheat. This equilibrium occurs if $K_A \geq 0.788$. In equilibrium 2.2, which occurs if $K_A \leq 3.985$, the citizens depose leaders who cheat. As this example makes clear, there is a range of removal cost parameters under which both equilibria exist, specifically $3.985 \geq K_A \geq 0.788$. We now examine the citizens' decision to replace leaders who cheat. In this model, leaders do nothing except play the PD game. Since it is costly to replace a leader, unless the leader has cheated and hence cannot cooperate in the PD game again, the citizens have no incentive to replace their leader. If, however, their leader has cheated in the past, then by replacing her, the citizens can restore cooperation. Whether the citizens choose to do so depends upon the cost of leader replacement and the quality of the cooperation they restore. In equilibrium 2.2 the restoration of cooperation is valuable. Indeed, once restored, cooperation continues nearly indefinitely. By replacing a leader who has cheated, the citizens can obtain the reward payoff R in practically every future period. Provided that $K_A \leq 3.985$, the citizens are willing to pay to restore cooperation.

In equilibrium 2.1 the citizens are less willing to pay to replace a leader in order to restore cooperation because cooperation is much less valuable. As discussed above, in equilibrium 2.1 cooperation is much less robust and can be expected to last only on average about two periods. Since the citizens gain less by restoring cooperation in equilibrium 2.1 than in equilibrium 2.2, even a relatively modest removal cost deters the citizens from replacing their leader. As we shall vehemently argue in the final chapter, this result suggests that even if citizens do not currently remove leaders who cheat on agreements because the value of the agreements is insufficiently large, if leaders emphasized the leader specific nature of punishment in future agreements, then they could commit to much deeper and more reliable cooperation, and the citizens would then want to punish leaders who cheated.

The pattern of cooperation and leader turnover differs between equilibrium 2.1 and 2.2. In equilibrium 2.1 cooperation breakdown is common.

Further, once cheating has occurred, the punishment phase continues until the leader who cheated is removed. Since in this setting the citizens do remove the leader to restore cooperation, this means cooperation ceases until the offending leader dies or is removed through some other exogenous mechanism. With leader replacement, cooperation restarts. In contrast, in equilibrium 2.2 instances of cheating are extremely rare. Should cheating occur, the citizens quickly replace their leader to maintain cooperation. Any breakdown in cooperation is likely to be short.

In summary, when the citizens do not replace leaders who cheat, cooperation breakdowns are likely to be relatively frequent and leader turnover reinitiates cooperation. When citizens replace leaders who cheated, instances of cheating are relatively rare. What is more, such cheating does not lead to the breakdown of cooperation, since the citizens depose the responsible leader to maintain cooperative relations. Hence, paradoxically, it is in the high cost case where citizens do not replace leaders that we are most likely to observe leadership turnover restore cooperation. When citizens would replace leaders to restore cooperation, instances of cheating are rare and often do not lead to cooperation breakdown because the responsible leader is quickly replaced.

So far we have compared only the cases of both nations removing leaders who cheat with the case of neither nation removing a leader who cheats. We now discuss equilibrium 2.3, the mixed case where the citizens in nation A replace their leader if she cheats, but the citizens in nation B do not. The cut point thresholds for cheating in this case are $\tau_A = 34.257$ and $\tau_B = 4.320$. Interestingly, both these thresholds are higher than in the corresponding symmetric cases. Although in equilibrium 2.3, leader β does not risk her tenure in office for cheating, she does jeopardize future cooperation. Relative to the case of equilibrium 2.1, the value of this future cooperation is higher since now its cooperative partner is extremely unlikely to cheat. Since cooperation is more valuable, it requires a larger temptation to induce cheating. As a result β cheats with only probability 0.013 per period.

From leader α's perspective, the quality of cooperation in the mixed case is worse than in equilibrium 2.2 because although β cheats only about 1.3 percent of the time, in equilibrium 2.2 leader β practically never cheated. However, this relative decline in the quality of cooperation has little effect on α's decision to cheat because for leader α the cost of cheating is the loss of office, not the loss of cooperation. The reason for α's even greater reluctance to cheat in equilibrium 2.3 relative to equilibrium 2.1 is that in equilibrium 2.3 there is a 1.3 percent chance that β simultaneously cheats, and under this contingency leader α receives only the P payoff for defecting.

Next we consider the citizens' decision to replace their leader should she cheat. In equilibrium 2.1, the lower bound on the cost of leader removal that induced the citizens to retain their leader even though she cheated is $K_B \geq 0.788$. In equilibrium 2.3 the comparable bound is $K_B \geq 4.320$. The cost required to deter citizens from replacing their leader in equilibrium 2.3 needs to be much higher than in equilibrium 2.1. The reason is that the quality of cooperation in equilibrium 2.3 is much higher than it is in equilibrium 2.1. The upper bound on the cost of leader removal in equilibrium 2.2 is higher than the corresponding bound in equilibrium 2.3. From the perspective of nation A, the quality of cooperation is worse in equilibrium 2.3 than in equilibrium 2.2, and therefore the citizens are willing to pay only a relatively smaller amount to restore cooperation. These differences in the bounds of removal costs suggest some implications as to when leaders would be removed for cheating.

A leader in a low removal cost nation is more likely to be removed for cheating another nation with low removal costs than she is to be removed for cheating a nation with high removal costs. Similarly, in a nation with high leader removal costs, a leader is more likely to be removed for cheating a low removal cost nation than for cheating a fellow high removal cost nation.

In equilibrium 2.3 it is leader β from a high replacement cost nation who is the more likely leader to cheat. Specifically, β cheats with probability 0.013, while α cheats with only probability 1.326×10^{-15}. Hence the likely pattern of cooperation between mixed systems is occasional cheating by the high removal cost nation with cooperation restored following leader turnover in the high cost nation.

Through our analysis of the stochastic PD game with leader mortality, we generate predictions as to how domestic political institutions shape the dynamics of cooperation and leader turnover. Cooperation is far more robust between nations where leader removal is easy. Unfortunately, these analyses only examined the robustness of a fixed level of cooperation; they did not speak directly to the depth of possible cooperation. Although the current model and the basic game in chapter 1 give us some intuition as to cooperation depth, we now address this issue directly.

A CONTINUOUS CHOICE PRISONERS' DILEMMA

Although the PD is a useful metaphor for international cooperation, many policy decisions are a question of degree rather than a straightforward cooperate or defect decision. (This section draws heavily on McGillivray and Smith 2005.) For instance, in international trade, nations decide the extent to which they discriminate against foreign goods. In the context of a common pool resource problem, such as a fishery, nations choose how many fish to allow their nationals to catch. In the context of externality problems, such as the release of pollutants, nations decide on how closely to regulate their industries.

Decisions on these policy areas, and many others, cannot easily be conceptualized as dichotomous choices. However, these issues share many features of the basic PD setup. Nations wish to cooperate on such issues. They desire open trading regimes, abundant fish stock, and a clean environment. Yet, while nation A wants nation B to lower its barriers to trade, catch fewer fish, and release fewer pollutants, nation A does not want to completely reduce its trade barriers, fish catches, or pollution levels. Nation A prefers nation B to make the greater contribution to the public benefit. Similarly, nation B prefers that nation A shoulders the greater proportion of the load. In this context, these problems of collective action resemble the prisoners' dilemma. Each nation prefers to free ride on the efforts of others, but nations are better off if they agree to cooperate.

As in the PD framework, reciprocal punishment strategies can enforce cooperation in the context of continuous choice problems. We utilize Downs and Rocke's (1995) framework. Nation A chooses P_A and nation B chooses P_B. These levels of P might be thought of as each nations' catch of fish or the level of pollutants released. However, for convenience of language, we will often refer to P in the context of trade as a level of protection. Without any cooperation, each nation is myopically protectionist and sets trade to $P = 100$. This is the Nash equilibrium level. Both sides benefit if they both reduce protection, but as in the PD game, if A reduces its protection but B does not, then B is even better off (the temptation payoff) and A is worse off than if no cooperation had occurred (the sucker's payoff).

Nations can use reciprocal strategies to enforce cooperation. Suppose the nations agree to cooperate by both reducing protection to $P = 90$. Once nation A reduces its barriers to trade, nation B wants to renege on the agreement. However, if nation A adopts the strategy of entering the punishment phase and refusing to cooperate with B for T periods if nation B ever sets protection above 90, then by failing to honor the agreement and obtaining the temptation reward for one period, nation B forgoes the benefits of cooperation for T periods. The logic for reciprocal punishments in continuous games is similar to the logic in the PD game.

Unfortunately, the real world is a noisy place. Nation A cannot perfectly observe the level of protection that nation B sets. Neither can A perfectly observe how many fish nation B catches or the amount of pollution B releases. A's estimates of B's actions are noisy. Although nation B chooses policy P_B, nation A observes $Q_B = P_B + \varepsilon$ where ε is random noise that is distributed with distribution $F(x) = Pr(\varepsilon \leq x)$. In particular, we assume $F(x)$ is the normal distribution with mean 0 and variance σ^2. In this

TABLE 2.2

Payoff from Various Levels of Cooperation in the Continuous Choice
Prisoners' Dilemma

		Nation B's Protection Level, P_B		
		100	*50*	*0*
Nation A's	100	0, 0	300, $-2{,}500$	1,100, $-10{,}000$
Protection	50	$-2{,}500$, 300	50, 50	3,100, $-5{,}200$
Level, P_A	0	$-10{,}000$, 1,100	$-5{,}200$, 3,100	100, 100

setting reciprocal strategies become problematic because if A observes Q_B
more than 90, A does not know if B really violated the agreement or A
simply saw a noisy signal of B's honest behavior. The ambiguity this noise
creates places a severe limit on the level of cooperation that nations can
obtain. However, when leader replacement is easy, leader specific punishments allow an enormous improvement in the level of cooperation that
can be obtained between nations relative to the maximum possible level
of cooperation between unitary actor states.

To explain the logic of the argument we build on a model of cooperation by Downs and Rocke (1995; see also Downs and Rocke 1990; Porter
1983; Green and Porter 1984). Downs and Rocke axiomize the properties
of the PD game in the continuous choice setting. Using a Taylor series
approximation around the noncooperative Nash equilibrium, they state
the shape of utility functions that satisfy these properties (1995, pp. 101–
104). They also state a specific utility function to construct their examples.
Although our arguments readily generalize to a broad range of utility
functions, throughout we focus on their specific example. In particular,
nations A and B pick levels of production P_A and P_B ($P_i \in \Re^+$) and receive
payoffs of $U_A(P_A, P_B) = -(P_B - 100) - (P_A - 100)^2 + 0.9(P_A - 100)(P_B -
100) + 0.1(P_B - 100)^2$ and $U_B(P_A, P_B) = -(P_A - 100) - (P_B - 100)^2 + 0.9(P_A -
100)(P_B - 100) + 0.1(P_B - 100)^2$ in each round. The game is infinitely
repeated and payoffs are discounted according to a common discount factor δ. Table 2.2 illustrates the properties of the utility functions for some
selected values of protection levels P_A and P_B.

In single shot play the unique subgame perfect equilibrium is
$P_A^* = 100$ and $P_B^* = 100$, which results in payoffs of $U_A(P_A^*, P_B^*) = 0$ and
$U_B(P_A^*, P_B^*) = 0$. As table 2.2 shows, both nations gain from a mutual reduction in protection. Yet, as cooperation deepens and P is lowered, each
side gains enormously from defecting. In general for any given level of
P_B, A's best response is $BR_A(P_B) = 55 + 0.45\, P_B$. Hence at maximum cooperation (0,0), A's optimal defection is to set $P_A = 55$, which produces

payoffs of 3,125 and −5,702.5. As cooperation deepens, the temptation to cheat and the cost of being exploited become huge.

We now embed the continuous choice PD within a model of domestic competition. The game is infinitely repeated, with the following stage game:

1. α and β, the leaders of nations A and B respectively, play the continuous choice prisoners' dilemma. In particular, they pick a level of protection P_A and P_B, respectively. The actual production P_A and P_B remain private information for α and β. However, their observed actions Q_A and Q_B become publicly observable to all players.

2. At cost K_A and K_B respectively, the citizens of A and B can replace their respective leaders. These choices are made independently.

3. All players receive payoffs. In addition to the payoff from the continuous choice PD, leaders receive a payoff of Ψ if they retain office.

Enforcing Cooperation through the Threat of Withdrawing Future Cooperation

The basic logic of reciprocal punishments remains the same in the continuous choice game as in the binary choice PD. Each nation specifies a threshold beyond which it treats the other nation as cheating. For example, nation A states, perhaps implicitly, that if it observes nation B's policy Q_B above the threshold H_A, then it will regard nation B as having cheated and enter the punishment phase and withdraw cooperation for the next T periods of play. Note that in contrast to earlier games, here we consider a potentially finite punishment period.

Although nation A cannot perfectly observe B's policy choice, its threat to withdraw future cooperation if B's observed policy choice is above the threshold shapes B's policy choice. Leader β faces a dilemma. As leader β increases policy, P_B, nation B gains greater rewards. Increasing P_B, however, increases the risk that nation B's policy will violate the threshold: $Q_B > H_A$. Leader β sets policy to tradeoff these risks and benefits. When leader replacement is difficult, being caught in violation of the threshold leads to T periods of noncooperation. In contrast, if leaders use LSP strategies and the cost of leader removal is low, then once leader β is caught in violation of the threshold, her citizens remove her to maintain cooperation. Since officeholding is the primary motive of leaders, the consequences of being caught cheating are much more severe in the latter case than in the former. If leader β is easily removed and faces LSP from the other nation, then β sets policy P_B well below the threshold H_A to reduce the probability of being caught cheating. This desire to set policy low to avoid being caught cheating enables large coalition leaders to credibly commit to high levels of cooperation.

Again, it is convenient to introduce the notation I_A^t to indicate the integrity or standing of nation A's leader at the end of period t. We utilize the idea of leader specific punishments. If α, the incumbent leader in nation A, is caught cheating, nation B refuses to cooperate with this leader for T periods. However, punishments are leader specific. Nation B will immediately restart cooperation with nation A if the incumbent who cheated is replaced.

At the start of the game or following the replacement of A's leader, nation A is in "good standing," $I_A^t = 0$. The evolution of A's integrity is as follows:

$$
I_A^t = \begin{cases}
0 & if & \text{leader } \alpha \text{ is replaced in period } t \\
0 & if & I_A^{t-1} = 0, \text{ and } Q_A \leq H_B \\
0 & if & I_A^{t-1} = 0 \text{ and } I_B^{t-1} > 0 \\
T & if & \alpha \text{ retained, } I_A^{t-1} = 0, I_B^{t-1} = 0 \text{ and } Q_A > H_B \\
I_A^{t-1} - 1 & if & \alpha \text{ retained, } I_A^{t-1} > 0.
\end{cases}
$$

In words, this means that A maintains a good standing ($I_A^t = 0$) if its leader is replaced, if A is observed to have cooperated $Q_A \leq H_B$, or if B is in poor standing, ($I_B^t > 0$). If both leaders are in good standing and α is observed to cheat ($Q_A > H_B$), then for the next T periods A is in poor standing, $I_A^t > 0$.

As is common in infinitely repeated games, although the statement of the equilibrium is complex, the path of play is straightforward. Therefore we briefly describe the key features of the path of play for each of two scenarios: high and low cost of replacing leaders.

When the cost of replacing leaders is high, the citizens do not replace leaders in poor standing since the benefits of immediately restoring cooperation are too small to justify the cost of changing the leader. This case effectively reduces to the unitary actor scenario, and the only incentive to maintain cooperation is the loss of T future periods of cooperation.

When the cost of replacing leaders is low, citizens replace leaders who are caught cheating. By doing so, the citizens ensure continued cooperation. Since leaders primarily care about keeping their jobs, they are careful to avoid being caught cheating. This desire to avoid cheating allows leaders to commit to maintain a level of commitment that the citizens themselves could not maintain.

We now characterize MPE that use LSP. We state the strategy for nation A and leader α. B's strategy is analogous. These equilibria characterize, $\tilde{P}$, the level of protectionism that is maintained in equilibrium. We start by considering the cases where the cost of leader removal is high.

Proposition 2.3: *(High removal cost)*

If

$$K_A \geq U_A(\tilde{P}_A, \tilde{P}_B)\frac{\delta - \delta^{T+1}}{1 - \delta + (\delta - \delta^{T+1})p_A}$$

and $\tilde{P}$ satisfies equation 2.3 below, where

$$p_A = 1 - F(H_B - \tilde{P}_A) \quad \text{and} \quad p_B = 1 - F(H_A - \tilde{P}_B),$$

then the following is a Markov perfect equilibrium:

(1) If both leaders are in good standing ($I_A^{t-1} = 0$ and $I_B^{t-1} = 0$) then α plays $P_A = \tilde{P}$. If either leader is in poor standing ($I_A^{t-1} > 0$ or $I_B^{t-1} > 0$) then $P_A = P_A^* = 100$.

(2) The citizens retain leader α.

$$D\frac{dU_A(\tilde{P}_A, \tilde{P}_B)}{dP_A} - U_A(\tilde{P}_A, \tilde{P}_B)\frac{dp_A}{dP_A}(1 - p_B)(\delta - \delta^{T+1}) = 0 \quad \text{(EQ 2.3)}$$

where $D = (1 - (1 - p_A)(1 - p_B)\delta - (1 - (1 - p_A)(1 - p_B))\delta^{T+1})$

Proof: see Downs and Rocke 1995, 1990; Porter 1983; Green and Porter 1984. We discuss the key aspects of the proof below.

Proposition 2.4: *(Low removal cost)*

If

$$K_A \leq U_A(\tilde{P}_A, \tilde{P}_B)\frac{\delta - \delta^{T+1}}{1 - \delta + (\delta - \delta^{T+1})(1 - F(H_B - \tilde{P}_A))}$$

and $\tilde{P}_A$ satisfies equation 2.4, then the following strategy is a Markov perfect equilibrium:

(1) If both leaders are in good standing ($I_A^{t-1} = 0$ and $I_B^{t-1} = 0$) then α plays $P_A = \tilde{P}_A$. If either leader is in poor standing ($I_A^{t-1} > 0$ or $I_B^{t-1} > 0$), then $P_A = P_A^* = 100$.

(2) If both players are in good standing and α is not observed cheating ($I_A^{t-1} = 0, I_B^{t-1} = 0$ and $Q_A \leq H_B$), then the citizens in nation A retain leader α. If α and β are in good standing ($I_A^{t-1} = 0, I_B^{t-1} = 0$) but α is observed to cheat ($Q_A > H_B$), then A replaces α. If α is in poor standing ($I_A^{t-1} > 0$) then A deposes α if

$$K_A \leq \delta U_A(\tilde{P}_A, \tilde{P}_B)\frac{1 - \delta^{I_A^{t-1}}}{1 - \delta + \delta p_A(1 - \delta^{I_A^{t-1}})}$$

and retains α otherwise.

$$\tilde{P}_A \in \arg\max_{P_A \in \Re^+} U_A(\underline{P_A}, \tilde{P}_B) + F(H_B - \underline{P_A}) \frac{\Psi}{1 - \delta F(H_B - \tilde{P}_A)}$$

$$+ \frac{\delta}{1-\delta} U_A(\tilde{P}_A, \tilde{P}_B) \qquad\qquad \text{(EQ 2.4)}$$

Corollary: *For an interior solution* $\tilde{P}_A \leq H_B$, *equation 2.4 implies*

$$\frac{d}{d\tilde{P}_A} U_A(\tilde{P}_A, \tilde{P}_B) - \Psi\left(\frac{F'(H_B - \tilde{P}_A)}{1 - \delta F(H_B - \tilde{P}_A)}\right) = 0 \qquad\qquad \text{(EQ 2.5)}$$

We discuss the most salient feature of the proof below with the remaining details considered in the appendix.

The Logic of Cooperation in the Continuous Choice PD

Here we explore the logic behind the propositions stated above.

HIGH COST OF LEADER REPLACEMENT

The following analysis largely reproduces Downs and Rocke (1995, p. 97). We start by deriving the value of playing the game starting with both sides in good standing ($I_A^{t-1} = 0, I_B^{t-1} = 0$). Provided this good standing is maintained, α and β play $P_A = \tilde{P}$ and $P_B = \tilde{P}$. Given these levels of production, the probability of A accidentally being observed to cheat is $p_A = \Pr(Q_A > H_B) = \Pr(P_A + \varepsilon_A > H_B) = \Pr(\varepsilon_A > H_B - P_A) = 1 - F(H_B - P_A)$. Similarly, the chance B being caught "cheating" is $p_B = 1 - F(H_A - P_B)$.

Using recursion, the value of playing $P_A = \tilde{P}_A$ and $P_B = \tilde{P}_B$ can be calculated as

$$V_A = U_A(\tilde{P}_A, \tilde{P}_B) + (1 - p_A)(1 - p_B)\delta V_A$$

$$+ (1 - (1 - p_A)(1 - p_B))\left(\frac{\delta - \delta^{T+1}}{1-\delta} U_A(P_A^*, P_B^*) + \delta^{T+1} V_A\right).$$

The first term represents the value of the game in the current period. The second term is the discounted value of the game multiplied by the probability that neither side is observed cheating. The final term is the probability that one side is observed to cheat multiplied by the payoff of the noncooperative outcome for the next T periods before the restoration of cooperation. α also receives the office holding benefit Ψ in every period. Yet, since

α receives this payoff regardless of her action, we have excluded it from the calculation. Utilizing the normalization that $U_A(P_A^*, P_B^*) = 0$, the expression for V_A reduces to

$$V_A = \frac{U_A(\tilde{P}_A, \tilde{P}_B)}{(1-(1-p_A)(1-p_B)\delta-(1-(1-p_A)(1-p_B))\delta^{T+1})}.$$

In its choice of $\tilde{P}_A$, A faces a trade-off. Nation A increases its immediate payoff by increasing P_A; doing so, however, increases the risk of cooperation breakdown. The following first order condition ensures these incentive are exactly balanced and is the basis of equation 2.3:

$$\frac{dV_A}{dP_A} = \frac{1}{D^2}\left(D\frac{dU_A(P_A, \tilde{P}_B)}{dP_A} - U_A(P_A, \tilde{P}_B)\frac{dp_A}{dP_A}(1-p_B)(\delta-\delta^{T+1})\right) = 0,$$

where D is the denominator in the expression of V_A. While this FOC is complicated, Downs and Rocke have calculated the best possible treaties under a variety of parameters.

Next we examine the citizens' decision to retain their leader. If the incumbent is caught cheating in the current period (assuming both leaders are otherwise in good standing), then the citizens can expect T period of noncooperative behavior before the restoration of cooperation. Thus, the value of retaining a leader who has just been caught cheating is

$$\frac{\delta-\delta^{T+1}}{1-\delta}U_A(P_A^*, P_B^*)+\delta^{T+1}V_A = \delta^{T+1}V_A.$$

Alternatively, if the citizens remove their leader (at a cost of K_A), they can immediately restore their nation's good standing. The payoff from this is $-K_A + \delta V_A$. Provided that $K_A > V_A(\delta-\delta^{T+1})$, the citizens never replace their leader.[2]

LOW COST OF LEADER REPLACEMENT

When the cost of leader replacement is low, citizens depose leaders caught cheating in order to avoid the suspension of cooperation. Given the

---

[2] Note that since the citizens do not replace their leader facing T periods of punishment, they would not want to remove their leader when facing fewer than T periods of punishment. That is, if the citizens were to replace their leader, they would do so immediately.

threshold, H_B, if leader α chooses an output level of P_A, then she is observed to cheat with probability $p_A = Pr(Q_A > H_B) = Pr(\varepsilon_A > H_B - P_A) = 1 - F(H_B - P_A)$. Similarly, β's chance of being caught cheating is $p_B = 1 - F(H_A - P_B)$. Given the citizens' replacement strategy if a leader is caught cheating then she is immediately removed and cooperation continues.

Hence, in equilibrium if α and β choose effort levels $\tilde{P}_A$ and $\tilde{P}_B$ then α's expected value of playing the game (starting with a good standing) is

$$V_\alpha = \frac{1}{1-\delta} U_A(\tilde{P}_A, \tilde{P}_B) + \sum_{t=1}^{\infty} (1 - p_A)^t \delta^{t-1} \Psi$$

$$= \frac{1}{1-\delta} U_A(\tilde{P}_A, \tilde{P}_A) + \frac{F(H_B - \tilde{P}_A)}{1 - \delta F(H_B - \tilde{P}_A)} \Psi.$$

We define V_α more precisely in the appendix. The first term represents the payoff from the cooperative outcome of the continuous choice PD in every period. Remember that even if the leader is removed, she still continues to receive the payoff from cooperation under the next leader. The second term represents the net present value from officeholding given that the leader retains office with probability $(1 - P_A)$ in each period.

We now examine α's choice of optimal P_A in the immediate period. We do so mindful that in all future periods α or any successor will play $\tilde{P}_A$. If $\tilde{P}_A$ is an equilibrium strategy, then it must be the optimal strategy to pick it in the immediate round given it will be played in all future rounds and given the strategies of other players. Specifically, we need to ensure there is no one period defection that α prefers in the immediate round given that she (or any replacement) intends to play $\tilde{P}_A$ in the future. α's payoff from playing $P_A = \underline{P}_A$ in the immediate period is

$$EU_\alpha(\underline{P}_A; \tilde{P}_A, \tilde{P}_B) = U_A(\underline{P}_A, \tilde{P}_B) + F(H_B - \underline{P}_A)[\Psi + \delta V_\alpha]$$

$$+ (1 - F(H_B - \underline{P}_A)) \left[\frac{\delta}{1-\delta} U_A(\tilde{P}_A, \tilde{P}_A) \right].$$

The first term represents α's immediate payoff from the current period's play of the continuous PD, given α's choice of P_A. The second term is the probability that α is not observed cheating (given her choice $\underline{P}_A$) multiplied by the value of retaining office this period and the expected value of playing the game in future periods (V_α). The final term is the probability that α is caught cheating (given her choice $\underline{P}_A$) multiplied by the value of cooperation in all future periods under new leadership. Substituting V_α into this expression yields

$$EU_\alpha(\underline{P}_A; \tilde{P}_A, \tilde{P}_B) = U_A(\underline{P}_A, \tilde{P}_B) + F(H_B - \underline{P}_A)\frac{\Psi}{1 - \delta F(H_B - \tilde{P}_A)}$$

$$+ \frac{\delta}{1-\delta}U_A(\tilde{P}_A, \tilde{P}_A).$$

If $\underline{P}_A = \tilde{P}_A$ is a best response given B's strategy, the citizens' strategy and play in future rounds, then there is no one round defection that improves α's payoff:

$$\tilde{P}_A \in \arg\max\nolimits_{\underline{P}_A \in \Re^+} EU_\alpha(\underline{P}_A; \tilde{P}_A, \tilde{P}_B).$$

This represents equation 2.4.

For an interior solution, equation 2.4 implies the first order condition given in equation 2.5 and the following second order conditions:

$$\frac{d^2}{d\tilde{P}_A^2}U_A(\tilde{P}_A, \tilde{P}_B) + F''(H_B - \tilde{P}_A)\frac{\Psi}{1 - \delta F(H_B - \tilde{P}_A)} < 0.$$

For the case of ε_i being normally distributed, $P_A \leq H_B$ is a sufficient condition to ensure the SOC is met; hence the corollary.

We now move to the citizens' decision to remove their leader. We start by calculating the citizens' value for having a leader in good standing:

$$V_{cA} = \frac{1}{1-\delta}U_A(\tilde{P}_A, \tilde{P}_B) - \frac{K_A}{1-\delta}p_A.$$

The first term is the expected reward from the continuous choice PD game. The second term represents future expected costs of removing leaders caught cheating, which in each period occurs with probability

$$p_A = 1 - F(H_B - \tilde{P}_A).$$

Suppose A's leader has just been caught cheating ($Q_A > H_B$). If the citizens of A retain their leader, then they anticipate T periods of noncooperation before the restoration of cooperation, the net present value of which is

$$\sum_{t=1}^{T} \delta^t U_A(P_A^*, P_B^*) + \delta^{T+1} V_{cA} = \delta^{T+1} V_{cA}.$$

If alternatively the citizens replace their leader at a cost of K_A, then cooperation immediately resumes, which is worth $-K_A + \delta V_{cA}$. Substituting for V_{cA}, this implies that, provided that

$$K_A \leq U_A(\tilde{P}_A, \tilde{P}_B) \frac{\delta - \delta^{T+1}}{1 - \delta + (\delta - \delta^{T+1}) p_A}$$

$$= U_A(\tilde{P}_A, \tilde{P}_B) \frac{\delta - \delta^{T+1}}{1 - \delta^{T+1} + (\delta^{T+1} - \delta) F(H_B - \tilde{P}_A)},$$

the citizens of nation A replace α if she is caught cheating. While this condition is illustrative of the cost at which citizens replace leaders, the formal characterization of the equilibrium requires a more careful exposition, which we present in the appendix.

POLITICAL INSTITUTIONS AND THE DEPTH OF COOPERATION

When leaders use LSP, the incentives to cooperate depend upon the cost of leader removal. When the cost of leader removal is high, leaders jeopardize T periods of future cooperation if they are caught cheating. When leader removal is easy, citizens replace leaders caught cheating to restore cooperation. In this setting leaders jeopardize their tenure in office if they cheat. Since officeholding is the primary motive of leaders, the threat of losing office is far more salient than the threat of losing future cooperation. This enables leaders who are easily removed to commit to a far greater depth of cooperation than can leaders who cannot be easily replaced. Figure 2.2 graphically demonstrates how political institutions shape the maximum depth of cooperation.

Figure 2.2 plots the minimum level of protection that can be supported in equilibrium under different contingencies as the amount of noise becomes small: $\sigma \rightarrow 0$. The upper two lines represent the high removal cost scenario, with punishment periods of a single period ($T = 1$) and indefinite punishment ($T = \infty$). The two lower lines correspond to cases of easy leader removal with differing values for officeholding: $\Psi = 100$ and

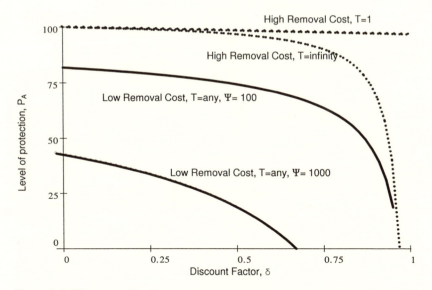

Figure 2.2. The ease of leader removal and the depth of cooperation in the continuous choice PD game.

$\Psi = 1,000$. The length of the punishment period does not affect the leader's ability to commit to cooperate in the latter cases because the leader is removed immediately by the citizens. The lines represent the minimum level of protection (i.e., the maximum level of cooperation) that the nations can agree to credibly implement given the discount factor. The Nash equilibrium level of protection is $P_A = 100$. Cooperation is agreement to reduce protection below this base level.

The top line considers the case of a single period punishment and high leader replacement costs. In this setting if A's protectionism is observed above H_B, then B withdraws cooperation for a single period. As the figure shows, the threat of losing a single period of cooperation is insufficient to support all but minimal cooperation. As shown, the lowest protection level P_A, supportable even by very patient nations, is only slightly less than the noncooperative Nash case of $P_A = 100$. When the threatened punishment is small, leaders can commit to only minimal reductions in protection.

Increasing the length of the punishment phase increases the size of the threatened punishment. This allows for greater reductions in protection. The second line on figure 2.2 corresponds to the indefinite withdrawal of cooperation in response to observed cheating. Since cheating in this scenario permanently jeopardizes cooperation, leaders can commit to reduce protection further than in the first case. Indeed, as leaders become extremely patient, $\delta \geq 0.968$, then leaders could commit to completely remove protection and fully cooperate,

$$\tilde{P}_A = 0.$$

Unfortunately, maintaining high levels of cooperation in the high removal cost case requires long punishment and patient nations.

Leader specific punishments in the low removal cost setting allow high levels of cooperation even when leaders heavily discount the future, as shown by the two lower lines in figure 2.2. The two lines differ by the value of officeholding: $\Psi = 100$ (third line down) and $\Psi = 1,000$ (lowest line). While these officeholding values might appear large, they are of the order of magnitude of the value of agreements. Remember, complete cooperation by each side ($P_A = P_B = 0$) is worth 100 per period relative to the single shot Nash equilibrium, and the temptation to defect under this circumstance is worth 3,125. When leaders care about officeholding and citizens can remove leaders easily, then far deeper cooperative arrangements can be reached and achieving these deals does not require extremely high patience.

Figure 2.2 shows clearly that in the low noise world, leader specific punishments allow for much deeper cooperation when leaders are easily replaced. These results hold even as we increase the amount of noise. For our simulations, we assume the observational errors are normally distributed with variance $\sigma^2 = 1$. Downs and Rocke (1995, pp. 98–99) provide tables on the limits of cooperation. For instance, with a discount factor of $\delta = .9$, they find no cooperative agreement is possible for short punishment periods; however, with an infinite punishment ($T = \infty$), the limit on cooperation is $P_A = P_B = 75.8$. In contrast, leader specific punishment supports full cooperation, $P_A = P_B = 0$, at $\delta = 0.9$ if $\Psi = 1,000$. This full cooperation is achieved by setting a threshold of $H = 2.667$.[3] Under this circumstance, leader α will accidentally be caught "cheating" 0.4 percent of the time. To ensure that the citizens depose their leader if she is caught

---

[3] Here we characterise fully cooooperative agreements with the minimal risk of accidental failure of cooperation. Alternatively one might ask what the optimal agreement is from the perspect of the leader or the citizens:

$$\max_{P,H} V_\alpha$$

subject to the equilibrium constraints or

$$\max_{P,H} V$$

subject to the equilbrium constraints.

cheating requires that the cost of leader replacement not be too high. In particular, the limiting cost in this scenario is

$$K_A \leq \frac{\delta - \delta^{T+1}}{1 - \delta^{T+1} + (\delta^{T+1} - \delta)F(2.667)}100,$$

which converges to 870 as $T \to \infty$.[4]

If, as we believe, officeholding is the dominant motive for leaders, then full cooperation can be achieved with even lower risks of breakdown. For instance, if $\Psi = 100{,}000$, then a threshold of $H = 4.049$ achieves full cooperation ($P_A = 0$) with a risk of accidental breakdown of only $p_A = 0.000026$. In order that citizens replace their leader, the limiting cost of removal (for $T = \infty$) is $K_A \leq 899.8$, nearly nine times the value of full cooperation. As these simulations show, leader specific punishments allow full cooperation even in the presence of noise.[5]

Leader specific punishments allow deeper cooperation between nations whose political institutions make leader removal easy. Breakdowns in cooperation are rare when leader removal is easy for two reasons. First, should any cheating be observed, the responsible leader is immediately removed to ensure an uninterrupted flow of cooperation. Second, to avoid being deposed, leaders set their policies well below the threshold that triggers punishment. In contrast, leaders who are hard to remove from office have less to fear from being caught cheating since it does not cost them their jobs, and therefore they set policies closer to the threshold for cheating.

The analysis of leader specific punishments in the continuous choice PD game predicts that two nations with political institutions that make leader removal easy can commit to deeper and more robust cooperation than can other pairs of nations.

The models in this chapter show how leader specific punishments shape the relationships between patterns of cooperation, leader turnover, and the ease of leader removal. While the theory of leader specific punishment generates numerous hypotheses about the transitions between cooperative and punishment phases of interstate relations, it has several deficiencies that need addressing. First, the theory is phrased in terms of the ease of leader removal. This is not a dimension on which one typically classifies political institutions. Second, the development of the theory thus far assumes the preferences of all citizens in a nation are perfectly aligned. This

---

[4] If $T = 1$ then the limiting cost is $K_A \leq 89.7$.

[5] Full cooperation can still be supported even as the amount of noise increases. If $\sigma^2 = 100$, for instance, full cooperation with $\delta = 0.9$ and $\Psi = 100{,}000$ requires a threshold of $H = 34.324$.

is clearly a gross simplification. In chapter 3 we turn to correcting these deficiencies by examining the selectorate model of political institutions. In addition to providing a metric for the ease of leader replacement, selectorate politics provides a series of additional hypotheses about how domestic political institutions affect the variability of policy change associated with leader change and the impact of this volatility on interstate relations.

APPENDIX

The Stochastic Prisoners' Dilemma

In the main text we characterized symmetric equilibria in which the citizens in both states made the same decision with regard to retaining or removing leaders. In the text we also discussed a mixed case where the citizens in state A replace their leader if she cheats, but the citizens in nation B do not remove their leader. Here we formally characterize this mixed case.

Proposition 2.5: The Stochastic PD with Leader Mortality: Mixed Case (Equilibrium 2.3)

The following strategies are an MPE if

$$K_A \leq \frac{-\left(P\delta\rho_A + P\delta\rho_B - P\delta\rho_A\rho_B\right)}{1-\delta\rho_A} + \frac{V_A^{01}\left(\delta\rho_B - \delta^2\rho_B^2\right)}{1-\delta\rho_A}$$

$$+ \frac{V_A^{00}\delta(1-\rho_B)\left(\rho_A - \delta\rho_A - \delta\rho_B\right)}{1-\delta\rho_A}$$

and

$$K_B \geq \delta V_B^{00} - \delta\rho_B V_B^{01} - \delta(1-\rho_B)V_B^{00}$$

where $\tau_A \geq 0$ is defined as the solution to equation 2.6 (and defined as $\tau_A = 0$ if no positive solution exists) and $\tau_B \geq 0$ is defined as the solution to equation 2.7 (and defined as $\tau_A = 0$ if no positive solution exists):

Leader α plays C if

$$I_A^t = 0,\ I_B^t = 0 \text{ and } \varepsilon_{At} \leq \tau_A;$$

and plays D if either

$$I_A^t = 1,\ I_B^t = 1 \text{ or } \varepsilon_{At} > \tau_A.$$

Leader β plays C if

$$I_A^t = 0,\ I_B^t = 0 \text{ and } \varepsilon_{Bt} \leq \tau_B;$$

and plays D if either

$$I_A^t = 1,\ I_B^t = 1 \text{ or } \varepsilon_{Bt} > \tau_B.$$

The citizens in nation A replace leader α if either

$$I_A^t = 1 \text{ or } (I_B^t = 0 \text{ and } \alpha \text{ plays } D);$$

otherwise they retain α.

The citizens in nation B never replace β.

$$F(\tau_B)(R + \Psi + \delta\rho_A V_a^{00}) + (1 - F(\tau_B))(S + \Psi + \delta\rho_A \rho_B V_a^{01} + \delta\rho_A(1 - \rho_B)V_a^{00})$$
$$= (1 - F(\tau_B))(\Psi + P) + F(\tau_B)(R + \Psi) + F(\tau_B)\tau_A \qquad \text{(EQ 2.6)}$$

$$\delta\rho_B \frac{P + \Psi}{1 - \delta\rho_B} + F(\tau_A)(R + \tau_B - P) + P = \delta\rho_B V_\beta^{00} + F(\tau_A)(R - S) + S \qquad \text{(EQ 2.7)}$$

where (continuation values for α)

$$V_\alpha^{01} = P + \Psi + \delta\rho_A \rho_B V_\alpha^{01} + \delta\rho_A(1 - \rho_B)V_\alpha^{00} \text{ and}$$

$$V_\alpha^{00} = F(\tau_A)F(\tau_B)(R + \Psi + \delta\rho_A V_a^{00})$$
$$+ F(\tau_A)(1 - F(\tau_B))(S + \Psi + \delta\rho_A \rho_B V_a^{01} + \delta\rho_A(1 - \rho_B)V_a^{00})$$
$$+ (1 - F(\tau_A))(1 - F(\tau_B))(P + \Psi) + (1 - F(\tau_A))F(\tau_B)(R + \Psi)$$
$$+ F(\tau_B)\int_{\tau_A}^{\infty} f(\varepsilon)\varepsilon d\varepsilon;$$

(continuation values for β)

$$V_\beta^{00} = F(\tau_A)F(\tau_B)(R + \Psi + \delta\rho_B V_\beta^{00}) + (1 - F(\tau_A))F(\tau_B)(S + \Psi + \delta\rho_B V_\beta^{00})$$
$$+ F(\tau_A)(1 - F(\tau_B))\left(R + \Psi + \delta\rho_B \frac{P + \Psi}{1 - \delta\rho_B}\right) + F(\tau_A)\int_{\tau_B}^{\infty} \varepsilon f(\varepsilon)d\varepsilon$$
$$+ (1 - F(\tau_A))(1 - F(\tau_B))\left(P + \Psi + \delta\rho_B \frac{P + \Psi}{1 - \delta\rho_B}\right);$$

(continuation values for A)

$$V_A^{01} = P + \delta\rho_B V_A^{01} + \delta(1 - \rho_B)V_A^{00}, \text{ and}$$
$$V_A^{00} = F(\tau_A)F(\tau_B)(R + \delta V_A^{00}) + (1 - F(\tau_A))F(\tau_B)(R - K_A + \delta V_A^{00})$$
$$+ F(\tau_B)\int_{\tau_A}^{\infty} \varepsilon f(\varepsilon)d\varepsilon + (1 - F(\tau_B))F(\tau_A)(S + \delta\rho_B V_A^{01} + \delta(1 - \rho_B)V_A^{00})$$
$$+ (1 - F(\tau_A))(1 - F(\tau_B))(P - K_A + \delta\rho_B V_A^{01} + \delta(1 - \rho_B)V_A^{00});$$

(continuation values for B)

$$V_B^{01} = P + \delta \rho_B V_B^{01} + \delta(1 - \rho_B)V_B^{00}, \text{ and}$$

$$
\begin{aligned}
V_B^{00} &= F(\tau_A)F(\tau_B)(R + \delta V_B^{00}) + F(\tau_A)(1 - F(\tau_B))(R + \delta \rho_B V_B^{01} + \delta(1 - \rho_B)V_B^{00}) \\
&+ F(\tau_A)\int_{\tau_B}^{\infty} \varepsilon f(\varepsilon)\,d\varepsilon + F(\tau_B)(1 - F(\tau_A))(S + \delta V_B^{00}) \\
&+ (1 - F(\tau_A))(1 - F(\tau_B))(P + \delta \rho_B V_B^{01} + \delta(1 - \rho_B)V_B^{00}).
\end{aligned}
$$

Proof:

We start by defining α's continuation values and examining the optimality of α's decisions. If α has cheated in the past ($I_A^t s = 1$) then $V_\alpha^{10} = V_\alpha^{11} = P + \Psi$. If leader α has not cheated in the past but leader β has, then

$$V_\alpha^{01} = P + \Psi + \delta \rho_A \rho_B V_\alpha^{01} + \delta \rho_A (1 - \rho_B)V_\alpha^{00}.$$

If neither leader has ever cheated then

$$
\begin{aligned}
V_\alpha^{00} &= F(\tau_A)F(\tau_B)(R + \Psi + \delta \rho_A V_a^{00}) \\
&+ F(\tau_A)(1 - F(\tau_B))(S + \Psi + \delta \rho_A \rho_B V_a^{01} + \delta \rho_A (1 - \rho_B)V_a^{00}) \\
&+ (1 - F(\tau_A))(1 - F(\tau_B))(P + \Psi) + (1 - F(\tau_A))F(\tau_B)(R + \Psi) \\
&+ F(\tau_B)\int_{\tau_A}^{\infty} f(\varepsilon)\varepsilon\,d\varepsilon.
\end{aligned}
$$

If either α or β has previously cheated, then α's integrity is unaffected by the play of the PD game and β plays D. Therefore α's best response is to play D. Suppose neither leader has previously cheated. If α plays C then her payoff is

$$
\begin{aligned}
&U_\alpha(C \mid I_A = 0, I_B = 0, \varepsilon_{At}) \\
&= F(\tau_B)(R + \Psi + \delta \rho_A V_a^{00}) + (1 - F(\tau_B))(S + \Psi + \delta \rho_A \rho_B V_a^{01} + \delta \rho_A (1 - \rho_B)V_a^{00}).
\end{aligned}
$$

If, alternatively, α plays D, then her payoff is

$$U_\alpha(D \mid I_A = 0, I_B = 0, \varepsilon_{At}) = (1 - F(\tau_B))(\Psi + P) + F(\tau_B)(R + \Psi) + F(\tau_B)\varepsilon_{At}.$$

Since the latter payoff is linearly increasing in ε_{At} and the former is constant, then either for all

$$\varepsilon_{At} \geq 0 \quad U_\alpha(D \mid .) > U_\alpha(C \mid .)$$

(in which case τ_A is defined as 0) or there exists $\tau_A \geq 0$ such that $U_\alpha(D \mid .) = U_\alpha(C \mid .)$. This latter equality defines the equation. If $\varepsilon_{At} > \tau_A$ then α

plays D; otherwise α plays C. Given the strategies of the other players, α plays a best response in every state.

Next we consider leader β's continuation values. If leader β has previously cheated, then

$$V_\beta^{11} = V_\beta^{01} = P + \Psi + \delta\rho_B(P + \Psi) + \delta^2\rho_B^2(P + \Psi) + \cdots = \frac{P + \Psi}{1 - \delta\rho_B}.$$

If β has not cheated but leader α has then

$$V_\beta^{10} = P + \Psi + \delta\rho_B V_\beta^{00}.$$

If neither leader has previously cheated, then

$$V_\beta^{00} = F(\tau_A)F(\tau_B)(R + \Psi + \delta\rho_B V_\beta^{00}) + (1 - F(\tau_A))F(\tau_B)(S + \Psi + \delta\rho_B V_\beta^{00})$$

$$+ F(\tau_A)(1 - F(\tau_B))\left(R + \Psi + \delta\rho_B\frac{P + \Psi}{1 - \delta\rho_B}\right) + F(\tau_A)\int_{\tau_B}^\infty \varepsilon f(\varepsilon)\,d\varepsilon$$

$$+ (1 - F(\tau_A))(1 - F(\tau_B))\left(P + \Psi + \delta\rho_B\frac{P + \Psi}{1 - \delta\rho_B}\right).$$

If either leader has previously cheated, then β's best response is to play D. If neither leader has ever cheated, then β's payoff for playing D is

$$U_\beta(D \mid I_A = 0, I_B = 0, \varepsilon_{Bt})$$

$$= F(\tau_A)(R + \Psi + \delta\rho_B V_\beta^{01}) + F(\tau_A)\varepsilon_{Bt} + (1 - F(\tau_A))(P + \Psi + \delta\rho_B V_\beta^{01})$$

$$= \Psi + \delta\rho_B V_\beta^{01} + F(\tau_A)(R + \varepsilon_{Bt} - P) + P.$$

If, alternatively, β plays C, then

$$U_\beta(C \mid I_A = 0, I_B = 0, \varepsilon_{Bt})$$

$$= F(\tau_A)(R + \Psi + \delta\rho_B V_\beta^{00}) + (1 - F(\tau_A))(S + \Psi + \delta\rho_B V_\beta^{00})$$

$$= \Psi + \delta\rho_B V_\beta^{00} + F(\tau_A)(R - S) + S.$$

Since the former is linearly increasing in ε_{Bt} and the latter is constant, we define $\tau_B \geq 0$ to equate

$$U_\beta(C \mid I_A = 0, I_B = 0, \varepsilon_{Bt}) = U_\beta(D \mid I_A = 0, I_B = 0, \varepsilon_{Bt})$$

if a solution exists (this defines equation) and define $\varepsilon_{Bt} = 0$ else. Hence β's strategy is optimal in each state given the strategies of the other players.

Next we examine the decisions of citizens in nation A. We start by calculating the continuation value associated with each state.

$$V_A^{11} = P - K_A + \delta \rho_B V_A^{01} + \delta(1 - \rho_B)V_A^{00}, \quad V_A^{10} = P - K_A + \delta V_A^{00},$$
$$V_A^{01} = P + \delta \rho_B V_A^{01} + \delta(1 - \rho_B)V_A^{00}, \text{ and}$$
$$V_A^{00} = F(\tau_A)F(\tau_B)(R + \delta V_A^{00}) + (1 - F(\tau_A))F(\tau_B)(R - K_A + \delta V_A^{00})$$
$$+ F(\tau_B)\int_{\tau_A}^{\infty} \varepsilon f(\varepsilon) d\varepsilon + (1 - F(\tau_B))F(\tau_A)(S + \delta \rho_B V_A^{01} + \delta(1 - \rho_B)V_A^{00})$$
$$+ (1 - F(\tau_A))(1 - F(\tau_B))(P - K_A + \delta \rho_B V_A^{01} + \delta(1 - \rho_B)V_A^{00}).$$

It is important to note that the equilibrium specifies that the citizens of A replace α for cheating even if β has also cheated. Replacement under this condition does not guarantee the immediate restoration of cooperation, which requires leader β to also be replaced. We examine the citizens in A's decision to depose α under this least attractive contingency. Obviously if the citizens replace α when it only leads to the probabilistic restoration of cooperation, then they certainly replace α when it leads to cooperation with certainty:

$$U_A(depose) = -K_A + \delta \rho_B V_A^{01} + \delta(1 - \rho_B)V_A^{00},$$

and

$$U_A(retain) = \rho_A \rho_B \delta(P - K_A + \delta \rho_B V_A^{01} + \delta(1 - \rho_B)V_A^{00})$$
$$+ \rho_A(1 - \rho_B)\delta(P - K_A + \delta V_A^{00})$$
$$+ (1 - \rho_A)\rho_B \delta(P + \delta \rho_B V_A^{01} + \delta(1 - \rho_B)V_A^{00})$$
$$+ (1 - \rho_A)(1 - \rho_B)\delta V_A^{00}.$$

The citizens in A depose leader α if $U_A(depose) \geq U_A(retain)$ which implies

$$K_A \leq \frac{-(P\delta\rho_A + P\delta\rho_B - P\delta\rho_A\rho_B)}{1 - \delta\rho_A} + \frac{V_A^{01}(\delta\rho_B - \delta^2\rho_B^2)}{1 - \delta\rho_A}$$
$$+ \frac{V_A^{00}\delta(1 - \rho_B)(\rho_A - \delta\rho_A - \delta\rho_B)}{1 - \delta\rho_A}.$$

In nation B the citizens' continuation values are

$$V_B^{11} = P + \delta \rho_B V_B^{01} + \delta(1-\rho_B)V_B^{00}, V_B^{10} = P + \delta V_B^{00},$$
$$V_B^{01} = P + \delta \rho_B V_B^{01} + \delta(1-\rho_B)V_B^{00}, \text{ and}$$
$$V_B^{00} = F(\tau_A)F(\tau_B)(R + \delta V_B^{00}) + F(\tau_A)(1-F(\tau_B))(R + \delta \rho_B V_B^{01} + \delta(1-\rho_B)V_B^{00})$$
$$+ F(\tau_A)\int_{\tau_B}^{\infty} \varepsilon f(\varepsilon)d\varepsilon + F(\tau_B)(1-F(\tau_A))(S + \delta V_B^{00})$$
$$+ (1-F(\tau_A))(1-F(\tau_B))(P + \delta \rho_B V_B^{01} + \delta(1-\rho_B)V_B^{00}).$$

If β has not cheated, replacing her only imposes costs and does not affect the prospects of future cooperation. Therefore, β is not deposed.

Suppose leader β has cheated (either $I_B^t = 1$) or ($I_A^t = 0$ and β plays).

If the citizens in B depose β then $U_B(depose) = -K_B + \delta V_B^{00}$. If they retain β then

$$U_B(retain \mid I_B = 1) = \delta \rho_B V_B^{01} + \delta(1-\rho_B)V_B^{00}.$$

Since

$$K_B \geq \delta V_B^{00} - \delta \rho_B V_B^{01} - \delta(1-\rho_B)V_B^{00}$$

retaining β is a best response.

Since no players have a single period deviation that is expected utility improving in any state, the specified strategy is MPE. QED.

For reasons of comparability, we examine the cooperation in stochastic PD game between unitary actor nations. Specifically we examine a Grim Trigger strategy where nation A plays C if $\varepsilon_{At} \leq \tau_A$ and neither nation has ever played D and plays nation A plays D if either $\varepsilon_{At} > \tau_A$ or either nation has ever played D. B's strategy is defined analogously.

Proposition 2.6: The Stochastic PD between Unitary Actors: Nations A and B playing the Grim Trigger strategy is an MPE of the stochastic PD game where $\tau_A \geq 0$ is defined as the solution to equation 2.8 solution exists, and $\tau_A = 0$ otherwise. τ_B is analogously defined.

$$F(\tau_B)(R + \delta V_A^{00}) + (1-F(\tau_B))\left(S + \delta \frac{P}{1-\delta}\right)$$
$$= F(\tau_B)\left(R + \delta \frac{P}{1-\delta}\right) + F(\tau_B)\tau_A + (1-F(\tau_B))\left(P + \delta \frac{P}{1-\delta}\right)$$

$$\text{(EQ 2.8)}$$

where

$$V_A^{00} = \frac{1}{(1-\delta F(\tau_A)F(\tau_B))}\left(F(\tau_A)F(\tau_B)R + F(\tau_A)(1-F(\tau_B))\left(S+\delta\frac{P}{1-\delta}\right)\right.$$

$$+ (1-F(\tau_A))F(\tau_B)\left(R+\delta\frac{P}{1-\delta}\right) + F(\tau_B)\int_{\tau_A}^{\infty}\varepsilon f(\varepsilon)d\varepsilon$$

$$\left. + (1-F(\tau_A))(1-F(\tau_B))\left(P+\delta\frac{P}{1-\delta}\right)\right).$$

Proof:

If either nation has ever cheated then A's continuation values are

$$V_A^{10} = V_A^{11} = V_A^{01} = \frac{P}{1-\delta}.$$

If neither side has cheated then

$$V_A^{00} = F(\tau_A)F(\tau_B)(R+\delta V_A^{00}) + F(\tau_A)(1-F(\tau_B))\left(S+\delta\frac{P}{1-\delta}\right)$$

$$+ (1-F(\tau_A))F(\tau_B)\left(R+\delta\frac{P}{1-\delta}\right) + F(\tau_B)\int_{\tau_A}^{\infty}\varepsilon f(\varepsilon)d\varepsilon$$

$$+ (1-F(\tau_A))(1-F(\tau_B))\left(P+\delta\frac{P}{1-\delta}\right).$$

Therefore,

$$V_A^{00} = \frac{1}{(1-\delta F(\tau_A)F(\tau_B))}\left(F(\tau_A)F(\tau_B)R + F(\tau_A)(1-F(\tau_B))\left(S+\delta\frac{P}{1-\delta}\right)\right.$$

$$+ (1-F(\tau_A))F(\tau_B)\left(R+\delta\frac{P}{1-\delta}\right) + F(\tau_B)\int_{\tau_A}^{\infty}\varepsilon f(\varepsilon)d\varepsilon$$

$$\left. + (1-F(\tau_A))(1-F(\tau_B))\left(P+\delta\frac{P}{1-\delta}\right)\right).$$

If either side has ever cheated, then clearly playing D is a best response. Suppose neither side has ever cheated. If A plays C then its payoff is

$$U_A(C) = F(\tau_B)(R+\delta V_A^{00}) + (1-F(\tau_B))\left(S+\delta\frac{P}{1-\delta}\right).$$

If alternatively A plays D then its payoff is

$$U_A(D) = F(\tau_B)\left(R + \delta\frac{P}{1-\delta} \right) + F(\tau_B)\varepsilon_{At} + (1 - F(\tau_B))\left(P + \delta\frac{P}{1-\delta} \right).$$

We define τ_A as the value of $\varepsilon_{At} \geq 0$ the equations these two terms:

$$F(\tau_B)(R + \delta V_A^{00}) + (1 - F(\tau_B))\left(S + \delta\frac{P}{1-\delta} \right)$$

$$= F(\tau_B)\left(R + \delta\frac{P}{1-\delta} \right) + F(\tau_B)\varepsilon_{At} + (1 - F(\tau_B))\left(P + \delta\frac{P}{1-\delta} \right).$$

If no such τ_A exists, then $\tau_A = 0$.

Nation A playing C if $\varepsilon_{At} \leq \tau_A$ and playing D if $\varepsilon_{At} > \tau_A$ is a best response. B's strategy is analogous.

The Continuous Choice PD

Here we examine those aspects of the propositions that were inadequately dealt within the main text. In particular we focus on the citizens' decision to remove their leader. Porter (1983) and Green and Porter (1984) proved a detailed and thorough account of the derivation of first order conditions and continuation values for the high removal cost case.

LEADER REMOVAL

We examine leader removal in the low cost case. The high cost case follows trivially from these results. We consider the incentives to remove leader α in period t as a function of her standing, given the strategy of nation B and α's strategy. First, if the incumbent is in good standing, there is no benefit in replacing her. The citizens' expected payoff from replacing α is K_A less than the payoff from keeping her.

Second, suppose $I_A^{t-1} = 1$; this is to say the incumbent is in poor standing but the current period is the last period of punishment. Since in the next period cooperation is restored whether or not the leader is replaced, there is no reason to replace α.

Next consider $I_A^{t-1} = 2$; this is to say there is one more period of punishment (after the current period) before the restoration of the incumbent's good standing. If the citizens depose α in period t, then their payoff is $-K_A + \delta V_{cA}$. If alternatively they retain α, then their payoff is

$$\delta U_A(P_A^*, P_B^*) + \delta^2 V_{cA} = \delta^2 V_{cA}.$$

Hence, the continuation value for playing the game with a standing of

$$I_A^{t-1} = 2$$

is

$$Z_2 = \max\{-K_A + \delta V_{cA}, \delta^2 V_{cA}\}.$$

Next consider $I_A^{t-1} = 3$. If A replaces α then their payoff is $-K_A + \delta V_{cA}$. If alternatively A retains α, then their payoff is

$$0 + \delta Z_2.$$

Suppose that

$$Z_2 = -K_A + \delta V_{cA},$$

that is, A will depose α in the next period. A deposes α if

$$-K_A + \delta V_{cA} \geq \delta(-K_A + \delta V_{cA}),$$

which occurs when

$$K_A \leq \delta V_{cA}.$$

Yet since

$$Z_2 = -K_A + \delta V_{cA}$$

we know that

$$K_A \leq \delta V_{cA} - \delta^2 V_{cA}.$$

Since

$$\delta V_{cA} < \delta V_{cA} - \delta^2 V_{cA},$$

therefore

$$K_A \leq \delta V_{cA},$$

so A deposes

$$\alpha \text{ at } I_A^{t-1} = 3.$$

Suppose instead that

$$Z_2 = \delta^2 V_{cA};$$

that is, A will not depose α in the next period. A deposes α in the current period only if

$$K_A \le \delta V_{cA}(1-\delta^2).$$

Let the continuation value for playing the game with a standing of

$$I_A^{t-1} = 3 \text{ be } Z_3 = \max\{-K_A + \delta V_{cA}, \delta^3 V_{cA}\}.$$

We now reiterate these arguments inductively. First, if

$$Z_i = -K_A + \delta V_{cA}$$

(i.e., A will depose α given standing $I_A^{t-1} = i$), then A will depose α given standing

$$I_A^{t-1} = i+1;$$

therefore

$$Z_{i+1} = -K_A + \delta V_{cA}.$$

Second, suppose

$$Z_i = \delta^i V_{cA},$$

and consider A's deposition decision given a standing of

$$I_A^{t-1} = i+1.$$

If A deposes α, then their payoff is

$$-K_A + \delta V_{cA}.$$

If A retains α, then their payoff is

$$\delta Z_i = \delta^{i+1} V_{cA}.$$

Hence,

$$Z_{i+1} = \max\{-K_A + \delta V_{cA}, \delta^{i+1} V_{cA}\}.$$

Given this induction,

$$Z_T = \max\{-K_A + \delta V_{cA}, \delta^T V_{cA}\}.$$

This characterizes the optimal deposition decisions as specified in the low removal cost proposition for

$$I_A^{t-1} = 1,...,T \text{ and } (I_A^{t-1} = 0 \text{ and } \alpha \text{ is not caught cheating}).$$

Now consider the situation where α (in good standing, $I_A^{t-1} = 0$) is caught cheating. If A deposes α, then its payoff is

$$-K_A + \delta V_{cA}.$$

If A retains α, then its payoff is δZ_T. If

$$Z_T = -K_A + \delta V_{cA},$$

then A deposes α when she is caught cheating, since

$$Z_T = -K_A + \delta V_{cA}$$

implies

$$-K_A + \delta V_{cA} > \delta Z_T.$$

If $Z_T = \delta^T V_{cA}$ then A deposes α only if

$$K_A \le \delta V_{cA}(1 - \delta^T)$$

This implies the limiting cost for the low cost case is

$$K_A \le \delta V_{cA}(1 - \delta^T),$$

which implies

$$K_A \le U_A(\tilde{P}_A, \tilde{P}_B)\frac{\delta - \delta^{T+1}}{1 - \delta + (\delta - \delta^{T+1})p_A},$$

as stated in the main text. If

$$K_A > U_A(\tilde{P}_A, \tilde{P}_B)\frac{\delta - \delta^{T+1}}{1 - \delta + (\delta - \delta^{T+1})p_A},$$

then A never deposes α, which characterizes the high cost scenario.

α's Continuation Value

In the text we report α's continuation on the equilibrium path. Here we provide a more careful consideration of V_α. Assuming both α and β are in good standing, then α chooses P_α in each period. Should α be replaced, the new leader (and any subsequent leaders) produce P_A in each period. Then

$$V_\alpha = U_A(P_\alpha, P_B) + (\delta U_A(P_A, P_B))\sum_{t=1}^{\infty}\delta^{t-1}(1 - (F(H_B - P_\alpha)^t)$$

$$+ (\Psi + \delta U_A(P_\alpha, P_B))\sum_{t=1}^{\infty}\delta^{t-1}(F(H_B - P_\alpha))^t.$$

The first term represents α's immediate payoff for the continuous choice PD; the second is the net present value of paths in which α is deposed and the final term is the net present value of paths in which α retains office. In equilibrium,

$$P_A = P_\alpha = \tilde{P}_A$$

so this equation reduces to that reported in the main text. Maximizing this equation with respect to P_α provides an alternative method to derive equation 2.5.

CHAPTER 3

Political Institutions, Policy Variability, and the Survival of Leaders

WE USE BUENO DE MESQUITA, Smith, Siverson, and Morrow's (2002, 2003; henceforth BdM2S2) selectorate politics model as the basic organization for our discussion of domestic political institutions. Through this conceptualization of political institutions we fulfill two goals. First, we derive a metric for the ease of leader replacement, a vital component of leader specific punishment theory. Second we describe the types of policies enacted under different political systems. In particular we relax the assumption that all players within a single nation receive the same rewards from government actions and examine how institutions affect the extent to which leaders pander to the particularistic interests of their supporters. In institutional settings that encourage leaders to focus on rewarding individual supporters rather than enacting policies that benefit the nation as a whole, the rearrangement of coalitions that often accompanies leadership change can lead to large shifts in policy. Such switches in policy can, and often do, disrupt relations between states.

LEADER SURVIVAL

The effect of political institutions on the survival of leaders is, we believe, a highly understudied topic. Some aspects of political survival have been systematically analyzed. For instance there is a large literature on cabinet survival in parliamentary systems (for example, Bienen and van de Walle 1992; Browne, Freindreis, and Gleiber 1986; Diermeier and Stevenson 1999; Grofman and Van Roozendaal 1994; Warwick 1995). Similarly, there are numerous studies that examine the factors, such as economic performance, that influence voting in democracies and therefore by extension government survival (for example, Lewis-Beck 1986; Powell and Whitten 1993). Yet other facets of leader survival have been relatively understudied, and this neglect leads to deficiencies in our understanding of other aspects of politics. For instance, although there is a long intellectual debate on the idea of diversionary war (see Levy 1989 for a review), until recently scholars had not systematically examined the impact of war and war outcomes on the survival of leaders. An understanding of the consequences of war on leader survival greatly enhances our ability to explain when leaders "gamble for resurrection" and the general timing relationships that relate conflict involvement and length of time in office (Gaubatz 1991; Smith 2004; BdM2S2 2001).

Bueno de Mesquita, Siverson and Woller 1992 and Bueno de Mesquita and Siverson 1995 were perhaps the first articles to systematically collect data on the tenure of leaders across countries and test the impact of international events on leader survival. These studies found that institutions have both a direct impact on the survival of leaders and an indirect impact by moderating the consequences of international outcomes. For instance, democratic leaders are not only more likely to be deposed overall, they are also more susceptible to deposition as a result of losing a war or suffering high causalities. In contrast, war outcomes have relatively little impact on the survival of autocratic leaders. Chiozza and Goemans (2003, 2004; see also Goemans 2000a, b) simultaneously assess the decision to start a conflict and the impact of the war on survival. They suggest that there is a big selection effect in the decision to fight and that this dissipates much of the effect of conflict on survival. Flores (2005) similarly finds that the survival of foreign ministers is relatively unaffected by international outcomes. Put succinctly, leaders avoid those conflicts that jeopardize their tenure.[1]

The most comprehensive study of comparative leader survival is Bueno de Mesquita and his colleagues' *Logic of Political Survival* (2003, also 1999, 2001, 2002). In addition to empirically assessing the survival of leaders, they provide a theory of selectorate politics that explains how political institutions shape which policies best enable leaders to survive in office. We use their theory to derive the metric for the cost of leader replacement, an essential feature of leader specific punishment theory. Selectorate theory also directly implies several hypotheses about the effects of leader change on interstate relations that derive from the extent to which policy changes are associated with leadership change under different institutional arrangements.

Having first described the basic features of selectorate theory, we explain why it provides a metric for the cost of leader survival. We then examine why the policy variability associated with leadership change varies according to selectorate institutions and why this affects interstate relations.

---

[1] In a particularly innovative paper, Jones and Olken (2004) want to assess the impact new leaders have on economic performance. However, recognizing a similar endogeniety problem between economic policy and survival, they utilize a natural experiment by looking at instances of sudden death (in a nonpolitical manner) of leaders. As a side note, we recommend against taking the same airplane as a head of state!

SELECTORATE POLITICS

BdM2S2 assume politicians use two types of policies to reward their supporters: public goods and private goods. Public goods are enjoyed by all the citizens of a state. In contrast, private goods are enjoyed only by those to whom they are allocated. Of course, in reality no policy is a pure public or pure private benefit, but real world policies have either a public or private focus. For instance, environmental protection is a public good; every citizen benefits from clean air. However, the provision (or nonprovision) of this public good is often private in nature. Those paid to clean the environment or regulate industries receive private benefits. A leader might choose to put all environmental cleanup contracts out for competitive bidding and install a professional bureaucracy to enforce environmental regulations. Alternatively, a leader might allocate bloated cleanup contracts to her cronies and allow corrupt bureaucrats to take bribes to "turn a blind eye." The former has a public goods focus, while private goods dominate in the latter. All policy dimensions contain elements of public and private goods. A free and open trading environment is a public good. In contrast, trade protection provides private goods to a few at the expense of the many. The key is that political institutions determine which type of policy focus best enables a leader to survive in office.

BdM2S2 classify political system on two dimensions: winning coalition size (W) and selectorate size (S). The winning coalition (W) is the minimal set of supporters that a leader needs to retain power. This is to say, if the leader cannot retain the support of these W individuals, she is deposed. The selectorate is the pool of potential supporters from which the leader draws her winning coalition. BdM2S2 provide about forty pages developing these concepts and show how these concepts map into real world institutions. They also provide an empirical metric to estimate these concepts, which we will introduce and utilize later. Here we briefly illustrate the concepts of W and S.

Democracies are typically large coalition systems. For instance, a directly elected president requires the support of half the voters, which often constitutes the entire adult population, to ensure survival. That is to say, the selectorate is the size of the population and a winning coalition is half the selectorate. As a practical matter, winning coalition sizes are often much less that half the population. In the Westminster parliamentary system, with two-party competition in single-membered districts, a winning coalition is about 25 percent of the voters; that is, to ensure survival the incumbent needs to win half the votes in half the districts.

Monarchies and military juntas have much smaller selectorates composed of aristocrats and military brass, respectively. Winning coalitions in these systems are typically some specified fraction of the selectorate. For instance, in England in 1199 there were 236 barons who controlled 7,200 knights' fees. To be elected and subsequently maintain his position as king of England—and it was a contested election—, John Lackland (I) required the support of sufficient barons to constitute a majority of the knights' fees (BdM2S2 2003, chap. 2). Both the selectorate and winning coalition were extremely small.

Dictatorships and other autocratic systems of government typically have winning coalitions, which although larger than those of King John's England, are much smaller than those in democratic systems. Within these systems, selectorate size can vary enormously from a small group, as in an oligarchy, to the entire population in a corrupt electoral system. Political institutions shape the policy priorities of leaders and the ease with which they retain office.

SELECTORATE INSTITUTIONS, POLICY CHOICE, AND LEADER SURVIVAL

Political institutions shape the private/public focus of a leader's policy choices. Suppose a leader has R resources with which to buy support. Since a leader's primary goal is to remain in office and survival depends upon maintaining the support of her coalition, she wants to purchase those policies that maximize her survival prospects. Having formed a coalition of size W, she could divide out the R resources as private goods to each member of her coalition. If her coalition is small, such an allocation gives each of her supporters a huge reward, R/W. However, as W grows in size, the welfare that each supporter receives diminishes as the private goods are diluted over more and more supporters. When W is large, a leader can more effectively provide her supporters with rewards through the provision of public goods, which benefit everyone in society, whether they are supporters or not.

Winning coalition size (W) shapes the policy focus of leaders. When coalition size is large, policies focused on public goods provide a more effective means of rewarding supporters than do policies focused on private goods. As coalition size diminishes, policies become increasingly focused on rewarding the few with private goodies rather than providing effective governance that benefits the many. It is not an accident that large coalition democratic systems are wealthier and healthier than small coalition autocracies. BdM2S2 provide numerous tests of the relationship between W and the provision of public and private goods.

In addition to determining policy choice, coalition size—in conjunction with selectorate size—shapes the ease of leader survival, an essential component of leader specific punishment theory. Coalition size determines the mix of private and public goods that most efficiently rewards supporters. When the coalition size is small, leaders predominately use private goods to reward supporters; the provision of public goods is relatively low. Under such circumstances, the welfare of those in the coalition (who receive both public and private goods) is much higher than the welfare of those outside the coalition, who receive only public goods. Being a member of the winning coalition is very valuable. In contrast, if the winning coalition size is large, membership of the coalition is relatively less valuable. When the coalition is large, the majority of rewards are supplied in the form of public goods that reward citizens whether they are in the coalition or not. Although members of the coalition receive greater benefits than those outside of the coalition, because of the small private benefits they receive, these differences are relatively modest.

For a supporter to defect from the incumbent's winning coalition to support a challenger is risky. When a challenger attempts to come to power, he will promise virtually anything to obtain essential support. Yet, once he has come to power and is no longer dependent on the support of key defectors, he may choose to rearrange his power base. BdM2S2 assume leaders have tiny idiosyncratic preferences over whom they would prefer in their coalition. They refer to these idiosyncrasies as affinity. In an attempt to come to power, the challenger needs to attract members of the incumbent's winning coalition, and this constraint largely dictates where the challenger draws supporters from. Once firmly ensconced in office, the challenger would like to rearrange his coalition by dropping some members of the coalition that brought him to power and replacing them with supporters with whom he has higher affinity. As many disgruntled supporters can attest, providing key support to bring a candidate to office does not guarantee a desirable administrative position.

The incumbent has a significant advantage in promising future private rewards to her coalition than does the challenger. Since the incumbent has already been in office and therefore already had the chance to rearrange her coalition, those selectors in her winning coalition can be fairly certain of their inclusion in the incumbent's coalition in the future. If a supporter were not among the leader's top W affinity ranked selectors, the incumbent would already have replaced them. The incumbent can effectively promise continued membership of the winning coalition and access to the future private goods that coalition members receive. The challenger cannot make such guarantees. When a member of the incumbent's coalition defects and brings the challenger to power, the supporter risks exclusion from future winning coalitions. The cost and risk of this exclusion are shaped by political institutions.

The cost of exclusion from future winning coalitions increases as coalition size contracts. When W is small, leaders predominately rely on private goods to reward their supporters and, as explained above, the welfare difference between those in the coalition and those outside the coalition is large. The risk of exclusion from future winning coalitions increases as the requisite number of supporters becomes smaller. This risk is further exaggerated when the leader gets to pick her coalition from a large selectorate.

To survive in office the incumbent needs to ensure that the rewards she provides and the future rewards she can commit to provide are greater than the net present value of what the challenger can promise. The ability of the incumbent to credibly commit to include a supporter in future coalitions creates an incumbency advantage. While the challenger might, in the current period, offer to spend all the R available resources optimally, he cannot credibly promise access to future private goods. The incumbent can. It is this ability to commit to retain her current supporters as coalition members in the future that generates the incumbency advantage. The size of this advantage is greatest when coalition size is small and selectorate size is large. It is this configuration of institutions that creates a high cost and a high risk of exclusion from future access to private goods.

BdM2S2 predict that leaders from small W, large S political systems find it easiest to survive in office. Their empirical tests strongly support these predictions.[2] Further, they argue that tenure in office affects the likelihood of further survival. The advantage held by incumbents is rooted in their ability to promise access to future private goods. The longer a leader has been in office, the more time and opportunities she has had to rearrange her coalition. As the tenure of a leader increases, members of her coalition become increasingly reassured of future coalition membership. As a consequence, the incumbency advantage rises over time (although at a decreasing rate), so leaders find it easier to survive in office as their tenure grows. However, this tenure effect on the ease of survival is moderated by political institutions.

The relative importance of private goods provision depends upon political institutions. The incumbency advantage derived from being able to promise future private goods is small in large W systems, since private goods are relatively unimportant under such institutional configurations. The ease of surviving in office grows with tenure most in small W systems and least in large W systems. Empirically BdM2S2 observe that the hazard rate with which leaders are deposed decreases only very slightly with tenure for leaders in large coalition systems but decreases rapidly for small coalition leaders.

Although our discussion of BdM2S2's selectorate theory omits formal proofs, it should be apparent that the selectorate conceptualization of

---

[2] BdM2S2 also predict that it is these leaders that find it easiest to steal societal resources for their own gain. While kleptocracy is by its very nature hard to systematically measure, anecdotal accounts appear consistent with this prediction.

political institutions provides a measure for the ease of leader removal. In a large W system there is little incumbency advantage. Although members of the incumbent's coalition risk being excluded from access to future private goods if they defect to the challenger, both the cost and risk of such exclusion are small. The cost of exclusion is small because when W is large, leaders provide proportionately few private goods. Further, the risk of exclusion from future private goods is also small, since the challenger needs many supporters. If an incumbent can no longer provide the public good of international cooperation, then supporters readily defect to a challenger who can.

In a small coalition system, the incumbent's supporters are much less likely to defect as a result of the incumbent's inability to sustain international cooperation. In a small W system the majority of rewards are provided in the form of private goods. Deposing the incumbent jeopardizes access to these valuable private goods. Removing a small coalition leader is costly for her supporters.

It is worth pausing to note that in the development of the leader specific punishment theory, we denoted the cost of leader replacement as the cost paid by the citizens. The discussion of the selectorate theory makes it clear that the costs of leader change are primarily opportunity costs for securing future private goods by those in the incumbent's coalition, rather than on the citizenry as a whole. Since political survival depends upon the decision of this group, rather than on the citizens as a whole, the selectorate theory provides the appropriate metric for the cost of leader removal for the relevant segment of the population.

POLICY VARIABILITY AND THE TURNOVER OF LEADERS

The selectorate theory predicts how the institution of winning coalition size determines the types of policies leaders pursue. When coalition size is large, leaders predominantly supply public goods. The leader needs to "buy" too many supporters to be able to rely on giving each of her supporters their desired particularistic wants. The leader instead relies on policies that benefit all of society, although of course they still want to ensure that the mechanism that facilitates these public goods provides private benefits for the "right" selectors. A leader from a small coalition system relies proportionately more on private goods for rewarding her supporters. Policy is focused on providing goodies rather than good policy.

The formal models of leader specific punishment in earlier chapters all assumed a single policy issue that benefited every member of a nation to the same extent. For instance, in the stochastic PD game in chapter 2, every citizen in nation A received either P, R, S, or T, according to the outcome of the PD game. The assumption of perfect alignment of preferences is unrealistic. The selectorate model provides insights as to the consequences of relaxing the national preference assumption.

Trade policy is a convenient device through which to explore the consequences of divergent preferences. Free trade and the absence of protectionist barriers to trade reduce the price consumers pay for goods. Since all citizens consume goods, free trade provides benefits to all members of society. Protectionism has redistributional consequences which provide private benefits for those associated with the protected industry at the expense of foreign workers and society in general.

The survival goal for a small coalition leader is best obtained through policies that provide high levels of private goods to supporters. In terms of trade policy, a small coalition leader wants to provide high levels of assistance to those industries associated with her supporters. Such a policy of intense private goods for the limited interests of supporters has several implications for international cooperation. First, the leader puts the interests of her supporters in front of those of international cooperation. Attaining international cooperation is not as useful a way to reward her supporters. If protecting a supporter's industry violates an international trade agreement, it is more likely that a small coalition leader will break the agreement, than a large coalition leader.

Second, the policies of small coalition systems are liable to change radically with leader turnover. For instance, suppose an incumbent leader formed a coalition around supporters in the agricultural export sector. Given the political incentives, the leader is likely to implement policies that vigorously promote this sector, such as subsidies and preferential access to fertilizer. Suppose the leader is replaced. The new leader needs to form a coalition. The new leader might base his coalition around the same set of supporters that his predecessor did. However, he is free to find his favorite W supporters from any of the S selectors. He might, for example, base his coalition on an ethnic group outside of the agricultural export section. When the shift in leadership is accompanied by a shift in coalition, a radical shift in policy can be expected. For instance, the new leader has no incentive to continue the policies that enriched the agricultural export sector. Indeed, he is likely to want to pillage these rich resources. Policy shifts to a different set of intensely private goods oriented policies.

This example is not simply a hypothetical story. Following independence Jomo Kenyatta became Kenya's first president in 1963. He was from the Kikuyu tribe that populated the rich agricultural lands of the Central Highlands that surround the Kenyan capital, Nairobi. Unlike most postindependence African leaders, who preferred to promote industrialization by using agricultural regions to subsidize cheap food for urban workers, Kenyatta chose policies to promote agricultural development, particularly in Kikuyu regions. In Western Province and Nyanaz he promoted the export of sugar, and sugar growers prospered under his rule. His policies included the effective use of farm marketing boards that ensured farmers received stable prices for their crops.

Although Kenyatta was acclaimed as a popular leader who was elected president on several occasions, it would be difficult to describe Kenya as democratic system. Kenyatta suppressed popular opposition, intimidated opponents and voters alike, and ensured the polls reported the results he wanted. His successor, Daniel Arap Moi, abused the electoral system yet further. He banned opposition parties and introduced a two-stage electoral process known as queuing. Under this system voters would stand behind their chosen candidate. The electoral returning officer would then count the number of supporters for each candidate. If any candidate achieved 70 percent of the vote, they were immediately declared the winner. If no candidate received 70 percent of the vote, a second "secret ballot" occurred.

While in principle it should take half the voters in the district to secure victory, and 70 percent of the voters to do it in the first round, in practice the returning officer's support was frequently enough. Whatever the size of the lines, the returning office might simply report numbers indicating victory for the government candidate. Throup and Hornsby (1998, p. 43) describe the case of an election between the government chosen candidate Kiruhi Kimondo and an independently minded member of Parliament, Charles Rubia. Rubia on two occasion pointed out to the returning officer that the numbers he was reporting did not reach the 70 percent threshold. Rubia suggested changing the reported numbers once more to give the Kimondo 70.5 percent of the vote to avoid the farce of a pointless second round election. While nominally democratic, Kenya is in effect a small coalition system.

Kenyatta died in 1978. Moi, who had been serving as his deputy, was not Kikuyu. Although when he initially came to power he ruled with the support of interests from Kenyatta's coalition, he rapidly sought to replace these supporters with those from his own ethnic background, particularly Kalenjin tribesmen of the Central Rift Valley region. With his supporters' interests no longer based in agriculture, his policies turned to looting the previously successful agricultural sector for the benefit of himself and his supporters.

In common with many other African leaders, Moi used farm marketing boards to reward supporters (Meredith 2005, chap. 16). Although Kenyatta used these boards to provide stable prices and ensure profitability for his supporters, Moi reversed the process and used the boards to extract resources from rural areas by forcing farmers to sell to the boards at prices fixed way below world market prices.

In the case of sugar, Moi set an external tariff to ensure that Kenya's domestic price was more than three times world prices. However, the high price did not benefit Kenyan sugar farmers, who were forced to sell their products to the Kenyan Sugar Authority at below world prices. Moi's cronies made even more profits by importing sugar duty-free, on the pretext that it was in transit to Tanzania and Uganda, and selling it on the open market. The sugar industry was devastated, and Kenya shifted from a sugar exporter to a sugar importer.[3]

The shift in coalitions that accompanied Kenyatta's departure led to huge shifts in policies as winner became losers and some losers became winners. Robert Bates describes the transition.

> I recall working in western Kenya shortly after Daniel Arap Moi succeeded Jomo Kenyatta as President of Kenya. With the shift in power, the political fortunes of elite politicians had changed. As I drove through the highlands, I encountered boldly lettered signs posted on the gateways of farms announcing the auction of cattle, farm machinery, and buildings and lands. Once they were no longer in favor, politicians found their loans cancelled or called in, their subsidies withdrawn, or their lines of business, which had once been sheltered by the state, exposed to competition. Some whom I had once seen in the hotels of Nairobi, looking sleek and satisfied, I now encountered in rural bars, looking lean and apprehensive, as they contemplated the magnitude of their reversal. (2001, p. 74)

This example reminds us of our own experiences of traveling in Kenya just prior to the 1992 election. While naively believing we were relatively politically informed, we discussed the upcoming election with a sanitation worker traveling on the bus between Malindi and Kalifi. While possessing little formal education, he regaled us with the ethnicities of all the various candidates in the local districts, potential coalitions, the likely outcome in each of the local voting areas, and, most importantly from his perspective, which outcomes would allow him to keep his prestigious city job of managing Kalifi's garbage dump. Changes in leadership in small coalition systems shift who receives rewards and who does not.

The Bate's Kenyan example illustrates the radical shift from one set of intense private goods-oriented policies to a different set of private goods oriented policies that often accompany leadership change. The turnover of leaders in small coalition systems creates high policy variability. Further, these shifts in policy are taken without regard to their consequences for international cooperation. The transition from Kenyatta to Moi resulted in a 3% decline in Kenyan trade with the United States.

---

[3] "Kenyan Sugar Growers Taste Corruption's Bitter Fruits," *Times Media Limited*, August 26, 1997.

Leadership turnover in large coalition systems leads to shifts in policy too. The George W. Bush presidency has been a polarizing event for many Americans. Yet, in comparative terms, the shift from the Clinton to Bush administration had nothing like the profound effects Bates describes in Kenya. Neither did it jeopardize American's role in international organizations. While Bush attempted to reward supporters in the steel industry through a 30 percent steel tariff, when the World Trade Organization deemed these tariffs illegal, Bush withdrew these private benefits to preserve the public benefit of a free-trade regime. The citizens of Kenya were less fortunate. Moi's actions always favored himself and his cronies, rather than the Kenyan people. Following years of misappropriations of funds (a.k.a. theft), foreign nations and international organizations cut off aid to Kenya. As Meredith (2005, pp. 402–3) states, "From being one of the West's favoured African countries, Kenya had sunk to pariah status." After Moi's departure, Western aid again began to flow into Kenya, in part to finance President Mwai Kibaki's campaigns against corruption. While Kibaki, as a new leader coming to power in December 2002, was not accountable for his predecessor's thefts, his administration soon embarked on their own campaign of theft.[4] The political imperative of staying in office ensures that leaders in the United States and Kenya trade off the relative importance of private and public goods very differently.

Large coalition leaders survive in office through the effective provision of public goods. To the extent that international cooperation is a public good, leaders place the maintenance of international cooperation above the particularistic interests of their supporters. While violating an international agreement may ingratiate a leader with a small group of her supporters, she needs the support of a large coalition to survive in office. Compensating all the other member of her coalition for the termination of international cooperation is a difficult task and one best avoided by maintaining cooperation in the first place. In contrast, leader change in small coalition systems is often accompanied by radical shifts in intense private goods policies. For such leaders, ensuring the supply of private goods to cronies dominates concerns about public welfare.

These differences in policy focus lead to predictions as to how relations between states are affected by leader change. Leader change in large coalition systems does not in general endanger international cooperation. Both predecessor and successor value the maintenance of cooperative relations, and the basic public goods focus of policy remains unchanged. Leader change in small coalition systems weakens cooperative relations between

---

[4] "Timeline: Kenya: A Chronology of a Key Event, Saturday, 5 March, 2005"; "Corruption Haunts Kenya's Leader Wednesday, 23 February 2005"; and "Poll blow for Kenya's New Rulers, Friday, 31 December, 2004." All http://news.bbc.co.uk/.

states. Radical policy shifts often accompany leader change. Kenya went from a sugar exporter to a sugar importer following the transition from Kenyatta to Moi. This shift harmed those trading sugar with Kenya and made investing in Kenya risky. Until the full extent of Moi's policies could be assessed, other states did not know whether it would be profitable to continue trading sugar, or any other good. Such increases in risk and uncertainty reduce the incentive for productive economic activities such as trade and investment.

The theory of leader specific punishments made predictions about transitions between cooperative and punishment phases of the game and consequences for leader survival. Selectorate theory provides additional predictions about the policy consequences of leadership turnover during the cooperative phrase. Leader turnover in large coalition systems leaves the primary policy objectives relatively unchanged. The new leader survives by promoting policies that enrich the many, as did his predecessor. In contrast, the policy objectives of small coalition leaders are to enrich the few at the expense of the many. However, since the few to be rewarded often change with leader turnover, so too do the policies a small coalition nation pursues.

In the preceding chapter, we developed a theory of leader specific punishments in which individual leaders, rather than the nation they represent, are held accountable for their actions. The theory generated a number of hypotheses that predicted that the level of cooperation that could be achieved between nations and the dynamics of the pattern of cooperation and leader change depend upon the ease with which leaders can be replaced. In this chapter we use the selectorate model of politics to generate a metric for the ease of leader replacement. Selectorate theory also allowed us to relax the assumption that every person in a nation received the same benefits from government policy. This generated another hypothesis that the magnitude of policy changes associated with leader change was larger in small coalition systems than in large coalition systems. With respect to maintaining domestic political support, small coalition leaders are also less concerned about maintaining international cooperation. This combination of high policy volatility and relatively low concern for the maintenance of good external relations means that other nations have legitimate concerns about what actions a newly installed small coalition leader is likely to take. Having developed the theoretical side of the argument, we now move to testing its implications.

CHAPTER 4.

Leader Specific Strategies in Human Subject Experiments

LEADER SPECIFIC PUNISHMENT arguments provide an internally consistent theory that relates leadership change to policy choices. While the theory is logically defensible, does it reliably explain and predict behavior? Logical coherence does not make a theory useful unless it helps us understand the world in which we live. This chapter is the first of several that tests the predictions derived in the previous chapters. We build our evidence from human subject experiments and statistical analyses of real world data on trade and sovereign debt.

Here we examine the intuitive plausibility that people condition punishments against individual leaders rather than the team (group or nation) that they represent. To do so we use human subject experiments and create conditions as close as possible to those outlined in the theory. Human subjects are divided into two teams, which we think of as nations. These teams play the repeated prisoners' dilemma, with each team led by a leader who is solely responsible for making their team's choice as to whether to cooperate (C) or defect (D). There is a voter in each team. Periodically the voter has the opportunity to replace the team leader. The cost of leader replacement, k, is varied across experiments to reflect how institutional differences affect the ease of leader replacement. This experimental setting closely resembles the theoretical model considered in the opening chapter.

Although, as with all human subject experiments, the results are noisy, our main finding is that leader replacement influences the pattern of cooperation between teams. In particular, leader replacement reduces the dependence between strategy choice and the history of past play. While this can jeopardize cooperation between teams that have previously been cooperating, it can also rejuvenate relations between teams that have not been cooperating. This result is a major finding in that it demonstrates the intuitive plausibility of our theory that leaders, as much as nations, are the relevant proper nouns of international relations.

HUMAN SUBJECT EXPERIMENTS

The prisoners' dilemma is one of the most widely studied human subject experiments.[1] Great importance has been placed on the PD game. This emphasis is justified, as the PD is a basic building block in the study of cooperation. Scholars, such as Axelrod (1984), have analyzed optimal strategies to play PD through computer tournaments. The PD game has been used to study, among other things, how learning, uncertainty, reputation and information affect cooperative behavior. While PD experiments abound, to our knowledge no one has ever examined the PD game between teams lead by representative leaders. We believe that such a setup is a more realistic representation of the incentives created by political competition.[2]

Human subject experiments have been applied in international relations contexts.[3] Typically, however, such experiments have a human subject represent a nation. We believe these experiments mischaracterize the incentives of players. The standard underlying assumption is that a national preference exists and the player is trying to maximize the nation's payoff. Given this set of assumptions, personification of a nation is an appropriate way to set up an experiment. Unfortunately, no nation is a unitary actor. Nations are led by political leaders who make decisions on behalf of their nation. The leader makes decisions to maximize her interests, which we assume are officeholding, rather than the interests of the nation.

We conceptualize a nation as a team of players with a representative leader. Two teams play the basic prisoners' dilemma game. A leader makes decision on behalf of the team. If the team is unhappy with the leader's performance, they can replace her. This is precisely the setup in which we theoretically analyzed the implications of leader specific punishments. We also believe it better captures the political incentives of real world cooperative interactions.

---

[1] There is a large literature on dilemma and coordination games. See, for example, Andreoni and Miller 1993; Andreoni and Varian 1999; Axelrod 1970, 1984, 1986; Bornstein, Erev, and Goren 1994; Cooper, Dejong, Forsythe, and Ross 1992, 1994, 1996; Davis and Holt 1993; Dolbear Jr. et al. 1968; Hardin 1971; Ahn, Ostrom, and Walker 1998; Lave 1962, 1965; Ledyard 1993; Lichbach 1996; Moreno and Wooders 1998; Ochs 1995; Offerman, Sonnemans, and Schram 1996; Palfrey 1991; Palfrey and Rosenthal 1985, 1994; Rapoport 1988; Rapoport and Chammah 1965; Tullock 1999; Wu and Axelrod 1995.

[2] There is a literature on team games and intergroup cooperation, but as far as we know, none of these games have leaders who can be "ousted" from office. For example, see Bornstein, Erev, and Green 1995.

[3] See, for example, Bixenstine, Levitt, and Wilson 1966; Bonacich 1970; Cooper, DeJong, Forsythe, and Ross 1996.

Team Beta

Team Alpha		C	D
	C	60cents, **60cents**	20cents, **100cents**
	D	100cents, **20cents**	40cents, **40cents**

Figure 4.1. Jointly determined payoffs from the prisoners' dilemma game.

Experimental Setup

We examine three variations on the basic prisoners' dilemma game. The first set of experiments, which we refer to as *the representative leader experiment,* is of direct theoretical interest as a means of testing the theory of leader specific punishments. This version is based directly on the prisoners' dilemma game between representative leaders analyzed in chapter 1. Each team is led by a leader who plays the PD game on behalf of her team. Periodically a voter in the team can depose the leader.

The second variation on the experimental setting is *the direct democracy experiment.* In this experiment all members of each team vote on their team's choice of C or D, with the decision the majority choice. The third variation is *the basic PD game between individuals.* Both of these variants are "control" experiments against which we gauge the results of the *representative leader experiment.* We now detail the precise conditions of each experiment. We shall describe this experimental setup for the representative democracy version and explain how the other versions of the experiments differ.

In the representative democracy experiment subjects were randomly assigned a role in one of two teams, *A* and *B*. There are three people in each team. Each team has a leader, a challenger, and a voter. All players were given a copy of the payoff matrix and made aware of the structure of the game (see figure 4.1). The terms *prisoners' dilemma, cooperate, defect, C* and *D* were never used in describing the game.

In each round of the experiment, each team leader chooses between actions 1 and 2, which correspond to the actions *C* or *D* in a standard PD. Voters and challengers observe the actions of both leaders. The leaders' joint decision determines the payoff for each member of the team. In addition the leader receives $1.50 each round for as long as he or she remains leader. This benefit of office is common knowledge to all players. Given our emphasis on the officeholding motives of leaders, it is essential that this leadership reward is large relative to the PD payoffs.

Every fourth round, the voter decides whether to retain their team leader or replace her/him with the challenger. These votes are staggered, occurring in rounds 4, 8, 12, . . . for team *A* and rounds 6, 10, 14, . . . for team *B*. If the voter decides to remove the leader, then he/she pays a cost, k—which equals 5 cents, 20 cents or 200 cents—to do so. These costs reflect the relative difficulty of removing leaders—an important component of the leader specific punishment theory. The cost of leader removal is common knowledge. All members of both teams are informed of any leader replacements. If a leader is replaced by the challenger, then the deposed leader becomes the new challenger and can be reelected in future rounds of the game.[4] The game is repeated for 40 rounds; thereafter the game continues with 2/3 probability in each round. The subjects are aware that the game is repeated but are unaware of the stopping rule. At the end of the experiment, subjects are prompted to fill in a brief questionnaire.

All the experiments were carried out at New York University's Center for Experimental Social Science (CESS) and were reviewed and approved by the University Committee on Activities Involving Human Subjects (UCAIHS). Participants for the experiments were recruited via the CESS Web site.[5] Upon completion of the experiment each participant was given a voucher to be converted to cash at the university bursar's office. We kept no record of the subjects' names or any other identifying information.

New York University's experimental lab has capacity for twenty participants. Thus, three experiments were typically carried out simultaneously. The eighteen subjects in the three experiments were invited to take a seat in front of any computer in the experimental lab. Each computer is surrounded by a privacy screen. Team membership and assignment of role within a team were randomly allocated. The subjects had no way of knowing which other individuals in the room were assigned to which team and which roles. The entire experiment was run using Z-tree software[6] and the programming was carried out by Severin Weber, for which we are very grateful.

We ran eleven groups of the representative democracy experiment. The data from these experiments are shown in table 4.6 at the end of this chapter. In addition we ran three experiments using the direct democracy setup and six experiments using the individual setup, tables 4.7 and 4.8 respectively. In these other experiments the prisoners' dilemma game is identical, but the institutional setting differs. In the direct democracy experiment all three team members vote directly on whether to play action 1 or 2, with the choice being made by majority rule. In this context there is no representative leader. There is also no leader in the individual setup, in which teams are of size one, that is, individuals. In addition to the quantitative

---

[4] It would be preferable to have a larger pool of potential candidates for office so that deposing the new leader does not mean reinstalling the former incumbent. Unfortunately, this would greatly increase the cost of the experiment. Similarly, while increasing team size to include more that one voter is desirable, it also greatly increases cost.

[5] http://experiments.cess.fas.nyu.edu.

[6] Z-tree was written by Urs Fischbacher at the University of Zurich.

results from these experiments, which we shall now describe, qualitative evidence from the postexperiment questionnaire also suggests subjects condition their behavior on leader turnover.

RESULTS

We now examine the outcomes of the human subject experiments. The full data from the experiments are shown in tables 4.6, 4.7, and 4.8 at the end of this chapter. We examine the key theoretical predictions developed in the previous chapter. We start with a brief discussion of reciprocal strategies. We then examine the impact of leader turnover and how it enhances or diminishes cooperation. Following that, we analyze the replacement of leaders. Finally, we examine how the institutional regime affects the overall level of cooperation. With regard to each of these topics, the results of the human subject experiments are generally consistent with theoretical expectation. That said, any conclusions drawn need to be treated with caution due to the small sample size.

General Reciprocity

In all three versions of the experiments players' decisions to cooperate are influenced by previous play. Players are more likely to defect when either they or the opposing player played defect in the previous round. In all experiments players were most likely to play cooperate in the current period if the outcome in the previous period was CC. Since such results are highly consistent with theoretical expectations and previous evidence we do not present the statistical evidence.[7]

The Impact of Leader Turnover

In this section we examine the impact of leader change on the pattern of play in the representative democracy version of the experiment. The theory developed in the previous chapter indicated that leadership change interrupted the pattern of reciprocal behavior between nations. That is to say, leadership turnover reduces the extent to which current play is dependent upon previous play. This reduction in dependence has different implications according to the nature of prior relations. If prior relations were good and the teams had consistently achieved mutual cooperation

---

[7] For an excellent review of this literature see Davis and Holt 1993.

TABLE 4.1

Probit Analyses of Our Leader's Choice to Defect given
Previous Play and Leader Change

	Model 4.1	Model 4.2
(Our Previous Play = D)	1.219**	.369**
	(.104)	(.111)
(Their Previous Play = D)	1.288**	1.426**
	(.104)	(.111)
(Our Team has New Leader)		1.060**
		(.382)
(Their Team has New Leader)		.842*
		(.351)
(Our Team has New Leader)*		−1.887**
(Our Previous Play = D)		(.434)
(Their Team has New Leader)*		−1.481**
(Their Previous Play = D)		(.410)
Constant	−1.273	−1.382
	(.083)	(.089)
Observations	988	988

** Statistical Significant at the 1% level in a two tailed test.
* Statistical Significant at the 5% level in a two tailed test.

(CC), then leader change reduces the probability of continued good relations. In contrast, if prior interactions between the teams had not resulted in mutual cooperation, leadership turnover reduces the dependency between past and current play and enhances the probability that the teams will start mutual cooperation.

To analyze the reciprocity of strategies and the impact of leader change we use a probit model of the decision of leaders to play defect as a function of previous play and leadership change. The experiments examine the interaction between teams A and B. However, since the team labels are arbitrarily assigned, there is no systematic reason to anticipate that leader A behaves differently from leader B. Therefore, we analyze the data from the prospective of "our" team relative to "their" team. That is, our statistical tests treat how leader A plays relative to B and how leader B plays relative to A as the same decision, specifically as "our" team's choice. Thus while we have 505 rounds of play in the eleven representative democracy experiments, we have $2*505 = 1{,}010$ decisions by "our" team as a function or "our" previous play and "their" previous play. In table 4.1 we examine our leader's choice to defect as a function of the previous play of both teams and any leadership change.

Model 4.1 (see table 4.1) examines general reciprocity. It shows that our leader is more likely to play D in the current period when either team played D in the previous period. The variable (Our Previous Play = D) is a dummy variable indicating whether our team played C (0) or D (1) in the previous period. There is parallel notation for the opposing team. Model 4.2 (see table 4.1) reexamines these relationships controlling for leadership turnover. The variable (Our Team Has New Leader) is a dummy variable indicating whether our team replaced its leader at the end of the previous period. The model also contains interaction effects between previous defection and leader change. As with model 4.1, the significant positive coefficients on the first two variables indicate that if our team or their team played D in previous period, then our leader is likely to play D in the current period. A consequence of this result is that, absent leader change, teams are likely to maintain the previous pattern of play. So if the teams previously played CC, they are likely to again do so in the future. Similarly, if they previously played DD, they are likely to continue doing so. However, leadership change weakens this dependency on previous play.

The coefficients on both leader change variables are positive, and the coefficients on both the interaction terms between leader change and past play are negative. The substantive significance of leader change depends upon play in the previous period. If, for example, previous play had been cooperative, the positive coefficients on the leader change variables suggest that our leader is more likely to defect than would have been the case absent a leader change. In contrast, since the sum of the leader change variables and the interaction variables is negative (and statistically significantly so), if previous play had been noncooperative, then leader change reduces the probability that our leader will defect.

The interaction of past play and leader change is readily seen by calculating the predicted probabilities that our leader plays D under different contingent circumstances under the estimates from model 4.2. These predicted probabilities are shown in table 4.2. The four cells in table 4.2 correspond to the four possible outcomes in the previous period. The three figures in each cell are the predicted probability that our leader plays D following no leader change, leader change in our team, and leader change in their team, respectively.

Table 4.2 clearly shows the impact of leader change on the pattern of play. If in the previous period both teams cooperated (CC), then, absent leader change, the predicted probability that our leader defects is only 8 percent. In contrast, if our leader or their leader was replaced at the end of the previous period, the predicted probability of defection jumps to 37 percent and 29 percent, respectively. Leadership change appears to reduce established trust, making it less likely that cooperative relations continue.

The bottom right cell of table 4.2 corresponds to the case where both leaders played defect (DD) in the previous period. The predicted probabilities indicate that in the absence of leader change following this eventuality,

TABLE 4.2
Predicted Probabilities That Our Leader Plays *D* from
Model 4.2

		Opposing Team's Previous Play	
		C	D
Our Team's Previous Play	C	.08	.52
		.37	.87
		.29	.28
	D	.49	.92
		.20	.72
		.80	.78

Note: The first figure corresponds to no leader change, the second to leader change in our team, and the third to leader change in their team.

there is a 92 percent chance that our leader will defect again in the current period. Leader change offers a substantial opportunity to restart cooperation. In particular, model 4.2 predicts that the prospects of our leader cooperating following mutual defection improve by 20 percent and 14 percent following leader change in our team and their team, respectively. Leader change offers the opportunity to rejuvenate cooperative relations.

The upper right cell of table 4.2 calculates the predicted probability that our leader defects if in the previous period our team played *C* and their team played *D*. Having been cheated in the previous period, our leader has a predicted probability of 52 percent of subsequently defecting. If our leader was replaced at the end of the previous period, this predicted probability of defection rises to 87 percent. This is consistent with the pattern observed in the *CC* cell that new leaders are more suspicious and hence more likely to play *D*. Most interesting for the theory is the effect of leader change on their team. The 0.28 figure in the *CD* cell indicates that if their leader, who cheated our team in the previous period, is replaced, then our leader is less likely to defect than if their leader is not replaced, 28 percent versus 52 percent. Their team's removal of a leader who cheated us substantially increases the prospects of future cooperative relations.

The final bottom left (*DC*) cell examines the eventuality that our leader cheated in previous period. The predicted probabilities show that absent any leader change, our leader has a 49 percent chance of again playing *D*. If their leader is replaced, then our leader becomes even more likely to defect again, 80 percent. Given the evidence that incoming leaders are more likely to be suspicious and play *D*, this willingness to defect again appears a likely best response. More interestingly, should our leader be replaced, our new leader is more likely to behave cooperatively, with only a 20 percent predicted probability of defection.

The experimental design provides the voter the opportunity to replace their leader every fourth period. We found no evidence that the presence of an election had any systematic influence on leaders' decisions during that period. That is, statistically leaders appear to behave identically whether they face reselection in that period or not.

Although our study is limited by sample size and we have insufficient data to analyze the comparative statics with respect to the cost of leader replacement, we find leader turnover has a highly significant impact on the interactions between teams. If previous relations between the teams had been cooperative, it appears that following leader change, both the incoming leader and the leader already in place are more likely to defect than they would absent any leader turnover. Although the tendency to be suspicious of new leaders can disturb existing cooperative relations, this negative effect is counteracted by the possibility of restoring cooperation. If a leader who played D in the previous period is replaced, the teams are more likely to play cooperatively then they would have otherwise. Although leader change introduces an element of the unknown, it also provides an opportunity to restore cooperation.

Leader Replacement

Leader turnover influences the pattern of cooperative interactions between teams. We now examine what factors influence leadership turnover. The experimental design provides an opportunity for A team to change their leader in periods 4, 8, 12, . . . and for team B to replace their leader in periods 6, 10, 14, . . . The experiments provide a total of 232 opportunities for the voter in a team to replace their leader.

Our analyses indicate that the decision to replace a leader is driven by the performance of the leader—in terms of providing mutual cooperation—and the cost of leader replacement. Table 4.3 shows leader replacement by whether leaders managed to achieve mutual cooperation (CC) in the election period and the cost of leader replacement. The table shows that leaders who produce mutual cooperation are far less likely to be replaced than leaders who do not. Indeed, in experiments 4 and 10, which result in mutual cooperation in every period, there are no instances of leader change. The differences between mutual success and other outcomes in determining the replacement of leaders are statistically significant for $k = 5$ and $k = 200$. We cannot reject the null hypothesis that outcomes have no effect on leader replacement for the $k = 20$ experiments. However, since for the $k = 20$ there was only one case of mutual cooperation during an

TABLE 4.3
The Determinants of Leader Replacement

	Leader Replacement Cost, $k = 5$		Leader Replacement Cost, $k = 20$		Leader Replacement Cost, $k = 200$	
	Mutual Cooperation (CC)	Other Outcome	Mutual Cooperation (CC)	Other Outcome	Mutual Cooperation (CC)	Other Outcome
Retain Leader	54 (90%)	36 (52%)	1 (100%)	35 (63%)	27 (100%)	16 (84%)
Replace Leader	6 (10%)	33 (48%)	0 (0%)	21 (37%)	0 (0%)	3 (16%)

The Pearson Chi squared statistics for $k = 5$, 20, and 200 are 21.77, 0.5938, and 4.560, respectively, which are statically significant at the 5% level of $k = 5$ and $k = 200$ only.

electoral period, the test lacks any power as the null could never be rejected. Taken as a whole, the evidence in table 4.3 strongly suggests that whether a leader succeeds in providing mutually cooperative outcomes is an important determinant of leader replacement.

The cost of leader replacement also influences the likelihood of leader replacement, with leader replacement being more likely when the cost is low. As table 4.3 shows, as leader replacement cost increases, leaders are less likely to be replaced. For instance, when leaders fail to achieve mutual cooperation in an electoral periods, they are replaced 48 percent of the time when the replace cost is $k = 5$, compared with 37 percent and 16 percent when the costs are $k = 20$ and $k = 200$.

Table 4.4 presents probit analyses that reinforce these conclusions. Model 4.3 examines the cost of leader replacement and whether there was mutual cooperation in the election period. Model 4.4 replaces the variable for the outcome of the current period with the average level of mutual cooperation over the previous 4 periods. Again the conclusion is similar. Leaders who are cheap to replace and who have failed to provide mutual cooperation are replaced. When leaders produce cooperative outcomes or the cost of replacement is high, they are likely to be retained.

We examined whether instances of cheating—that is cases of CD or DC—systematically affected leader retention. The effects of these outcomes, either in the immediate election period or averaged over the preceding periods, were not statistically significant. Although the limited amount of data make it difficult to be definitive, it appears that in these experiments voters used the performance of the leader at producing good (i.e., mutually cooperative) outcomes as the standard by which to judge leaders rather than a sophisticated analysis of what led to the failure to cooperate. The experimental evidence suggests that voters use the broad

TABLE 4.4
Probit Analyses of the Leader Replacement

	Leader Change	
	Model 4.3	Model 4.4
Mutual Cooperation (CC) (last period)	−1.201**	
	(.240)	
Average Level of Mutual Cooperation (CC) (previous 4 periods)		.303**
		(.063)
Replacement Cost, k	−.0051**	−.0049**
	(.0018)	(.0018)
Constant	−.098	−.097
	(.119)	(.120)
Observations	232	232

** Statistically significant at the 1% level in a two tailed test.

measure of policy success (that is, achieving mutual cooperation, CC) rather than the specific pattern of play when deciding whether to retain or replace leaders. A casual glance at the experimental data reveals the difficulty in identifying whose actions lead to a failure to achieve mutual cooperation. Given this complexity, it is perhaps not surprising that the voter uses the unambiguous signal of policy success or failure.

Occurrence of Mutual Cooperation

Do institutional arrangements influence the ability of teams to achieve mutual cooperation? Our experimental design allows us to compare decision making within three different institutional arrangements. Although we are severely hindered by small sample size, in this section we compare the average level of cooperation achieved under representative democracy, direct democracy, and individual choice.

The theory developed in the previous chapters suggests that LSP allows teams that function as representative democracies to cooperate more readily than individuals because the threat of removal for a failure to cooperate enables leaders to commit themselves to cooperate. Although we did not formally develop a model of direct democracy, the direct democracy does not provide a team with the LSP commitment mechanism available in the representative democracy. Therefore we suspect that representative democracies cooperate more than direct democracies. We have no prediction as to whether individuals or a direct democracy cooperate more. Informally, we suspect that the patterns of mutual cooperation or mutual defection are

TABLE 4.5
Occurrence of Mutual Cooperation (CC)

| | Number of Experiments | Occurrence of CC Outcomes (Proportion of Total Outcomes) | | | | Proportion of Mutual Cooperation |
		Mean	Standard Deviation	Max	Min.	
Representative Democracy	11	0.35	.39	1	0	0, .45, .02, 1, .40, .68, .05, .02, .05, 1, .18
Direct Democracy	3	0.21	.21	.46	.08	0.46, .1, .08
Individual Choice	6	0.09	.11	.23	0	0, .02, .23, .04, 0, .23

likely to persist longer in the direct democracy setting because no single player is decisive in forming the team's strategy. This latter speculation is readily confirmed by causal observation of the direct democracy data in table 4.7.

Table 4.5 summarizes the average level of cooperation in each experiment in each of the three institutional settings. The final column contains that proportion of times that mutual cooperation (CC) occurred in each experiment. The column labeled "mean" is the average of these proportions. The columns labeled "standard deviation," "max," and "min" provide other summary statistics of the proportion of mutually cooperative outcomes across institutional arrangements.

The highest levels of mutual cooperation are achieved within the representative democracy institutions. In this setting, in both experiments 4 and 10 the teams cooperated in every period. However, experiment 1 under the representative democracy exhibits zero occurrences of mutual cooperation. The representative democracy experiment exhibits the highest average level of mutual cooperation, 35 percent versus 21 percent and 9 percent. These differences appear substantively large. Unfortunately, statistically we can reject the null hypothesis that all mean levels of cooperation are the same. For instance, a simple t-test that the mean level of cooperation in the representative democracy and individual settings are identical gives a t value of 1.61, which is statistically significant only at the 6 percent level in a one tailed test. Although the results are indicative of the theoretical predictions, small sample size prevents us from making a more definitive assessment of which institutional setting promotes the highest level of cooperation.

CONCLUSIONS

Human subject experiments allow researchers to re-create the incentives that people face in political circumstances. In this chapter we replicated the simple version of the prisoners' dilemma between two teams of players in which one player served as team leader and another served as a voter who could, at some cost, replace the leader in an experimental setting. We also contrasted this representative democracy game with a direct democracy version, in which each member of a team votes on their team's strategy, and a simple prisoners' dilemma between individuals.

Although we do not want to push the analysis too far given the limited sample size, even the limited number of experiments conducted show leader change has an important influence in shaping the interactions between teams. The evidence certainly demonstrates the plausibility of our arguments that strategies are conditioned against leaders rather than the team (group or nation) that they represent. This is indeed a remarkable finding, since the experiments were performed without the personification associated with real political leaders. Despite the fact that players performed the experiment through a computer—unable to associate actions with an individual—players still conditioned their play against leaders rather than their team.

The experiments yielded a number of findings that are important in understanding the evolution of cooperation. First, a team, be it a representative democracy, a direct democracy, or an individual, makes reciprocal strategy choices that are conditioned upon the pattern of previous play. This finding supports the Liberal approach to international cooperation. Second, leadership change weakens the dependence between past play and strategy choice. The implications of leader change depend upon the previous pattern of play. Given previously cooperative relations, leader change can jeopardize continued cooperation as leaders may distrust a new person with whom they have yet to build up a reputation or history of reciprocity. Leader change can interrupt cooperative play. Yet, when relations are poor and the pattern of previous play was largely noncooperative, leader replacement can lead to cooperation. Since leader change reduces the extent to which strategy choice depends upon past play, leaders are more likely to play C even if past play was not cooperative.

Third, leaders are more likely to be retained when either the cost of leader replacement is high or the leaders produce mutual cooperation. When leaders fail to achieve cooperative relations, the voter is likely to replace them, particularly when the cost of doing so is low. Finally, the experiments gave limited evidence that the institutional setting of representative democracy produced higher average levels of cooperation than the two other institutional settings.

The results of the human subject experiments suggest that many punishments are leader specific. This helps validate the concept of leader specific punishment theory. Leaders are important proper nouns in the game. That we find such a result in this game is a remarkable finding, since the players are not given any humanizing features. Players have no idea as to which individuals in the room represent them or the other team.

In addition to these quantitative results, qualitative evidence from the postexperiment questionnaire also suggests subjects condition their behavior on leader turnover. For instance, several subjects commented they "only changed tactics when a new leader was elected," or similar statements. Of course, it would be naïve to suppose that leader specific punishments were the only forces at work. Subjects are motivated by other incentives. For instance, several subjects reported replacing the leader with the challenger not because the leader was performing poorly, but out of a notion of fairness. One voter comments on why he/she changed his/her leader: "I did [it] because I didn't think it would be fair for one person to get $1.50 every round, while I could give it to someone else just as easily. Only I think I replaced twice, which defeats the fairness. . . . Oops. Oh well, someone is rich." These and other idiosyncrasies emphasize the need to increase sample size.

Although the results of the human subject experiments suggest leadership change plays an important role in the dynamics of cooperative relations, experiments cannot perfectly create the incentives present in real cooperative and political problems. Although the results here confirm the intuitive plausibility of our ideas, it remains to be shown whether leader specific strategies are features of real world interactions. It is to the task of assessing the impact of leader change on the relations between states to which we now turn.

TABLE 4.6
The Representative Democracy Human Subject Experiments

Experiment	1	2	3	4	5	6	7	8	9	10	11
Cost, k	5	5	5	5	5	5	20	20	20	200	200
1	CD	DD	DC	CC	DC	DD	DD	DC	DD	CC	CC
2	DC	DD	DC	CC	CD	DC	CD	DD	CC	CC	CC
3	CD	DC	DD	CC	CD	DD	DC	DD	CC	CC	CD
4	CD	CD	DD	CC	DD*	DD*	DC	DD*	CD	CC	CC
5	DD	DD	DC	CC	DD	DD	DC	DC	DD	CC	DC
6	DD	DC*	DD*	CC	DC*	DD*	DD*	CD	DC	CC	CC
7	CD	DC	CD	CC	DD	DD	CD	DC	DC	CC	CD
8	DD*	CD	DD*	CC	DC	DD*	DD	DD*	DC	CC	CD*
9	DD	DC	DD	CC	DC	DD	DD	CD	DD	CC	DD
10	CD	CD	DD*	CC	DC*	DD*	DD*	DD	DD*	CC	DC
11	DD	DC	CC	CC	DD	DD	DC	DC	DD	CC	CC
12	DD	CC	DC	CC	DC	DD*	CC	CD*	DC	CC	DD
13	DD	CC	DD	CC	DD	DD	CC	DC	DD	CC	DC
14	DD	CC	CD	CC	DD	DD	DC	DD*	DD	CC	DC
15	DD	CC	DC	CC	DD	CD	DD	DC	DD	CC	DD
16	DD*	CC*	DD*	CC	DD	CC	CD	DC	DD*	CC	DC
17	DD	DD	DD	CC	DD	CC	DC	CD	DC	CC	DC
18	DD	CD*	DD*	CC	DD	CC	DD*	DD	DD	CC	DD
19	DD	DD	DC	CC	DD	CC	DD	DD	CD	CC	DC
20	DD*	CC	DC	CC	DD*	CC	DC	DC*	DD	CC	DD
21	DD	DC	DD	CC	CC	CC	CD	DD	CD	CC	DC
22	DD*	CD	DD*	CC	CC	CC	DD	DD*	CD	CC	CC
23	DD	DD	DD	CC	CD	CC	DD	DD	DD	CC	DD
24	DD*	DD*	DD	CC	CD*	CC	DD	DD*	DD	CC	DD
25	CD	DD	DD	CC	DD	CC	CD	DD	DD	CC	DD
26	DD	CC*	DC*	CC	DD	CC*	DD	DD*	CD	CC	CD
27	DD	DC	DD	CC	DD	CC	DD	DD	CD	CC	CD
28	DD	CC	DD*	CC	DD*	CC	DD	DD*	CD*	CC	DD*
29	DD	CC	DD	CC	DC	CC	DD	CD	DC	CC	DD
30	DD	CC	DD	CC	DD*	CD*	DD*	DD*	DD	CC	DD
31	DD	CC	DD	CC	CC	CC	DD	DC	DD	CC	DD
32	DD	CC	DD	CC	CC	CC	DD	CD*	DD	CC	DD
33	DD	CC	DD	CC	CC	CC	DD	DC	DD	CC	DD
34	DD	CC	DD	CC	CC	CC	DD	DD	DD*	CC	DD
35	DD	CC	DD	CC	CC	CC	DC	DD	DC	CC	DD
36	DD*	CC	DD*	CC	CC	CC	DC	DD*	DD	CC	DD
37	DD	CC	CD	CC	CC	CC	DC	DC	DD	CC	DD
38	DD*	CC*	DD	CC	CC	CC	DD*	CD	DD	CC	DD*
39	DD	DC	DD	CC	CC	CC	DD	DC	DD	CC	CC
40	DD	CD	DD	CC	CC	CC	DD	CD	DD	CC	CC

(*continued*)

TABLE 4.6 (*continued*)

Experiment	1	2	3	4	5	6	7	8	9	10	11
Cost, k	5	5	5	5	5	5	20	20	20	200	200
41	DD	DD	DD	CC	CC	CC	DD	CC	DD	CC	CC
42	DD	DD*	DD	CC	CC*	CC				CC	DC
43	DD	CC	DD	CC	CC	CC				CC	DD
44	DD	CC	DD	CC	CC	CC				CC	DD
45				CC	CC	CC				CC	DD
46				CC	CC	CC				CC	DD
47				CC	CC	CC				CC	DD
48				CC	CC*	CC				CC	DD
49				CC	DC	CC				CC	DD
50				CC	DD	CC				CC	DD

Notes: Payoffs for team A: $CC = 60$, $CD = 20$, $DC = 100$, $DD = 40$. Leader replacement indicated by *. There are 40 basic periods with 2/3 probability in each round of continuing. Leader benefits = 150. Team A elections in periods 4, 8, 12 . . . . Team B elections in periods 6, 10, 14 . . . .

TABLE 4.7
The Direct Democracy Human Subject Experiments

Period	Ateam1	Bteam1	Ateam2	Bteam2	Ateam3	Bteam3
1	DDD	CCC	DCC	CDC	DCC	DDD
2	DDD	DCC	CDC	CDC	CDD	CDD
3	DDD	DCD	CDC	CDC	CDD	CDC
4	CDD	DCD	DDC	CDC	DDC	DDC
5	CDD	CDD	DDC	DDC	DDD	CDD
6	CDD	CDD	DCC	DDD	DCD	CCC
7	CDD	CCD	DCC	CDD	DCD	CCC
8	CDD	CDC	DCD	CCD	DCD	DDD
9	CDD	CDC	DCC	DDD	DCD	DCD
10	CDD	DCD	DDD	DDD	DCD	DDC
11	CDD	DCD	DDD	DDD	DCC	DCD
12	CDD	DDD	DDD	CDD	DCD	CDD
13	CDD	DDD	DDD	DDD	DCC	CDD
14	CDD	DDD	CCD	CDC	CCD	CDD
15	CDD	DDD	CCC	CCD	CCD	CDD
16	CDD	DDD	CCC	CDD	CDD	CDD
17	CDC	DDD	CCD	DDC	DDD	CCD
18	CDD	CDD	DCD	DDD	CDD	CCD
19	CDD	CDD	DDD	CDC	CCD	CDD
20	CDD	DDD	DDC	DDC	DCD	CDD
21	CDC	DDD	DDD	DCC	DCD	CCD
22	CDD	CDD	DDC	DDD	DCD	CDD
23	CDD	CDD	DDC	DDD	DCD	CCD
24	CDD	CDD	DDC	DDD	DDD	CDC
25	CDD	CDD	DCC	DDD	DCD	CDD
26	CDD	CDD	DCC	DDD	DCC	CDD
27	CDD	CDC	DCD	CDD	DCC	CDD
28	CDC	CDC	DDD	CDD	DCC	CDD
29	CDC	CDC	DDD	CDD	CCC	CDD
30	CCC	CDC	DCD	CDD	DDD	CDD
31	CCC	CCC	DDD	CDC	DDD	CDD
32	CCC	CCC	DCD	CDC	DDD	CDD
33	CCC	CCC	DDC	DDD	DDD	CDD
34	CCC	CCC	DCC	DDD	DDD	CDD
35	CCC	CCC	DDC	DDC	DDD	CCC
36	CCC	CCC	DCD	DDD	CDD	CDD
37	CCC	CCC	DDD	DDD	DDD	CDD
38	CCC	CCC	DCD	CDD	DDD	CDD
39	CCC	CCC	DDD	CDD	DDD	CDD
40	CCC	CCC	DCD	CDD	DDC	CDD
41	CCC	CCC	DDD	CDD	DDC	CCC

(*continued*)

TABLE 4.7 *(continued)*

Period	Ateam1	Bteam1	Ateam2	Bteam2	Ateam3	Bteam3
42	CCC	CCC	DDD	CDD	CDD	CDC
43	CCC	CCC	DCD	CDD	CDD	CDC
44	CCC	CCC	DCD	CDD	CCD	CDD
45	CCC	CCC	DCD	CCD	DDD	CDD
46	CCC	CCC	DDC	DDC	DDC	CCC
47	CCC	CCC	DDC	DDC	CCD	CDC
48	CCC	CCC	DCD	DDC	CCD	CDC
49	CCC	CCC	DCD	DDC	CCC	CDC
50	CCC	CCC	DDD	DDC	CCC	CDC

Notes: Payoffs for team A: $CC = 60$, $CD = 20$, $DC = 100$, $DD = 40$. There are 40 basic periods with 2/3 probability in each round of continuing.

TABLE 4.8
The Individual Human Subject Experiments

Period	1	2	3	4	5	6
1	CD	DD	CC	CC	DC	CD
2	CD	DC	DC	DD	DC	DC
3	CD	DC	DD	CD	DD	DC
4	DD	DD	CD	DC	CD	CD
5	DD	DC	DC	CD	DD	DD
6	DD	DD	DD	DD	DD	DD
7	DD	DC	CD	CC	DD	DD
8	DD	DD	CD	CD	DD	DD
9	DD	DD	CD	DD	CD	DD
10	DD	DD	DC	DC	CD	DD
11	DD	DD	DC	DD	DD	DD
12	DD	CC	DD	CD	DD	CC
13	DD	DC	CD	DC	DD	DC
14	DD	DD	CC	DD	CD	CC
15	DD	DC	CC	DD	DD	DC
16	DD	DD	DC	CD	DD	CC
17	DD	DD	DD	DC	DD	CC
18	DD	DD	CD	DD	DD	DC
19	DD	DD	CC	DD	DD	CC
20	DD	DD	DC	CD	DD	CD
21	DD	DD	CD	DC	DD	DC
22	DD	CD	DC	CD	DD	DD
23	DD	DD	CD	DC	DD	DD
24	DD	DD	CD	CD	DD	DD
25	DD	DD	DC	DC	DD	DD
26	DD	DD	DC	CD	DD	DD
27	DD	DD	CD	DC	DD	DD
28	DD	DD	CC	CD	DD	DD
29	DD	DD	CC	DC	DD	DD
30	DD	DC	DC	CD	DD	DD
31	DD	DC	CD	DC	DD	DD
32	DD	DD	CC	CD	DD	DD
33	DD	DD	DC	DC	DD	DD
34	DD	DD	DD	CD	DD	DD
35	DD	DD	CD	DC	DD	DD
36	DD	DD	CC	CD	DD	DD
37	DD	DD	CC	DC	DD	DD
38	DD	DD	CC	CD	DD	DD
39	DD	DD	DC	DC	DD	DD
40	DD	DD	DD	CD	DD	DD
41	DD	DD	CD	DC	DD	DD

(*continued*)

TABLE 4.8 *(continued)*

Period	1	2	3	4	5	6
42	DD	DD	DC	CD	DD	DD
43	DD	DD	DD	DC	DD	DD
44	DD	DD	CD	CD	DD	DD
45	DD	DD	DC	DC	DD	DC
46	DD	DC	DD	CD	DD	CC
47	DD	DD	CD	DC	DD	CC
48	DD	DD	CC	CD	DD	CC
49	DD	DD	DC	DC	DD	CC
50	DD	DD	DD	CD	DD	DC
51	DD	DD	DD	DC	DD	CC
52	DD	DD	CD	CD	DD	CC
53	DD	DD	CC	DC	DD	CC
54	DD	DD	CC	CD	DD	DC
55	DD	DD	DC	DC	DD	CC
56	DD	DD	DD	CD	DD	DC

Notes: Payoffs for team A: $CC = 60$, $CD = 20$, $DC = 100$, $DD = 40$. There are 40 basic periods with $2/3$ probability in each round of continuing.

CHAPTER 5

International Trade, Institutions, and Leader Change

WE HAVE VOCIFEROUSLY argued that individual leaders are the proper nouns of international relations. In the previous chapter we showed that people do indeed condition their behavior on leaders, at least in the experimental context. It is time to examine whether leadership change alters the relations between nations in the real world. To do so we examine dyadic trade flows between nations.

We combine data on political institutions, leadership turnover, and dyadic trade. We argue that merchants are more likely to trade internationally when they anticipate high levels of robust cooperation between the states in question. On this basis, dyadic trade flows serve as a proxy for bilateral cooperation. In this chapter we show the following empirical findings and explain them in the context of leader specific punishments.

1. Level of Cooperation
The level of trade between two large coalition systems is higher than trade between other dyadic pairings of states. This result is consistent with a prediction that follows directly from LSP theory. Pairs of nations in which leader replacement is easy, such as large winning coalition systems, can maintain higher levels of cooperation than pairs of nations in which at least one of the nations has institutions that make leader replacement more costly.

2. Instances of Failed Cooperation (Transition to the Punishment Phase)
We measure collapsed trading relations between nations as bilateral trade being less than half of the previous historical maximum level of trade. By this measure, dyads of large coalition systems are less likely to experience collapses in trade than other dyadic pairings of states. Again this result is consistent with a prediction of LSP theory. When leaders are the target of punishment strategies, the citizens of a nation being punished have an incentive to replace their leader to avoid the punishment. When leader replacement is relatively easy such that citizens act on this incentive, as is the case in large coalition systems, office-seeking leaders avoid those contingencies that are liable to lead to their removal from office. Therefore, leaders in large coalition systems avoid policies likely to incur the ire of other states and lead to diminished trade.

3. The Dynamics of Trade and Leader Turnover

a. Trade and Leader Change during the Cooperative Phase. During periods of regular relations—that is, not during periods of collapsed trade—leadership turnover in small coalition systems reduces trade. However, leadership change in large coalition systems has no appreciable effect on trade. This result is predicted by selectorate theory.

Leaders in small winning coalition systems generate policies that focus on the provision of private goods to satisfy the wants of their supporters. Shifts in leadership can result in large shifts in policy provision. Since protectionism and assistance to industry are common ways to provide private goods, leadership turnover can radically alter the terms of trade of certain goods, and this disrupts established trade. In large coalition systems, leaders focus predominantly on the provision of public goods. Leadership change does not fundamentally alter policy focus, and so trade is rarely affected by leader turnover.

b. Leader Turnover and the Restoration of Cooperation. When trading relations are sour, as measured by trade being only half its previous maximum value, then leadership turnover in small coalition systems improves trade. The effect of leader change in large coalitions is muted. LSP predicts the restoration of cooperation between nations following the removal of the leader whose policies led to the deterioration of relations between states and the decline in trade. While this restoration of relations occurs across all political systems, leaders who are likely to be removed for disrupting cooperative relations do not cheat in the first place. The effect of leadership change in improving sour relations is therefore observed only in small coalition systems.

Consistent with much of the literature on cooperation, to date, we have phrased our discussion of nations' behavior in terms of "cooperation." Yet what exactly does the term *cooperation* mean? In chapter 1 we used Keohane's (1984) conception of cooperation as "mutual adjustment." Certainly our use of the term has been consistent with this definition, but unfortunately, cooperation is not a primitive. It is not something that can be measured or quantified directly. Neither the World Bank nor the IMF collects figures on cooperation levels between states. Therefore we cannot empirically assess the idea of cooperation as a general premise. Instead we examine the specific policy issue of international trade, which is readily measurable.

Trade is based on the economics of scarcity. Nations export relatively abundant goods and import relatively scarce goods. While the underlying concepts of trade are economic, in practical terms mutual trust is an important determinant in deciding who trades with whom. Traders want reassurances that they will be paid promptly (and in the agreed upon manner) and that goods will be delivered in a timely fashion. The UK government could pass laws that greatly discriminate against French goods. Such an act would undoubtedly undermine Anglo-French trade. Few French entrepreneurs would invest in finding contacts, suppliers, or customers in the UK if they anticipated such a law. Although most international trade is between individuals and corporations rather than governments, intergovernment cooperation, at least partially, shapes the willingness of economic actors to participate and invest in trade. For the purposes of this chapter, we assume changes in dyadic trading patterns depend, at least partially, on the willingness of governments to cooperate.

DATA

To assess how domestic political institutions affect the relationship between trade and leader turnover requires three types of data: data on political institution, data on leader turnover, and trade data. In this section we describe these data, the compilation of the data and coding decision. Many of these data are also used in subsequent chapters. Throughout we use the nomenclature that subscript A refers to a variable related to nation A, subscript B refers to a variable related to nation B, and subscript $t-1$ refers to a variable lagged by one year. Table 5.1 summarizes the data sources and definitions of many of our key variables.

Domestic Political Institutions

In leader specific punishment theory institutions determine the cost of leader replacement. BdM2S2's selectorate theory operationalizes this cost. Further, independent of LSP, the selectorate theory argues that the types of policies a leader chooses depend upon selectorate institutions. Leaders in small coalition systems best survive by supplying private goods to their supporter rather than the provision of public goods. This private goods focus means that leader turnover entails high levels of policy volatility as new leaders shift policy away from the interests of their predecessor's coalition toward rewarding their supporters. Leader turnover creates high policy volatility in small coalition systems, compared to large coalition systems, and such volatility can jeopardize international cooperation and discourage trade.

BdM2S2 develop an index of winning coalition (W) using data from Polity IV (Marshall, Jaggers, and Gurr 2002) and Arthur Banks's (2001) data. Their index of coalition size contains four components that reflect the inclusiveness or noninclusiveness of the system: *REGTYPE, XRCOMP,*

XROPEN, and *PARCOMP*. The variable *REGTYPE* refers to regime type and is coded as 2 for military regimes and coded as 3 for military/civilian regimes. Since coalitions in military regimes are formed around a small group of military elites, a military regime is indicative of a small coalition. The BdM2S2 index *W* receives one point if *REGTYPE* is not coded as 2 or 3.

The variable *XRCOMP* measures the competitiveness of executive recruitment. This variable is coded as one when the chief executive is selected by heredity or in rigged, unopposed elections. Such rules are indicative of leaders being dependent upon only a small number of supporters. In contrast, higher values (2 or 3) of *XRCOMP* indicate a dependence on a greater number of supporters. When *XRCOMP* equals 2 or 3, *W* receives an additional point.

The openness of executive recruitment, *XROPEN*, contributes an additional point to *W* if the executive is recruited in a more open setting than heredity (that is, the variable's value is greater than 2). Executives who are recruited in an open political process are more likely to depend on a larger coalition than are those recruited through heredity or through the military.

Finally, one more point can be contributed to the index of *W* if *PARCOMP*, competitiveness of participation, is coded as a 5, meaning that "there are relatively stable and enduring political groups which regularly compete for political influence at the national level" (Polity IV, p. 26). This variable is used to indicate a larger coalition on the supposition that stable and enduring political groups would not persist unless they believed they had an opportunity to influence incumbent leaders; that is, they have a possibility of being part of a winning coalition. The indicator of *W* is then divided by 4 to create a five-point scale for *W* taking the possible values 0, .25, .5, .75, and 1.

Although democracies are large coalition systems, the concepts of winning coalition size and democracy are theoretically and empirically distinct. The definition of democracy is fraught with controversy. Criteria often asserted as necessary for democracy include free and fair elections, freedom of the press, civil liberties, and the turnover of political leaders (Przeworski et al. 2000). Winning coalition size is defined as the number of supporters whose continued support a leader requires in order to retain power. To our knowledge, no definition of democracy includes such a characteristic in its definition. Given the conceptual disagreements as to what constitutes democracy, it is not surprising that numerous empirical measures of democracy have been proposed. Polity, for instance, proposes ten-point scales for the level of democracy and the level of autocracy based upon various Polity measures. Consistent with other studies, we subtract the autocracy score for the democracy to create a 21-point index. We then normalize this variable to create the *DEMAUT* variable, which takes the value of 1 for the most democratic and least autocratic systems and takes value of 0 for the most autocratic and least democratic systems.

At the extremes, that is, in the most democratic and the most autocratic systems, measures of W and $DEMAUT$ are highly correlated. However, on the interior—, that is, when W does not equal 0 or 1—the correlation between W and $DEMAUT$ is much lower. BdM2S2 (2003, pp. 138–140) detail these differences. Given theoretical considerations, selectorate institutions are the appropriate institutions to consider. This said, we have repeated many of the analyses using $DEMAUT$ instead of W (although we do not report them here). These tests produce substantively similar results.

Leadership Data

We measure the turnover of leaders using BdM2S2 (2003) compilation of leaders. These data are based primarily on Bueno de Mesquita and Siverson's (1995) article on the survival of leaders. These data were cleaned by Goemans (see Chiozza and Goemans 2003, 2004), and were in turn updated by BdM2S2 (2003). For the purposes of studying bond markets in the next chapter, we updated these data through June 2004. These data record the date each leader entered and left office.

Within LSP the leader is defined as the decision maker who sets policy. For ease of language, throughout we have conceptualized the leader as an individual. However, we recognize that the decision maker who sets policy might represent a small group of individuals or the leaders of a political party rather than strictly a single individual. Theoretically, the appropriate level at which to conceptualize a "leader" is the level at which nations condition leader specific punishments. For instance, in a parliamentary system, one might imagine targeting punishments at the level of the prime minister, the cabinet, or the ruling party. While theory is consistent with the targeting of punishments at each of these levels, for the purposes of empirical testing we consider the decision maker who sets national policy to be the individual head of state.

In this chapter, our dependent variable, trade, is available only as annual data. Therefore, we require an annualized measure of leader turnover. In an earlier study (McGillivray and Smith 2004), we considered a dichotomous leadership turnover variable that was code 1 if any leader change occurred during a calendar year. While this variable coding is straightforward, it does not always accurately represent the impact of leader turnover. For instance if a leader was deposed in December 1960, the impact of the change is unlikely to be represented in trade figures for 1960 because most of the trade for that year was already concluded before the leader was replaced. The impact of the December 1960 leader turnover would most likely to be experienced in the 1961 trade figures.

We examine the impact of leader change for the twelve months following an instance of leader change. In the case of a December 1960 leadership change, we code one month of 1960 as experiencing leadership change and 11 months of 1961 experiencing leadership change. Had the leadership change occurred in January 1960, all twelve months of the leadership change would have been experienced in 1960. An instance of leadership change in June 1960 would contribute seven months of leader change to 1960 and five months of leader change to 1961. While this coding of leadership change is straightforward when leader turnover is rare, care is required when there are frequent leadership turnovers. In particular, in year t we take the month of the first leadership turnover during that year and calculate the number of leader change months this event contributes to the current year t. We then calculate the month of the last leader change during year t and use this to calculate the number of months to contribute to year $t+1$. We then limit the number of months of leadership change experienced in any year to a maximum of twelve. For instance, if leaders are deposed in December 1960 and January 1961, then the first event contributes eleven months of leader change to 1961 and the second event would contribute an additional twelve months, a total of twenty three months. Having constrained the maximum number of months of change to twelve, we normalize the number of months by dividing by twelve. Using these rules we create a leader change variable, (Leader Change), which codes the proportion of the year experiencing leadership change. This variable takes values $0, 1/12, 2/12, 3/12, \ldots, 1$.

Trade and Economic Data

Dyadic trade data measure the flow of trade between two nations, A and B. We use Oneal, Russett, and Berbaum's (2002) measures of dyadic trade flows. These measures draw on their earlier work (Oneal and Russett 1997, 1999a, b, 2000, 2001), as well as work by Gleditsch (2002). These data are measured in nominal U.S. dollars. We convert these data into constant U.S. (year 2000) dollars using an implicit price deflator (Johnston and Williamson 2002). The data are organized by dyad year, with the dyads organized according to Correlates of War (COW) country codes. The data range from 1885 to 1992 and include 409,918 observations on 16,561 dyads. However, due to the inclusion of lagged variables and missing data, our analyses contain considerably less data.

The Oneal, Russett, and Berbaum data also include measures of Gross Domestic Product, population, military disputes, alliance, and distances. Our data include additional controls for civil and interstate war taken from the correlates of war project, COW (Singer and Small 1972; Small and

TABLE 5.1
Summary of Key Variables

Variable	Concept	Data Source
ln(Trade)	Logarithm of dyad trade flows measured in constant U.S. dollars	Oneal, Russett, and Berbaum 2002
ln(Trade)$_{t-1}$	Logarithm of dyadic trade in the previous year	
W	Winning coalition size: 0, .25, .5, .75, 1	BdM2S2 (2003)
Leader Change	Leadership Change: proportion of the current year that falls within 12 months of instances of a leader deposition	BdM2S2 2003
LOW	Indicator of poor trading relations: a dichotomous variable that is coded as one if the current level of dyadic trade is less than half the maximum level of trade recorded between the dyad	Constructed
Ln(Population)	Logarithm of population size	Oneal, Russett, and Berbaum 2002
Ln(GDP)	Logarithm of Gross National Product	Oneal, Russett, and Berbaum 2002
Ln(Distance)	Logarithm of distance between nations *A* and *B*	Oneal, Russett, and Berbaum 2002
Contiguous States	Dummy variable to indicate if nations *A* and *B* are contiguous	Oneal, Russett, and Berbaum 2002
Interstate War	Dummy variable to indicate if nation is involved in an interstate war	COW
Civil War	Dummy variable to indicate if nation is involved in a civil war	COW

Notes: Subscripts *A*, *B* and *US* are used in future tables to indicate which variables correspond to which nations and the subscript $(t-1)$ refers to the value of the variable in the previous year.

Singer 1982; Sarkees 2000). Typically, we do not report analyses including these controls. Table 5.1 summarizes several key variables.

SETUP OF ECONOMETRIC TESTS AND MODEL SPECIFICATION

The principal dependent variable is the logarithm of dyad trade flows measured in constant U.S. dollars: *Ln(Trade)*. This variable captures the magnitude of trade flows between nations *A* and *B* in year *t*. The variable

$Ln(Trade)_{t-1}$ is the lagged dependent variable, that is to say, the magnitude of trade between states A and B in year $t-1$.

Several of the predictions of leader specific punishment theory deal with transitions between cooperative and punishment phases of play. Tests of these predictions require distinguishing between phases of play. In McGillivray and Smith 2004, we coded the collapse of good trading relations between nations by comparing trade flows in the previous year with recent historical averages. If trade last year was only half the average of the previous five year, then we refer to relations as "bad." While this variable is easy to code and captures recent declines in trade relations, it has some limitation. For example, following the Iranian revolution in 1979, U.S.-Iranian trade collapsed from a high of $15,371 million (2000 U.S.$) in 1978 to only $614.09 million by 1981. Although there has been variation in the level of subsequent trade, it would be fair to say U.S.-Iranian relations remain strained. By our earlier coding rules, U.S.-Iranian trade is "bad" for the years 1980–85. However, after this period, the variable "bad" does not distinguish the poor state of U.S.-Iranian relations because the recent historical average is generated during the punishment phase. Similarly, the "bad" coding would not recognize the poor state of U.S.-Cuban relations after the early 1960s. Therefore, we propose an alternative coding of the collapse of trading relations between states: *LOW*.

The dichotomous variable *LOW* measures severe declines in dyadic trade relations by comparing trade in the current year with the highest level of dyadic trade in any previous year. In particular, *LOW* takes a value of 1 if trade in the current year (measured in constant dollars) is less than half the previous highest recorded level of trade; otherwise *LOW* is coded as 0.

We use *LOW* as a proxy for poor relations between nations. Unfortunately, the *LOW* variable is not perfect. Our theoretical concerns are transitions between cooperative and punishment phases of play. Ideally we wish to identify instances when one nation cheats another, and this politically induced act leads to a diminution of trade. Anecdotally, we know that Castro's decision to nationalize U.S. interests in Cuba led to the sour U.S.-Cuban relations that continue today. *LOW* attempts to systematically identify such events. Yet, our variable misses some instances of cheating and falsely codes other dyad years as sour relations. Uruguay provides a typical example of the latter. From 1952 onward, U.S.-Uruguay trade is coded as low. Yet, this coding results from the collapse in the world wool price rather than from a political decision to cheat. Prior to the 1950s, Uruguay's economy was relatively closed with protection for domestic industry. The economy was driven by exports of wool and beef. In 1951 the world wool price peaked at about five times its regular price, in large part due to increased demand by the U.S. army in Korea. Once the Korean War wound down, the wool price slumped. The year 1951 was a huge boom for Uruguayan exports, and this boom year made those years after it appear like instances of sour relations, while to our knowledge U.S.-Uruguayan relations remained amicable. While we would like *LOW* to perfectly capture the state of political relations between nations, it unfortunately does not. Dyad years in which *LOW* is coded as 1 should be thought of as instances when the chance of politically induced sour relations between states is high. If *LOW* is coded as 0, then politically induced sour relations are less likely.

In the construction of *LOW*, the comparison of current trade is made against the previously highest level of trade. This creates a bias in the data that works against our hypotheses. All else equal, if the time series is short, then the highest previous value of trade is typically lower than if the time series is long. As a consequence of the variable construction, trading relations are less likely to be coded as *LOW* when the time series is short rather than long. In general, the dyadic trade time series are longest for Western democratic states.[1]

The theory makes a number of predictions. Testing these different hypotheses requires a number of different methods. To assess the impact of institutions on trade we use a gravity model (Deardorff 1995; Frankel and Roemer 1999; Helpman and Krugman 1985). This model uses the analogy of gravity to explain the flow of goods given the masses of nations (wealth and population) and their distance apart. Wall (1999) provides background on the gravity model. A standard specification for the gravity model is $Ln(Trade) = \beta_1 Ln(Distance) + \beta_2 Ln(GDP_A) + \beta_3 Ln(GDP_B) + B_4 Ln(POP_A) + \beta_5 Ln(POP_B) + \ldots + e_t$, where $Ln(Distance)$ is the distance between states, $Ln(GDP_A)$ and $Ln(POP_A)$ refer to the logarithms of GDP and population in nation A, and e_t is a stochastic error. The model is well suited to explaining cross-sectional differences in trade flows between pairs of states.

Tests of the dynamics between leader turnover and trade require a framework that measures the impact of independent variables on the proportionate change in trade. For this purpose we use a lagged dependent variable specification: $Ln(Trade) = \beta_1 Ln(Trade)_{t-1} + \beta_2 Institutions + \beta_3 leadertur nover + \ldots + e_t$, where the error term, e_t, is assumed normally distributed with mean 0 and variance σ^2. In this lagged dependent variable setting, the dependent variable (the magnitude of trade between A and B) depends upon the magnitude of prior trade ($Ln(Trade)_{t-1}$), political institutions, and leadership change. The coefficients on the political and leadership variables determine how the expected magnitude of trade

---

[1] To check if this creates a problem we record the LOW variable by looking only at instances of LOW trade compared to the highest level of previous trade over the last fifteen years. The results were substantively similar.

varies relative to trade last year. As a rough guide, appropriate for small changes, the coefficient can be thought of as the proportionate change in trade from a unit change in an independent variable.

We modify the basic lagged dependent variable model. We include fixed effects for each dyad. Effectively this assigns each pair of nations a unique intercept, which, all else equal, dictates the rate of growth of trade between the states. The appropriateness of fixed effects in cross-sectional studies of international relations has been heatedly debated in recent years (Beck and Katz 2001; Green, Kim, and Yoon 2001; King 2001; Oneal and Russett 2001). Fortunately, our results are similar whether we include fixed effects or not. Since fixed effects are generally the more demanding tests, we present those results.

Our analyses examine how institutional variables and leader change in nations A and B affect the volume of trade between them. The data are organized by COW country codes with the lowest indexed nation being state A and the higher indexed nation being state B. The COW country codes list each state in the international system, starting with the Americas and finishing with Australasia. Beyond the organization of the codes by region, there is nothing systematic about the list. Therefore, there is no basis for assuming the impact of independent variables in the lower listed nation systematically differs from the impact of independent variables in the higher listed state. That is, the impact of leader change on dyadic trade in state A should have the same impact as leader change in state B. To reflect this symmetry we constrain the coefficient estimates associated with nation A to be identical to the coefficient estimates associated with nation B.

For clarity, we present several of our results, looking first at only dyads that include the United States, which is coded as nation A. The United States, as the world's largest economic market for the majority of the sample, trades with practically every other state. Additionally, the United States has a large winning coalition system throughout the sample. The hypotheses predict that leader turnover has little effect in large coalition systems. By focusing on U.S.-only dyads, the effect of leader change and institutions in nation B can be examined with the institutions in nation A held constant.

Several hypotheses predict that institutions and leader change affect the volatility of trade as well as its level. To test these hypotheses we model the variance of the error term as a function of independent variables. Specifically, we assume the stochastic error term, e_t, is normally distributed with mean 0 and variance $\sigma^2_{i,t}$, where (i,t) refers to a particular dyad i at time t. If Z_{it} is a vector of independent variables, then $\sigma_{i,t} = \gamma_0 + \gamma Z_{i,t}$. Estimates of γ allow us to assess the extent to which the independent variables Z affect the volatility of trade.

To be specific, to model the fixed effects we use the following standard notation $y_{i,t} - \underline{y}_i = (x_{i,t} - \underline{x}_i)\beta = (e_{i,t} - \underline{e}_i)$, where $\underline{y}_i$ is the mean of the dependent variable for dyad i, and so forth. We convert all x and y variables to difference from mean format by dyad to implement the fixed effects. Our assumptions is that $E(e_{i,t} - e_i) = 0$ and $E(e_{i,t} - e_i)^2 = \sigma_{i,t}^2$, where $\sigma_{i\,t} = \gamma_0 + \gamma Z_{i,t}$. $Z_{i,t}$ is a vector of independent variables (not in difference from mean format). The fixed effects apply only to the β and not the γ parameters. As with other results, we maximized the likelihood function in *STATA 8*.

RESULTS

The Effect of Institutions on the Level of Dyadic Trade

There is already considerable evidence that political institutions affect the level of dyadic trade. As we summarized extensively in chapter 1, joint democracy promotes trade. Since winning coalition size, W, is highly correlated with democracy, it is not perhaps surprising that we also find large coalition systems promote trade.

Table 5.2 contains two gravity models examining the cross-sectional effects of institutions. Model 5.1 is a gravity model with the inclusion of the standard gravity variables of *Ln (Distance)*, *Ln (GDP)*, *Ln (population)*, and contiguity. Additionally model 5.1 has variables for institutions (W_A, W_B, and $W_A * W_B$) and time trend variables (*year* and *year²*). Model 5.2 replicates this analysis with the addition of variables for each state's involvement in interstate or civil wars. The models were estimated with variables relating to each state. However, since the variables relating to nation A are constrained to equal those associated with nation B, we report the coefficient estimates for one nation.

LSP theory and selectorate theory predicted that large coalition systems are more trustworthy and able to obtain higher levels of cooperation than small coalition systems. The coefficient on the coalition size variable (W_A) is −0.121 and the coefficient on the interaction of W_A and W_B is .556. Both coefficients are highly significant. The impact of institutions on trade depends upon the interaction of institutions in each nation. If nation A is a large winning coalition system ($W=1$) and nation B is a small coalition system ($W=0$), then the level of trade between them, all else equal, is about 11 percent lower than if they had both been small coalition systems ($W=0$). If both nations have large coalitions ($W=1$), then their trade is about 37 percent larger than it would have been if both states had small coalitions ($W=0$).

The theoretical analysis of the stochastic PD game predicted the ease of maintaining cooperation across different combinations of political systems. LSP theory predicts that dyads of two large coalition systems maintain deeper and more robust cooperation. This commitment makes an

TABLE 5.2
Gravity Models to Assess the Impact of Institutions on
International Trade

	Ln(Trade)	
	Model 5.1	*Model 5.2*
Winning Coalition, W_A†	−.121**	−.121**
	(.006)	(.006)
W_A*W_B	.556**	.556**
	(.010)	(.010)
Ln(Population)$_A$†	−.079**	−.076**
	(.001)	(.001)
Ln(GDP)$_A$†	.214**	.212**
	(.0009)	(.0009)
Contiguous States	.501**	.501**
	(.005)	(.005)
Ln(Distance)	−.182**	−.182**
	(.001)	(.001)
Year	−.337**	−.351**
	(.007)	(.007)
Year^2	.00009	.00009**
	(1.88e–06)	(1.90e–06)
Interstate War$_A$†		.020**
		(.004)
Civil War$_A$†		−.045**
		(.003)
Constant	334.23**	347.10**
	(7.182)	(7.227)
Observations	296,334	296,334

** Statistically Significant at the 1% level in a one tailed test.
* Statistically Significant at the 5% level in a one tailed test.
† The analyses include analogous variables for nation B. For
example the analysis includes W_B. However, since the estimates
constrain the coefficients on variables relating to nation B to
equal those relating to nation A, we do not report the (identical)
coefficient for nation B.

attractive trading environment as economic actors can anticipate long and
stable relationships and expect impartial enforcement of contracts. Consistent with these predictions, the amount of trade between two large coalition systems is greater than trade between other institutional pairings.

The analysis in chapter 2 suggested that although two large W systems
can cooperate much more successfully than either a pair of small W systems
or a mixed pair of systems, the mixed system was slightly more cooperative
than two small coalition systems. This suggests, perhaps, that we might

expect higher levels of trade between a large and small coalition system than between two small coalition systems. It is important to differentiate between interstate cooperation and trade, however. The former depends upon the ability of leaders to commit not to cheat. The latter is determined by the actions of many economic actors. Consider a trader in a large coalition system. When she decides which foreign nation to trade her goods in, she considers both economic and political factors. The relative scarcity of goods in different nations determines the economic incentives to trade, but if all else is equal on this dimension, the trader strongly prefers to trade with another large coalition system because of the stability of cooperative relations between large coalition systems. Traders in large coalition systems disproportionately trade with other traders from other large coalition systems. This diverts trade by merchants in large coalition systems away from small coalition systems toward other large coalition systems.

Although LSP predicts cooperation levels between mixed regime systems are slightly higher than between two small coalition nations, economic actors in large coalition systems prefer to trade with other large coalition systems. On balance, the empirics suggest that the latter diversion of trade from small to large coalition systems dominates arguments about the level of cooperation that states can maintain. All else equal, trade between a large and a small coalition system is lower than trade between two small coalition systems. The dominant result, however, is that two large coalition systems engender the highest level of trade.

The results are consistent with the argument of selectorate theory and LSP. They are also consistent with many other theoretical arguments, however, such as Russett and Oneal's (1997) Kantian arguments. As such they do little to extend our theoretical understanding of international cooperation because they do not help us distinguish between rival theories. Yet rival arguments do not predict the impact of leader turnover on trade and the frequency with which trade relations collapse.

Political Institutions and the Collapse of Trade

Leader specific punishments predict that small coalition systems are more likely to cheat on cooperative arrangements than are large coalition systems. Such cheating endangers dyadic trade because reciprocal punishment strategies often lead to the termination of trade. LSP predicts that politically induced collapses in dyadic trading relations are more common in dyads that involve a small coalition system.

Here we examine the relative frequency of collapsed trading relations as defined by the variable *LOW*. Remember this variable takes value 1 if dyadic trade in the current period is less than half the previous maximum level of trade; otherwise *LOW* equals 0. Trade between nations can decline for numerous nonpolitical reasons. In the long run, technology changes or changes in tastes can reduce the trade of particular goods. For example, prior to Haber's invention in the early 1990s, of a method to fix nitrogen by directly combining nitrogen and hydrogen over a catalyst, European nations imported nitrates. The demand for nitrates to improve agricultural yields was initially satiated by importing huge quantities of guano—bird droppings—from rainless islands off the coast of Peru. Between about 1850 and 1870 about 20 million tons of guano were collected, but with the exhaustion of these sources, deposits of caliche in the desserts of Chile accounted for the world's major trade in nitrates. The Haber process made this trade obsolete (Morrison and Morrison 2001). Acts of god, such as bad weather, can destroy harvests and significantly reduce trade in the short term. We might think of these effects as random shocks.

Dyadic trade can decline as a consequence of political actions. For instance, in 1960 Fidel Castro nationalized U.S. interests in Cuba without compensation. Since that time the United States has embargoed Cuba, and trade levels are a trickle of what they were in 1958. The United States and Cuba are in the punishment phase. While on a case-by-case basis it is easy to access the causes of a decline in trade, systematically it is difficult to tell whether *LOW* trade occurs because of political events leading to the punishment phase or random acts of god, such as failed harvests. While all nations are equally vulnerable to acts of god, LSP theory predicts that large coalition systems are significantly less likely to take political acts that lead to the punishment phase. While all dyads should experience *LOW* trade due to random shocks, dyads involving small coalition systems should experience a higher rate of politically induced poor trade than dyads involving only large coalition systems.

Table 5.3 tests this hypothesis by showing instances of *LOW* trading relations for dyads involving the United States. The focus on U.S.-only dyads is for both theoretical and practical reasons. The United States is a significant trading partner of virtually every nation in the world. Additionally the United States has constant, large *W* political institutions throughout the entire sample. The theory predicts that small coalition systems are most likely to cheat. By holding nation *A*'s institutions fixed, we assess the effect of institutions in nation *B*.

Table 5.3 reveals that instances of poor trading relations with the United States are relatively more frequent for small coalition systems than for large coalition systems. When coalition size is at its maximum, $W = 1$, only 4 percent of dyad years experience *LOW* trade relations. In smaller coalition systems, $W < .75$, the relative frequency of *LOW* trade is more than three times higher. These differences are highly statistically significant. Consistent with expectations, dyads of large coalition nations experience fewer

TABLE 5.3

Domestic Political Institution and Poor Trading Relations (U.S.-only dyads)

Nature of Trading Relations	Winning Coalition Size, W				
	W = 0	W = .25	W = .5	W = .75	W = 1
Good Relations (LOW = 0)	464	1,191	1,554	1,454	1,223
	86%	86%	84%	90%	96%
Poor Relations (LOW = 1)	73	187	286	155	51
	14%	14%	16%	10%	4%

Notes: Pearson chi2(4) = 114.8 (Pr = 0.000), Likelihood-ratio chi2(4) = 131.6 (Pr = 0.000).

instances of collapsed dyadic trading relations than do dyads involving a small coalition system.

The fifty-one cases of collapsed trade with the United States involving large coalition systems ($W = 1$) include cases relating to Uruguay from 1952 to 1970 and from 1985 to 1992; the UK from 1950 to 1954; the Netherlands in 1923; Switzerland in 1889, 1891, 1893, 1895, 1896, 1897, and 1927; Sweden in 1927; Norway in 1921, 1924, 1928, and 1929; and Malaysia in 1958 and from 1960 through 1965. One might argue that rather than Uruguay representing twenty-five cases, it is two instances of collapsed trade starting in 1952 and 1985. We construct an alternative version on table 5.3 on this basis, and the analysis reveals the same pattern. Large coalition systems still experience fewer instances of LOW trade. The distinction between $LOW = 1$ and $LOW = 0$ is calculated as half of previous maximum trade. We recalculated table 5.3 using other thresholds, such as trading being less than 1/2. 713 before $LOW = 1$. Similarly we have examined these data comparing current dyadic trade with the maximum level of dyadic trade in the past ten years or past fifteen-year period as the basis for assessing poor trading relations. In each case we obtain similar substantive results.

The table excludes data from the 1930s. The early 1930s saw a collapse in the world economy and severe recession across most economies in the world. This systemic impact of the depression reveals itself with nearly half the U.S.-dyad years during the 1930s appearing as LOW dyadic trade events. The purpose of coding LOW is to identify events where there is a high probability that politically induced cheating has led to a collapse in trade. We therefore exclude the depression era events for these and subsequent analyses.

The results are clear and robust. Dyads of large coalition nations have fewer instances of failed trading relations than do dyads involving a small coalition system.

The Dynamics of Leader Change and Trade

In this section we examine the role of leadership turnover on patterns of trade. Domestic political institutions moderate the effect of leader change. Leadership change in large coalition systems has little or no impact on trading relations. Leadership turnover in small coalition systems, however, substantially affects dyadic trade relations in two ways. First, during periods of regular cooperative trading, leader change in small coalition systems reduces trade. This prediction, which follows from selectorate theory, results from the possibility of high policy variability following leadership turnover in small coalition systems. Second, LSP predicts that if trading relations are poor, then leader replacement frequently reinvigorates trade.

LSP theory predicts that if nations are experiencing politically induced poor trading relations, leader turnover helps restore trade. In the context of the current analysis, LSP theory deals predominately with the rejuvenation of relations between nations. The selectorate theory, in addition to providing the metric for the cost of leader replacement, implies a relationship between the types of policies leaders choose and the coalition size. Leader change produces larger shifts in policies in small rather than large coalition systems. Such policy volatility reduces trade.

For presentational clarity we examine the effects of leader change in two steps. First, we test the implications of policy volatility implied by the selectorate theory. These tests can be thought of as the consequences of leader change during cooperative phases of play. Second, we examine leadership turnover during periods of sour trading relations. These latter tests look at transitions from punishment to cooperative phases of play. During each of these steps we examine two sets of analyses. First, we examine trade in U.S.-only dyads. Throughout the domain of the data, U.S. institutions remain constant and the United States has significant trade with most other nations. The United States is coded as nation A, and the constancy of its institutions makes it easy to assess the impact of institutions in nation B. Second, we examine dyadic trade between all dyads.

SELECTORATE INSTITUTIONS, LEADER CHANGE, AND POLICY VOLATILITY

Selectorate institutions shape the policy choices of leaders. If institutions are such that leaders are beholden to only a small coalition, then leaders can best reward their supporters through policies focused on private goods. That is, the leader satisfies the particularistic wants of her coalition. When leader change occurs in such systems, the leader often rearranges her coalition to a different set of supporters and shifts policies to be commensurate with the desires of the new supporters. Leader change produces shifts from one set of intense private goods policies to another. Since in the context of trade, private goods policies often include tariffs or other barriers to trade, assistance to industry, or nonimpartial application of bureaucratic and regulatory standards, shifts in policy can drastically alter the terms of trade for goods and lead to large shifts in which goods are traded. Since economic actors fear investing during such periods of policy turmoil, the expectation that such policies might be implemented harms trade.

In large coalition systems leadership turnover produces much more moderate shifts in policy. Leaders in large coalition systems must satisfy large numbers of supporters. The effective provision of public goods is a more efficient method to reward such a large group of supporter than trying to satisfy the particularistic wants of all supporters. The policies of large coalition leaders are predominantly aimed toward improving social welfare, with private goods being relatively unimportant. Changes in political leadership leave the policy focus relatively unchanged. Both successor and predecessor focus on public goods. The focus on public rather private goods means barriers to trade are relatively modest, such that even if barriers to trade shift to reflect the particularistic wants of a new coalition, the effects on trade are relatively small.

The selectorate theory implies that leader change in large coalition systems has relatively little effect on trading relations. In contrast, leader change in small coalition systems often leads to large scale shifts in policy. These polices can and sometimes do directly affect the trade of goods. Even the expectation that such changes might occur harms trade, however, Figure 5.1 shows U.S. trade with Cuba and the UK and figure 5.2 shows U.S. trade with Pakistan and New Zealand.

Both the UK and New Zealand are large coalition systems throughout the time period plotted. Their trade with the United States is shown by the x's. In contrast, Cuba and Pakistan, whose trade with the United States is shown by the circles, show considerable institutional variance, although neither ever became a large coalition system ($W=1$).

The figures graphically illustrate how domestic political institutions affect the pattern of trade. U.S.-Cuban trade exhibits much greater volatility than U.S.-UK trade. In contrast to the relatively smoothly progressing line of x's that show U.S.-UK trade, the circles showing U.S.-Cuban trade jump around radically before collapsing to almost 0 trade following Castro's 1959 accession to power. U.S.-UK trade exhibits comparatively little volatility; neither does leadership turnover have any visible impact on the pattern of trade. Not so in the case of U.S.-Cuban trade. Trade is overall more volatile, and leader change typically suppresses trade. Castro deposed Batista on January 2, 1959. Compared to 1958, U.S.-Cuban trade declined 16 percent during 1959. Following Castro's 1960s nationalization of U.S. interests without compensation, trade subsequently collapsed to practically nothing. While Castro's seizure of power

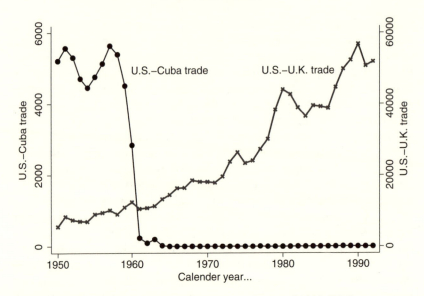

Figure 5.1. U.S. trade with Cuba and UK (in millions of 2000 US$).

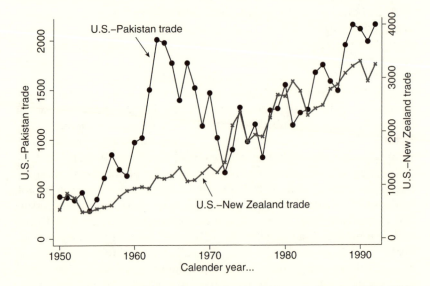

Figure 5.2. U.S. trade with Pakistan and New Zealand (in millions of 2000 US$).

had high international visibility, the immediate impact of his seizing office is comparable with that of other leaders. His predecessor, Batista, seized power in a coup on March 10, 1952. While Batista was to become a U.S. friend, U.S.-Cuba trade declined 15 percent between 1951 and 1953.

U.S. trade with the UK and Cuba clearly shows different patterns. It is easy to dismiss Cuba as a special case, however. The cynics among us might regard Cuba as having effectively been a U.S. colony prior to Castro's revolution. What is more, U.S.–Cuba trade was dominated by sugar, and so the value of trade was highly susceptible to shifts in the world price for sugar. Further, the UK's trade with the United States is orders of magnitude higher than that of Cuba and much more diverse. However, the differences between U.S. trade with large and small coalition systems are replicated in the graphs of U.S.-Pakistan and U.S.–New Zealand trade.

Both Pakistan and New Zealand have similar magnitudes of trade with the United States, and unlike the case of Cuba, neither trade is dominated by a single raw material. Yet the patterns persist. U.S.–New Zealand trade, although exhibiting some ups and downs, overall shows a consistent progression. In contrast, U.S. trade with Pakistan fails to show consistent growth and bounces around.

Systematic empirical tests show that these examples illustrate general features of leadership change under different institutional settings. First, we examine trade in U.S.-only dyads. In these tests, leadership turnover in the smallest coalition systems ($W=0$) reduces trade with the United States by about 7 percent relative to trade without leadership turnover. Leader turnover in the largest coalition systems ($W=1$) has no significant effect on trade. Second, we examine dyadic trade between all dyads. As with the U.S.-only dyads, leader turnover produces a decline in trade in small coalition systems but not in large coalition systems. The magnitude of the decline in trade associated with leader change in a small coalition system in the all-dyads analysis is about 1 percent.

The analyses in table 5.4 systematically tests the effects of leader turnover during cooperative periods of play for dyads that include the United States as nation A. The table contains three models. Model 5.3 is a simple representation of the selectorate model. It examines the trade of 176 nations with the United States. The dependent variable is the logarithm of trade flows between the United States and nation B. The variable $Ln(Trade)_{t-1}$ represents the lagged dependent variable—that is, the magnitude of trade in the previous period. As one expects, trade in the previous year is the best predictor of trade today. The model controls for fixed effects for each dyad.

The variable ($Leader\ Change_B$) represents leadership turnover in nation B. The negative coefficient of -0.076 indicates that leader turnover in the smallest coalition systems ($W=0$) reduces trade on average by about

TABLE 5.4
The Effects of Leader Turnover on Trading, U.S.-only Dyads

	Ln(Trade)		
	Model 5.3	*Model 5.4*	*Model 5.5*
Ln(Trade)$_{t-1}$	.961**	.879**	.871**
	(.004)	(.006)	(.006)
(Leader Change$_B$)	−.076**	−.059**	−.061**
	(.021)	(.020)	(.021)
WB*(Leader Change$_B$)	.069*	.059*	.063*
	(.030)	(.029)	(.027)
W$_B$	.024	−.013	−.012
	(.016)	(.016)	(.017)
Ln(Population)$_{US}$		−.766**	−.883**
		(.110)	(.105)
Ln(Population)$_B$		−.174**	−.180**
		(.019)	(.019)
Ln(GDP)$_{US}$		.318**	.358**
		(.046)	(.044)
Ln(GDP)$_B$		.152**	.169**
		(.014)	(.014)
Constant	.092	7.047	.000
	(.011)	(.912)	(.003)
Estimates of σ Ln(Trade)$_{t-1}$			−.011**
			(.001)
W$_B$			−.075**
			(.007)
Constant			.269
			(.006)
Observations (Dyads)	6,213	5,410	5,410
	(176)	(147)	(147)

** Statistically Significant at the 1% level in a one tailed test.
*Statistically, Significant at the 5% level in a one tailed test.

7 percent. The variable (*Leader Change*)$_B$*W$_B$ is the leadership turnover variable interacted with coalition size. The impact of leadership change in the largest coalition systems ($W=1$) is determined by the sum of this interaction variable and the (*Leader Change$_B$*) variable. The average impact of leader change in a large coalition system is $0.069 - 0.076 = -0.007$, which, statistically speaking, is indistinguishable from 0. Yet, a joint hypothesis test with a null hypothesis that the coefficients on both (*Leader Change*)$_B$ and W$_B$*(*Leader Change*)$_B$ equal 0 is strongly rejected. That is to say that while leadership change in nation *B* significantly affects trade with the United States if nation *B* is a small winning coalition system, if

nation B is a large coalition system, then leadership turnover has no appreciable effect on trade with the United States.

The variable W_B controls for coalition size in nation B. Remember that the U.S. coalition size equals 1 throughout the sample. The positive coefficient of 0.024 suggests that U.S. trade with a large coalition system grows faster than U.S. trade with a small coalition system. However, the effect of this variable is insignificant. This is perhaps unsurprising. The model controls for fixed effects. Therefore, the effect of the UK's large winning coalition in the U.S.-UK dyad is effectively assigned to the U.S.-UK specific intercept. Indeed in any case where nation B's institutions are constant throughout the sample, nation B's institutions do not contribute to the estimate of the coefficient on the W_B variable.

Model 5.4 repeats the analysis in model 5.3 but with the addition of the standard gravity model control variables for economic size and population size. We cannot use the gravity variable of distance between nations because this variable is constant for each dyad and our analyses include fixed effects. The results support the same conclusions as model 5.3. Leadership change has a significant impact in small coalition systems but has no appreciable impact in large coalition systems.

The selectorate theory predicts greater policy volatility in small rather than large coalition systems. Model 5.5 examines this prediction by explicitly modeling the variance of the stochastic error as a function of independent variables. In particular, we assume the variance depends upon the previous level of trade (Ln(Trade)_{t-1}) and nation B's winning coalition size (W_B). The estimates of the level of trade are similar to those of models 5.3 and 5.4. That is to say, leader change significantly reduces trade if nation B is a small coalition system, but leader change has no effect if nation B is a large coalition system.

σ, the standard deviation of the stochastic error, decreases as the prior level of trade increases and as nation B's coalition size increases. Suppose, for example, nation B's trade with the United States is \$1 billion, a fairly average amount. If nation B is a large coalition system, the variance in trade is approximately half what the variance would be if nation B was a small coalition system.

The above results establish that leadership change in small coalition systems affects trade with the United States. We now seek to show that the relationship between trade and leadership change is a general phenomenon and not one restricted to trade with the United States. Table 5.5 contains two models: 5.6 and 5.7. Each model examines trade flows for all dyads for which we have data. In this setup we include variables that relate to institutions and leadership change in nation A. We also include these same variables for nation B. Controlling for institutions, however,

TABLE 5.5
The Effects of Leader Turnover on Trading, All Dyads

	Ln(Trade)	
	Model 5.6	Model 5.7
Ln(Trade)$_{t-1}$	.935**	.944**
	(.0006)	(.0006)
(Leader Change$_A$)†	−.009**	.0002
	(.001)	(.0008)
W_A*(Leader Change$_A$)†	.006**	−.0008
	(.001)	(.0012)
W_A†	−.004*	−.000
	(.002)	(.0008)
W_A*W_B	.027**	.007**
	(.003)	(.002)
W_A*W_B*(Leader Change$_A$)†		.006**
		(.002)
WB*(Leader Change$_A$)†		−.003*
		(.001)
Constant	0.000	.001
	(.003)	(.00009)
Estimates of σ Ln(Trade)$_{t-1}$		.237**
		(.0009)
W_B†		.009**
		(.0005)
W_A*W_B		.011**
		(.0009)
Constant	.116**	.034**
	(.0001)	(.0003)
Observations	363,338	363,338

† The analysis contains analogous variables referring to the other nation ((Leader Change$_B$), W_B, etc). Since these coefficient estimates are constrained to be equal, we report only one set of estimates.
** Statistical Significant at the 1% level in a one tailed test.
*Statistical Significant at the 5% level in a one tailed test.

we have no reason to believe the impact of leadership change in nation *A* differs from the impact of leadership change in nation *B*. We therefore constrain the coefficients relating to nations *A* and *B* to be identical and report a single coefficient that applies to the variables associated with both nations *A* and *B*.

Model 5.6 is parallel to model 5.3. In contains 363,338 observations on 15,100 dyads. The coefficient on the leader change variable, (*Leader Change$_A$*), is − 0.0090. The variable W_A*(*Leader Change$_A$*) is an interaction variable between leadership change and political institution in each nation and the coefficient on this variable is 0.0062. The estimates on both variables are highly significant, as is a joint hypothesis test that both coefficient estimates are simultaneously 0. These coefficients suggest that leadership change in a small coalition system ($W=0$) reduces bilateral trade by about 0.89 percent. In large coalition systems ($W=1$), the impact of leader change on trade is much smaller: trade declines by about 0.28 percent. This difference is significantly different from 0.

The positive and significant coefficient on the W_A*W_B variable suggests dyadic trade grows faster between dyads of two large coalition systems than between other pairings of nations. This result is consistent with the earlier observation in the gravity model setting that trade volumes are highest between two large coalition systems.

Model 5.6 supports the results found earlier looking at U.S.-only dyads and the gravity models. Leadership change in small, but not large, coalition systems affects dyadic trade. Dyads composed of two large coalition systems experience a faster growth in trade than do other pairings of states. This latter result, however, suggests that the interaction of institutions impacts the dynamics of trade. In model 5.7 we examine this effect by interacting leadership change in nation B with the institutions in nation A. The variable $W_B*(Leader\ Change_A)$ is an interaction variable between nation B's coalition size and leadership change in nation A, and the variable $W_A*W_B*(Leader\ Change_A)$ is a triple interactive term of institutions in nations A and B and leadership change in nation A. There are analogous variables relating to leader change in nation A. Again we constrain coefficients on variables associated with leader change in nation A to equal those associated with leader change in nation B. We explicitly model the variance structure as a function of previous trade and political institutions. We have not induced the standard gravity control variables. Their inclusion, or the inclusion of other controls for things such as war and civil war, produces very similar results.

The large number of interaction terms in model 5.7 makes a direct interpretation of the coefficients difficult. Table 5.6 calculates the substantive effect of leadership change under different institutional configurations. Table 5.6 compares the rate of growth in trade for different combinations of large ($W=1$) and small ($W=0$) winning coalition systems. For ease of comparison we standardized the growth of trade between two small coalition systems to be 0. The top number in each cell refers to the predicted growth rate in trade if there is no leadership change. The lower number in each cell refers to the predicted growth rate in trade associated with leader change in nation B (($Leader\ Change_B$) = 1).

Looking first at the top number in each cell—that is, those associated with no leadership change—we see that trade between two large coalition systems grows faster than trade between other combinations of political

TABLE 5.6

The Impact of Leader Turnover under Different Institutional
Configurations (estimated from Model 5.7)

	$W_B = 0$	$W_B = 1$
$W_A = 0$	0%	−.004%
	.022%	−.064%
$W_A = 1$	−.004%	.068%
	−.278%	.883%

Notes: Nation A's coalition size, W_A; Nation B's Coalition Size, W_B.
Table reports the percentage growth in trade associated with different
combinations of institutional arrangements and the impact of leader
change. The first entry in each cell relates to no leader change and the
second entry corresponds to leader change in nation B.

institutions. This difference of 0.068 percent is highly statistically significant. If the dyad is mixed with one large coalition and one small coalition,
then the predicted growth in trade (−.004 percent) is statistically indistinguishable from 0.

The impact of leadership change depends upon institutional context.
When both nations have small coalitions, leader change does not alter the
growth in trade significantly. That is to say, the 0.022 percent in the top
left cell is indistinguishable from 0. Similarly in the top right cell, leader
change in nation B does not significantly alter trade when nation A is a
small coalition system and nation B is a large coalition.

Leadership change in nation B has a significant impact on trade when
nation A is a large coalition system. In particular, if nation B is a small
coalition system and nation A is a large coalition systems, leader change in
nation B reduces the growth in trade by 0.274 percent. If nations A and B
are large coalition systems, leader change increases trade growth by 0.815
percent. Both these differences are statistically significant.

 Political institutions moderate the impact of leader change. Consistent
with the arguments of selectorate theory, leadership change in large coalition systems does not harm trade. Indeed, the analyses in model 5.7 suggest leader change increases trade between large coalition systems. While
this result does not follow directly from selectorate arguments, it is worth
noting that leader turnover is an indicator of coalition size, since the
greater W is, the harder it is for leaders to survive. Large coalition systems
promote greater levels of cooperation.

Leadership change in small coalition systems harms trade. Model 5.6
suggest the impact of leader change in a small coalition system is to reduce trade by about 0.89 percent. Model 5.7 suggested the impact of
leader change in small coalition systems is most acutely felt in trading
relations with large coalition systems.

TRANSITIONS BETWEEN COOPERATIVE AND
PUNISHMENT PHASES

Leader specific punishment theory predicts that leadership change leads to a renewal of good relations between nations that are no longer cooperating. In particular, if the leader from nation A has cheated, then no leader from nation B will cooperate with nation A: the nations are in the punishment phase. Leaders from nation B, however, are willing to cooperate with any successor in nation A. Once the current leader in nation A is replaced, cooperation resumes. In the current context of dyadic trade flows, we cannot measure cooperation directly. However, if nations A and B are in the punishment phase and no longer cooperate, trade is significantly harmed. When the leader whose actions caused the transition to the punishment phase is removed, cooperation restarts and trade recovers.

If leaders are easily removed, as in large coalition systems, then they rarely cheat, since their citizens depose them to restore cooperation. On the equilibrium path, cheating by large coalition leaders is extremely rare. Most of the transitions to the punishment phase are brought about by small coalition leaders. Empirically, the replacement of a small coalition leader is more likely to result in the restoration of cooperation than is the replacement of a large coalition leader.

We test the effects of leader turnover between dyads that are experiencing a significant decline in trade. Remember, we defined LOW trade as a level of trade that is only half of the previous maximum level of trade for the dyad. These tests are necessarily noisy. Although we can observe declines in trade, we do not know if they are the result of some political action by one of the leaders or if the drop in trade results from some random event such as a harvest failure. We present our results in two steps, examining U.S.-only dyads before considering all dyadic trading relations. Since the effects of other variables are similar to those already described, we focus predominantly on variables relating to LOW.

Table 5.7 contains analyses relating to U.S.-only dyads. Model 5.8 is a fixed effects panel model. Consistent with earlier analyses, trade in the previous year is the best predictor of trade. The statistically significant coefficient estimates of $-.0878$ on the ($Leader\ Change_B$) variable and $.0735$ on the $W_B{}^*(Leader\ Change_B)$ variable support the previously reported relationship between leader turnover and trade. Specifically, during the cooperative phase of play ($LOW = 0$), leader change in a small coalition system reduces trade with the United States by about 8.4 percent, while leader change in a large coalition system has no significant impact on trade with the United State.

When trading relations between nation B and the United States are sour (as indicated by $LOW = 1$), the impact of leader change in nation B differs

TABLE 5.7
Leadership Turnover and the Restoration of Trading Relations,
U.S.-only Dyads

	Ln(Trade)	
	Model 5.8	Model 5.9
$Ln(Trade)_{t-1}$	.964**	.872**
	(.004)	(.007)
$(Leader\ Change_B)$	−.088**	−.074**
	(.021)	(.022)
$W_B*(Leader\ Change_B)$	.073*	.067**
	(.031)	(.028)
W_B	.019	−.014
	(.017)	(.017)
LOW_{t-1}	.022	−.002
	(.024)	(.028)
$LOW_{t-1}*(Leader\ Change_B)$	.125*	.138*
	(.069)	(.080)
$WB* LOW_{t-1}*(Leader\ Change_B)$	−.063	−.013
	(.103)	(.108)
$W_B* LOW_{t-1}$	.013	−.015
	(.045)	(.046)
$Ln(Population)_{US}$		−.883**
		(.105)
$Ln(Population)_B$		−.182**
		(.019)
$Ln(GDP)_{US}$		.358**
		(.044)
$Ln(GDP)_B$		.170**
		(.014)
Constant	.086	.000
	(.011)	(.003)
Estimates of $\sigma\ Ln(Trade)_{t-1}$		−.011**
		(.001)
W_B		−.077**
		(.007)
Constant		.270**
		(.006)
Observations	6213	5410
	(176)	(147)

** Statistical Significant at the 1% level in a one-tailed test.
* Statistical Significant at the 5% level in a one-tailed test.

TABLE 5.8
Sour Relations and the Impact of Leader Change on Trading Relations
for U.S.-only Dyads (Model 5.8)

	Nation B's Coalition Size, W_B	
	$W_B = 0$	$W_B = 1$
Normal Trading Relations, $LOW = 0$	0%	1.96%
	−8.40%**	0.52%
Sour Trading Relations, $LOW = 1$	2.19%	5.55%
	6.04%**	10.69%

Notes: Table reports the percentage growth in trade associated with different combinations of institutional arrangements and the impact of leader change. The first entry in each cell relates to no leader change and the second entry corresponds to leader change in nation *B*.

** The entries in the cells are statistically different at the 1% level.

from that experienced during normal cooperative phases. Assessing the impact of leader change when trading relations are poor ($LOW = 1$) requires the inclusion of variables for poor trading relations, leader change, institutions, and the interactions of these variables. This large number of interaction variables makes assessing the impact of leader change under conditions of poor trading relations directly from the regression output difficult. Therefore, we calculate the substantive impact of institutions, leader change, and sour relations on trade with the United States in table 5.8. The top figure in each cell corresponds to the predicted growth in trade with the United States with no leadership change. Again we standardize no leader change in the top left cell to equal 0. If relations are sour, as indicated by the *LOW* variable, then even in the absence of leader change, trade with the United States typically grows. It is worth remembering that some of these *LOW* events are caused by acts of god, such as harvest failures. If devastation of last year's harvest diminished trade then one expects trade, to improve, as the analyses suggest.

LSP theory predicts that leader change reinvigorates trade during the punishment phase. To the extent that *LOW* measures noncooperative phases of play, leader change when *LOW* equals 1 should improve trade. Selection effects suggest the impact of leader change should be strongest when nation *B* is a small coalition system. If nation *B* is a large coalition system, its leader is unlikely to cheat, since the citizens depose her to restore cooperation. The analyses support these predictions. If nation *B* is a small coalition system and trade relations were poor in the previous period ($LOW = 1$), then trade is expected to grow by 2.189 percent. If, however, the leader in the small coalition nation *B* changes (*Leader Change$_B$* = 1) then the expected growth in trade increases to 6.038 percent, a significant difference.

If nation B is a large coalition system and trade relations were poor in the previous year ($LOW = 1$), then leader change increases the expected growth in trade with the United States from 5.549 percent to 10.692 percent. Although this change is similar in magnitude to that experienced in small coalition systems, it is not statistically significant. As witnessed by table 5.2, there are significantly fewer instances of LOW trade when nation B is a large coalition system. To check the robustness of these results, model 5.9 includes gravity model control variables and explicitly models the variance of the stochastic error term. The results are similar.

Table 5.9 contains a single analysis (model 5.10), which examines the impact of leader turnover and poor relations for all dyads. Consistent with earlier analyses, we constrain the coefficients on variables associated with nation A to equal the coefficients on the analogous variables for nation B. Given the large number of interaction terms, a direct interpretation of the results is difficult. Table 5.10 calculated the predicted effects of leader change under different contingent circumstances.

Table 5.10 examines the interaction between combinations of large and small coalition systems. The top left cell, for instance, examines relations between A and B when both are small coalition systems ($W_A = 0$, $W_B = 0$). Each cell contains four entries that predict the expected growth in dyadic trade using model 5.10. The top entry in each cell corresponds to the expected percentage growth in dyadic trade if there is no leader change ($Leader\ Change_B = 0$) and trading relations are normal ($LOW = 0$). The second entry examines expected growth in trade associated with leader change in state B during periods of normal relations. The third and fourth entries both consider events when trade relations in the previous period were sour ($LOW = 1$). The third entry considers no leader change ($Leader\ Change_B = 0$) and the last entry considers leader change in nation B ($Leader\ Change_B = 1$).

When trading relations in the previous period are normal ($LOW = 0$, the top two entries in each cell of table 5.10) the effect of leader change in nation B is similar to that reported earlier. If nation B is a large coalition system leader change in nation B has no statistically significant impact on trade. When nation B is a small coalition system, however, expected trade with nation A is reduced 0.126 percent by leadership change.

When trade in the previous period was low relative to previous historical maximums ($LOW = 1$), then expected trade increases. That is, the third entry in each cell, that associated with $LOW = 0$ and no leader change, is significantly larger than the first entry in each cell. These differences are highly statistically significant. If trading relations in the previous period were poor as a result of an act of god—a harvest failure for instance—then trade should improve the following year. LSP theory predicts that large coalition leaders cheat rarely relative to small coalition leaders. Therefore,

TABLE 5.9
Leadership Turnover and the Restoration of Trading
Relations, All Dyads

	Ln(Trade)
	Model 5.10
$Ln(Trade)_{t-1}$	.954**
	(.0006)
$(Leader\ Change_B)$†	−.0013**
	(.0004)
$W_B{}^*(Leader\ Change_B)$†	.0017**
	(.0007)
W_B†	−.0002
	(.0007)
$W_A{}^*W_B$	.006**
	(.001)
LOW_{t-1}	.0177**
	(.003)
$LOW_{t-1}{}^*(Leader\ Change_B)$†	.025**
	(.004)
$W_B{}^*LOW_{t-1}{}^*(Leader\ Change_B)$†	−.031**
	(.006)
$W_B{}^*LOW_{t-1}$†	.021**
	(.003)
Constant	.002
	(.00009)
Estimates of σ	
$Ln(Trade)_{t-1}$	.240**
	(.0009)
W_B	.010**
	(.0005)
$W_A{}^*W_B$	.010**
	(.0008)
Constant	.034**
	(.0003)
Observations	377,144

**Statistical Significant at the 1% level in a one tailed test.
*Statistical Significant at the 5% level in a one tailed test.
†The analysis contains analogous variables referring to
the other nation (($Leader\ Change_A$), W_A, etc.). Since these
coefficient estimates are constrained to be equal, we report only
one set of estimates.

TABLE 5.10
The Impact of Institutions and Leader Change on the
Restoration of Trade, All Dyads (Model 5.10)

	$W_B = 0$	$W_B = 1$
$W_A = 0$	0.000	−.023
	− 0.126	.017
	1.784	3.927
	4.248	3.406
$W_A = 1$	−.023	.508
	−.149	.548
	3.927	6.703
	6.442	6.168

Nation A's coalition size, W_A; Nation B's coalition size, W_B
First entry: $LOW = 0$, $(Leader\ Change_B) = 0$
Second entry: $LOW = 0$, $(Leader\ Change_B) = 1$
Third entry: $LOW = 1$, $(Leader\ Change_B) = 0$
Fourth entry: $LOW = 1$, $(Leader\ Change_B) = 1$

the proportion of $LOW = 1$ events that are attributable to acts of god rather than the result of political actions is greater for dyads of large coalition systems than other pairings of states. We hypothesize the increase in expected trade between the third and first entries in each cell is greatest when both nations are large coalitions. This is precisely what we observe. When both nations are large coalitions ($W_A = 1$, $W_B = 1$) then expected trade increases by 6.195 percent if trade in the previous period was poor. In contrast, this difference is 1.784 percent if both nations are small coalition systems, and 3.950 percent if the dyad is mixed. These differences are highly significant. Following instances of sharp declines in trade, large coalition systems are most likely to experience a recovery in trade.

Leader turnover affects the prospects of restoring good trading relations during periods of poor trade ($LOW = 1$). To examine how leadership change affects the restoration of trade under different institutional configurations, we compare the third and fourth entries in each cell. We start by examining the interaction between two large coalition systems ($W_A = 1$, $W_B = 1$). LSP suggests instances of cheating between two large coalition systems should be rare. Therefore, collapses in trade between such systems are more likely to be random events than politically induced. Indeed, we saw evidence of this above. If, as the theory suggests, few instances of poor trading result from politically induced events, then leader turnover should have little impact on the restoration of trade, since the deposed leader is unlikely to have been responsible for the collapse of trade. If $LOW = 1$ and $(Leader\ Change_B) = 0$ then the expected growth in dyadic trade is 6.703 percent. If leader turnover occurs in nation B, the growth in dyadic trade is 6.168 percent. These numbers are not statistically different. Leadership change in a dyad of two large coalition systems experiencing poor trading relations does not significantly change the growth in trade.

Next we examine the impact of leadership change in nation B during poor trade relations when nation B is a large coalition system and nation A is a small coalition system. LSP theory predicts that under such a contingency, if the decline in trade results from cheating, then it is more likely that it was a leader in nation A rather than a leader in nation B who cheated. Therefore, leader change in nation B is unlikely to restore trade relations because the large coalition leader is unlikely to be the leader responsible for the collapse in trading relations. This is precisely the finding. There is no statistically significant difference between the 3.927 percent level of expected trade growth predicted without leader change and the 3.406 percent level of expected trade growth predicted with leader change. Leader change in large coalitions is unlikely to help restore poor trading relations. LSP theory predicts that such leaders are unlikely to be responsible for the collapse of trade in the first place.

If small coalition system B is experiencing a period of poor trading relations ($LOW = 1$), the replacement of the leader in nation B improves trade. The magnitude of the increase in trade growth associated with leader change is either 2.464 percent or 2.515 percent, depending upon whether nation A is a small or large coalition system. These differences are highly statistically significant. LSP theory predicts small coalition leaders cheat with a much greater frequency than large coalition leaders. We have already seen that the frequency of poor trading relations is higher for dyads involving a small coalition system than dyads of two large coalition systems. Relative to cases involving large coalition leaders, these $LOW = 1$ events are likely to have been induced by cheating by a small coalition leader. Since LSP predicts a restoration of trade when the leader responsible for the collapse in trade is replaced, the replacement of the leader from small coalition system B leads to the restoration of trade.

The results in tables 5.9 and 5.10 provide considerable support for LSP. The variable LOW codes instances of poor trading relations. We use this variable as a proxy for the likelihood of a politically induced collapse in trading relations. Events where $LOW = 1$ are relatively more likely to include instances of the punishment phase than events where $LOW = 0$. However, the LOW variable is a relatively poor discriminator of punishment phase events. This lack of discrimination works against our hypotheses. It is therefore remarkable that we find such significant results. The results in table 5.9 are robust to the inclusion of gravity control variables and relatively insensitive to the modeling of the variance in the error term. We have also reanalyzed model 5.10, including the higher order interactive terms of $W_A^*(Leader\ Change_B)$, $W_A^*W_B^*(Leader\ Change_B)$, $W_A^*LOW^*(Leader\ Change_B)$, $W_A^*W_B^*LOW^*(Leader\ Change_B)$, $W_A^*W_B^*$ LOW, and the analogous terms relating to leader change in nation A (we used the standard restriction that coefficients on variables relating to nations A and B are identical). This more complex model generally reproduces the results of model 5.10. It predicts a 10 percent increase in expected trade growth associated with leader change between two small coalition systems experiencing poor trading relations. However, this model also suggests that if $W_B = 0$, $W_A = 1$ and $LOW = 1$ then leader change in nation B reduces trade, a result inconsistent with the results presented here.

CONCLUSIONS

This chapter investigated the dynamics of trade relations and the institutionally determined impact of leadership change. To our knowledge, we are the first to investigate these dynamics. The results replicate earlier findings (for instance Russett and Oneal 2001) that nations with representative governments trade more with each other than do other pairings of nations. Additionally we found support for the hypotheses deduced from the LSP and selectorate politics theories concerning the dynamics of trade and leadership turnover, which were summarized at the start of this chapter.

Unfortunately these results are far from perfect. Many of the variables are imperfectly and noisily measured. For instance, BdM2S2's measure of winning coalition size with its five-point scale, although theoretically motivated, is at best no more than a blunt indicator of the magnitude of coalition size. Similarly, our attempt to identify instances of cooperation breakdown with the *LOW* variable is problematic. The measure cannot perfectly separate collapse in trust following politically motivated decisions from random fluctuations in trade due to, for example, the weather. It was for this reason that we used a different measure of poor trading relations than we used in earlier work (McGillivray and Smith 2004). While neither the current nor prior measure is perfect, the results are robust to a variety of measures of key concepts.

Overall we believe the results reported here reflect an honest and accurate portrayal of the dynamics between trade and leader change and the moderating effects of political institutions. Of course, there is bound to be disagreement about the appropriateness of one econometric technique or model specification relative to another. Such skepticism and desire to reexamine any result with alternative specifications, different techniques, and new data is healthy for the social science discipline. For this result our data are readily available (http://press.princeton.edu/titles/8712.html).

The importance of our empirical investigation lies not in the specific analyses that we provide, but rather in the novel questions we address. Numerous theoretical approaches suggest, and many empirical studies have found, that democracies actively trade and cooperate with each other. The pertinent question is why? By deriving the implications of LSP theory for the dynamics between trade and leader change and testing these predictions, we advance our understanding of international trade and cooperation by providing a new set of tests and metrics upon which to compare the explanatory power of different theoretical approaches.

CHAPTER 6

Putting the Sovereign Back into Sovereign Debt

THE TERM *SOVEREIGN DEBT* originates from a time when a monarch would borrow funds on behalf of his or her nation. Given the anarchy of the international system, the monarch could always default: lending and borrowing required trust. The terms on which leaders could borrow depended upon creditors' beliefs about the sovereign's ability and willingness to repay. In this chapter we build further on the ideas of leader specific punishments and examine how the institutional context in which a leader rules determines her access to credit and the consequence of leader turnover.

The term *sovereign debt* makes explicit the importance of an individual leader or sovereign in national borrowing. When Queen Elizabeth I of England borrowed funds, creditors directly identified her with the debt. In contrast, there is no pretense that the current English queen, Elizabeth II, personally assumes debt when the British government borrows money. Consistent with this transformation, many scholars have recently argued that it is institutions that enable nations to commit to repay debt, and therefore it is institutions that shape whether nations can borrow in the first place (North and Weingast 1989). Swimming against this tide, we put the sovereign back into sovereign debt and examine the consequences of sovereign (leader) specific punishments.

We establish theoretically that associating creditworthiness with specific leaders rather than nations per se reduces default risk, at least in institutional settings where leader removal is easy. We then test for evidence that sovereign specific punishment strategies are actually used by examining sovereign debt bond indices. These indices are constructed by measuring the price at which sovereign debt bonds are traded on secondary markets. If investors believe a nation is likely to default, its bonds trade at a discount. Changes in the value of the bond index provide a means to measure market actors' perceptions about the likelihood of default.

Using bond indices and other data, we show that large coalition systems are less likely to default than small coalition systems. We also establish empirically that there is much greater uncertainty associated with the debt of small coalition systems than large coalition systems, as measured by the price variance in sovereign debt. Leader change in large coalition systems does not affect investors' willingness to hold sovereign debt issued by large coalition systems. However, leader change in small coalition system leads to a large increase in price volatility and a reduction in price. Large and small coalition systems also differ in the extent to which economic fundamentals determine the value of debt. The value of debt issued by large coalition systems is relatively independent of economic fundamentals. In contrast, sovereign debt indices in small coalition systems are sensitive to economic conditions. Finally we examine the impact of leader change following prior default. When default has occurred during a leader's term in office, leader turnover improves a nation's creditworthiness, as measured by investors' willingness to hold bonds. We believe this is the first study to systematically assess the impact of leadership change on sovereign debt. Our empirical findings support the predictions of sovereign specific punishment theory.

We proceed as follows. First, we discuss extant arguments relating sovereign debt and political institutions. To motivate this discussion we examine the general relationship between default and access to credit. Second, we introduce a simple formal model of loans and repayment. Within the context of this simple game, we examine the impact of sovereign specific punishments. The term *sovereign specific* is used purely to identify the subject matter under discussion. We use *sovereign specific* and *leader specific* interchangeably. Such strategies drive a wedge between the behaviors of large and small coalition leaders. In particular, we show that the terms on which leaders beholden to only a small coalition of supporters can obtain loans depends upon their idiosyncratic preferences for debt repayment and the economic ease of repayment. In contrast, if leaders are beholden to a large coalition of supporters, and hence easily removed from power, then leaders can commit to repay loans under all but the most extreme of economic circumstances. Third, in our data section, we discuss the construction of sovereign debt indices and why they provide measures of default risk. Fourth, we derive the implications of the theoretical model and test them using bond indices and other data.

INSTITUTIONS, CREDIBILITY, AND EXPLANATIONS OF DEBT

Recently scholars have invested considerable effort into showing how domestic political arrangements shape a government's ability to credibly commit in both domestic and international spheres (Przeworski and Limongi 1993; Elster 2000; North and Weingast 1989; Bates 1996; De Long and Shleifer 1993; Firmin-Sellers 1994; Levy and Spiller 1996; North 1981, 1990; Olson 1993, 2000; Shepsle 1991; Tsebelis 2002; Weingast 1995, 1997b; Fearon 1994; Smith 1998; Schultz 1998). In general this literature suggests democrats can commit themselves more easily than autocrats. Since the ability to obtain a favorable loan stems from the ability to commit to repay, it is not surprising that given their lower default risk, democrats can obtain larger and lower interest rate loans than can autocrats (Brewer and Rivoli 1990; Abdullah 1985; Citron and Nickelsburg 1987; Balkan 1992; Feder and Uy 1985). While most scholars appear to agree that democrats can borrow at better terms than autocrats, there is considerable disagreement as to the details of why (see Stasavage 2003, chap. 1, for a summary).

Sovereign lending is a risky business. In the domestic setting, creditors can typically seize the assets of debtors who fail to repay loans. In the international setting, such recourses are rarely available to creditors. Unfortunately, while nations are willing to promise repayment when they need the money, when it comes time to raise taxes to make repayments, leaders would prefer to forget their promises. This time inconsistency makes lending problematic.

If leaders could commit to repay sovereign debt, then lenders would be willing to lend funds at favorable rates. Unfortunately, when leaders cannot make such commitments, lenders need to be compensated for the risk of default. Nations seen as likely to default face higher interest rates or, as was historically often the case, must rely on "forced" loans. Many factors affect the probability of default (see Eaton and Taylor 1985 for an overview). Obviously nations with small debts, healthy tax revenues, and an adequate supply of foreign currency via exports can service debt easily. As debts mount relative to revenues and exports, servicing debt becomes increasingly hard. However, it is not simply a question of ability to pay, but also willingness to pay.

A domestic lending analogy is useful. Historically, debtors who could not pay their debt could be thrown in debtors prisons until their debts were paid. Given that these prisons were extremely unpleasant and debtors had few prospects of paying their debts once inside, it is probably safe to assume that those sent to debtors prisons could not pay their debts. It was not that they lacked willingness; they lacked means. In many ancient societies, such as the Roman Republic, citizens were sold into slavery to settle their debts. When the penalty for default is the indefinite loss of one's freedom, people make every possible effort to pay their debts, and it is only those poor souls unable to make repayment who default.

In the United States the cost of default for individuals is much reduced. For instance, people who declare personal bankruptcy can protect many of their assets, such as their house and pension, from creditors. While bankruptcy is unpleasant, it does not typically involve prison or being sold into slavery. Not surprisingly, with the penalty for default reduced, some people who could service their debt choose instead to default. The less the penalty for default, the more reluctant people are to make repayment. The same is true for nations. The smaller the penalties for refusing to pay debts, the more likely nations are to default.

While the prospects of debtors prison or slavery are not appealing, they make obtaining a loan easier since creditors realize the probability of default is reduced. The ability to commit to repay means you can borrow more money at a lower interest rate. This is, of course, hugely advantageous.

In the history of English debt, many scholars point to the Glorious Revolution of 1688 as point at which debt shifted from sovereign debt to national debt. Weingast (1997a) argues that after the English parliament deposed the Catholic King James II and asked the Protestant William of Orange to assume the throne, parliament had established its supremacy. From 1688 onward English borrowing required the consent of parliament. There is substantial historical literature that compares political development and the creation of national debt in such countries as Britain, France, and the Netherlands (Root 1989; Schultz and Weingast 1998; Stasavage 2003; Velde and Weir 1992; North and Weingast 1989; Weingast 1997a, b; Eichengreen 1991). The key to these historical studies is the argument that parliament, or other legislatures, can commit to repay debt. In addition to providing an answer as to why democratic government can effectively commit to repay debt, leader specific punishment theory provides novel hypotheses regarding the effects of leader turnover on sovereign debt.

MODELING THE DEBT REPAYMENT

In general the greatest threat creditors have to punish default is to refuse future loans. With the exception of those rare circumstances when creditors can mobilize their government to intervene militarily to force repayment (and these are often unsuccessful), the removal of all future credit is the harshest punishment creditors can impose. In many cases creditors cannot even impose this level of punishment, since the wily sovereign can play off one creditor versus another, promising to make repayments to the party that advances further credit. In such circumstances the ability of creditors to co-ordinate has an important role in disciplining sovereigns (Weingast 1997a, b). As a starting point for modeling sovereign debt, we will assume the harshest threat creditors possess is the complete removal of future credit.

We present a simple model of the loan-repayment problem. In each period sovereigns might need a loan. The terms of the loan they can receive depend upon creditors' assessment of the risk of default. Once a loan is made, sovereigns must decide whether or not to repay their debt. The ease of repayment depends upon economic conditions. It is easier to raise revenues during economic booms than economic busts. The model treats the economic conditions under which repayment must be made as stochastic. Further, we introduce heterogeneity into the population of sovereign leaders by varying the extent to which a leader wishes to repay loans. As we shall see, while this idiosyncratic desire to repay debt is of little consequence in large coalition systems, it strongly accounts for prevailing interest rates in small coalition systems.

The Loan/Repayment Game

The game is infinitely repeated where the stage game is as follows:[1]

1. Nature decides with probability q whether the need for a loan arises. Access to a loan is worth V.
2. Should the need for a loan arise, there is a market of bankers/creditors who compete for the loan. We will not explicitly model this stage; however, either the sovereign making a take-it-or-leave-it offer (in which case she would offer the minimal price the bankers would accept) or Bertrand competition between bankers results in the competitive interest rate.
3. Nature decides the ease of repayment, c, where c is distributed with distribution $F(x)$ (with associated density $f(x)$). In what follows we focus our attention on the exponential distribution, $Pr(c < x) = F(x) = 1 - exp(-x)$.
4. The sovereign decides whether or not to repay.
5. Voters decide whether or not to retain the sovereign. The cost of removing the sovereign is k.

All players are risk neutral utility maximizers. Sovereign leaders receive a payoff of Ψ for each period in office, and all payoffs are discounted with a common discount factor δ. We normalize the banker's outside options, the risk-free interest rate, to 0.

To introduce heterogeneity into the model, we assume sovereigns differ in their desire to repay loans. Stasavage (2003), in his exploration of English borrowing following the Glorious Revolution, shows that the Whig and Tory parties differed in their desire to repay loans. The difference is largely accounted for by the fact that those lending to the government typically associated with the Whigs. To capture these differences in willingness to pay between leaders, leaders receive a payoff of s if they repay a loan and 0 if they do not. Leaders with high s values, such as late-seventeenth-century Whigs, regard repaying loans as important. Leaders with low s value see little reason to repay loans beyond its instrumental value that it enables them to borrow in the future.

While this model is highly stylized, it captures the prevailing incentives. Both creditors and sovereigns are better off if loans are made and repaid, but once the loan is made, the sovereign does not want to repay the debt.

---

[1] See Schultz and Weingast 1998 for a related model.

Reputation is the standard idea that encourages repayment (Bulow and Rogoff 1989; Dixit and Londregan 2000; Eaton and Gersovitz 1981; Grossman and Huyck 1988; Atkeson 1991; Cole and Kehoe 1994; Tomz 1999, 2001; Schultz and Weingast 1998; Glick and Kharas 1986). Since leaders want to be able to borrow in the future (and at favorable rates), they repay debt that myopically they would prefer to default on. Provided that the value of being able to borrow in the future is greater than the cost of servicing debt, leaders repay debts to preserve their reputations and access to credit. As debts mount and the cost of servicing debt escalates, leaders become more tempted to repudiate their debt. To offset this increase in default risk, creditors require higher interest rates before they will lend more funds. Unfortunately, this rise in interest rates doubly endangers the lender/borrower relationship. First, as interest rates rise, servicing debt becomes harder, further increasing the risk of default. Second, as interest rates rise, future borrowing becomes less attractive, and hence retaining a good reputation becomes less valuable. There is a real danger that creditors' fears of default become self-fulfilling expectations.

Sovereign Specific Punishments

Traditional reputation arguments assume creditors punish nations who default by reducing access to future credit. What are the consequences of shifting the target of these punishment strategies from the sovereign nation to the specific sovereign who defaulted? That is to say, should a leader default, then creditors cut her off from future credit. Creditors are, however, prepared to lend to her successor, who after all did not repudiate the debt. As we have already seen in other contexts, the imposition of such a leader specific lending strategy drives a wedge between the behavior of small coalition autocrats and large coalition democrats.

Sovereign specific punishments in the loan/repayment game utilize much of the formal technology introduced in chapter 2. Since this technology has been previously introduced, we analyze the consequences of sovereign specific punishments by answering a series of questions. By doing so, we informally derive equilibria for the game in an intuitive manner.

We start by calculating the interest rate at which a banker or creditor will lend to the sovereign. If the banker makes no loan, he keeps his money, worth 1. If, however, he makes a loan at interest rate r, then if the sovereign repays him, his return is $(1 + r)$, but if the sovereign defaults then his payoff is 0. If γ represents the probability of default, then the banker only agrees to the loan if $(1 + r)(1 - \gamma) + \gamma 0 \geq 1$. The competitive interest rate associated with the risk of default γ is $r = \gamma/(1 - \gamma)$. As we would expect, as the risk of default rises, creditors require higher returns.

Under a sovereign specific punishment scheme, once a leader defaults, she cannot secure future loans. Given that she cannot obtain another loan she should default on any outstanding debt, and given that she will renege on any future repayments, creditors should not be tempted to lend to her. The threat of refusing future loans to defaulters is credible.

The consequences of going into default differ by regime type. When leader removal is difficult, as in small coalition systems, then the defaulter retains office but can not secure additional loans. Once default occurs, the leader and nation miss the opportunity to earn V when the need for a loan occurs, which happened with probability q in each period. In contrast, if a leader avoids default, she can obtain future loans. We represent the value of being able to obtain future loans as Z_h. This continuation value is the expected value of the game starting without prior default. We will presently derive the value of Z_h; for present purposes, however, it is sufficient to assume it is valuable relative to playing the game following default, Z_d. The continuation value following default, Z_d, for a difficult to remove sovereign is $\Psi + \delta\Psi + \delta^2\Psi + \ldots = \Psi/(1-\delta)$: the net present value of receiving the officeholding benefit in every future period (remember, no future loan can be secured once default occurs).

We can now address the central question of repayment. Suppose having taken a loan, the sovereign (who was previously in good standing) defaults. Her payoff is $V + \Psi + \delta Z_d$, the value of receiving the loan (V) and the value of officeholding plus the discounted value of playing the game following default, δZ_d. Alternatively, if the sovereign repays the loan, then her payoff is $V - (1+r)c + s + \Psi + \delta Z_h$, where V is the value of having received a loan, $(1+r)c$ is the cost of repaying the loan given the difficulty of repaying c, s is the idiosyncratic desire of the leader to repay the loan, Ψ is the value of holding office, and δZ_h is the discounted value of being able to secure loans in the future. Provided that it is sufficiently easy to repay debt, $c \leq c_H = (s + \delta Z_h - \delta Z_d)/(1+r)$, then the sovereign repays her nation's debt. If paying the debt becomes more difficult, she defaults.

The level of difficulty in paying loans at which the leader is indifferent between repayment and default, $c_H = (s + \delta Z_h - \delta Z_d)/(1+r)$, is critical in describing equilibrium behavior. Given c_H, the probability of default is $\gamma = Pr(c > c_H) = 1 - F(c_H)$, and the corresponding interest rate is $r = \gamma/(1-\gamma) = (1 - F(c_H))/F(c_H)$. Given this critical level, we can also calculate the sovereign's continuation value, Z_h. Specifically,

$$Z_h = \Psi + (1-q)\delta Z_h + qV + qsF(c_H) + q\delta Z_h F(c_H)$$

$$- q(1+r)\int_0^{c_H} cf(c)dc + q\delta Z_d(1 - F(c_H)).$$

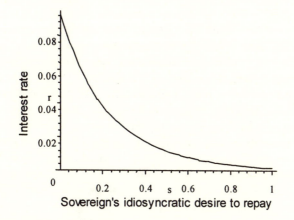

Figure 6.1. Prevailing interest rate given the sovereign's idiosyncratic desires to repay loan (s) when leader removal is difficult.

This expression is worthy of some description. The value of playing the game with an honest reputation has many components. First, the sovereign receives the value of holding office Ψ. With probability $(1 - q)$, no need for a loan arises, so the sovereign retains the ability to borrow in the future, the value of which is the discounted continuation value Z_h. With probability q the need for a loan arises, which is worth V. Having taken this loan, the sovereign repays the debt with probability $F(c_H)$. The expected cost of repaying the loan is given by the integral part of the expression above. In addition to these costs, the sovereign gains the payoff s and the ability to borrow again in the future (Z_h) with probability $F(c_H)$. If the cost of repayment is high, specifically $c > c_H$, which occurs with probability $1 - F(c_H)$, then the sovereign defaults. While this avoids the cost of repayment, it means the future value of play is only worth Z_d, rather than Z_h.

The definitions Z_h and Z_d, the competitive interest rate $r = (1 - F(c_H))/F(c_H)$, and the equation $c_H = (s + \delta Z_h - \delta Z_d)/(1 + r)$ characterize a subgame perfect equilibrium in which bankers play sovereign specific punishments, the citizens do not replace their sovereign even is she has defaulted, and the sovereign repays debts if and only if she has not previously defaulted and $c \leq c_H = (s + \delta Z_h - \delta Z_d)/(1 + r)$.

Figure 6.1 shows the interest rate bankers charge sovereigns according to their idiosyncratic preferences for repayment, s. This example is generated assuming c is distributed exponentially, $F(c) = 1 - exp(-c)$, the discount factor is $\delta = 0.9$, and the value of a loan is $V = 2$.

When leaders are hard to replace, figure 6.1 shows that the interest rate and the risk of default depend upon the sovereign's idiosyncratic desires to repay debt. Leaders with a strong desire to repay debt $(s = 1)$ can obtain loans at 0.17 percent, since they have risk of default of only 0.0017. Hence a leader who is strongly committed to repaying debt, and widely recognized as such, can obtain favorable terms. However, without this desire to repay loans, an absolute sovereign $(s = 0)$ must pay an interest rate of 9.2 percent, since her risk of default is 0.084. Idiosyncratic factors and economic conditions shape default risk and interest rates.

In his analysis of British borrowing following the Glorious Revolution, Stasavage shows that Whig and Tory governments differed considerably with respect to the terms under which they could obtain credit. Although the Glorious Revolution made parliament a far more important political institution than it had been in the past, the monarch still had considerable power in the appointment of ministers. Further, the franchise was small and "rotten boroughs" ensured extremely uneven representation. Although in comparison to other nations of the time, Britain had some of the most representative political institutions, it would be centuries before Britain became fully democratic.[2] Whig members of parliament were predominantly drawn from the merchant classes. For such individuals, and their supporters, maintaining creditworthiness and promoting trade were essential goals. Further, it was Whigs and their supporters who typically lent money to the government. The Tory party drew its members and support from the traditional landed interests. Such individuals were far less concerned with promoting trade and commerce. Further, few Tories were actively engaged in lending funds to the government. For the Tories, debt repayment was far less important than it was for the Whigs. Stasavage shows these differences between the parties significantly affected the terms under which the government could borrow money.

When leader removal is difficult, default ends access to credit. Under sovereign specific punishments, creditors refuse future loans to defaulters. Yet sovereign specific sanctions offer the possibility of restoring creditworthiness via the replacement of the sovereign. Since creditors punish the sovereign and not the nation she represents, leader turnover offers the possibility of restoring access to credit. If, following default, the citizens replaced their leader, they could once more borrow funds. The advantage of replacing the leader is that the nation can once more obtain credit, but it costs k to replace a leader. The citizens' payoff from deposing their leader is $-k + \delta Z_{Eh}$, where Z_{Eh} is the citizens' continuation value from playing the game with a leader who has not defaulted. Z_{Eh} is similar to the

---

[2] Many institutional codings do not rate Britain as a democracy until the passage of electoral reforms in the nineteenth century. For instance, POLITY's ten-point democracy scale scores Britain as a four prior to 1837, a six prior to 1880, and Britain is not scored as fully democratic (a score of ten) until 1920.

leader's value for playing the game absent the officeholding benefits and the idiosyncratic benefits of repayment, s. Specifically,

$$Z_{Eh} = (1-q)\delta Z_{Eh} + qV + q\delta Z_{Eh} F(c_H) - q(1+r)\int_0^{c_H} cf(c)dc.$$

If the citizens retain their leader, they avoid the cost k, but their nation loses all access to future credit, a payoff of 0. When k is high, specifically, $k \geq \delta Z_{Eh}$, then citizens retain leaders who default and the nation loses access to credit. When leader replacement is easy, however, citizens can restore access to credit by deposing their leader.

LOW COST LEADER REPLACEMENT

When the cost of leader replacement is low, citizens restore access to credit by removing defaulting sovereigns. Not only does this offer the prospects for restoring creditworthiness, but it also prevents default from occurring in the first place, since sovereigns are reluctant to default when it costs them their jobs. To analyze behavior in this low removal cost setting, we consider the same series of questions examined above.

Creditors require an interest rate sufficient to compensate them for any risk of sovereign default. As derived above, $r = \gamma/(1-\gamma)$, where γ is the risk of default. We now consider the key question of whether to repay a loan or to default. If the sovereign repays a loan then her payoff is $V - (1+r)c + s + \Psi + \delta Z_S$, where V is the value of the loan, $(1+r)c$ is the cost of repaying the loan, s is the sovereign's idiosyncratic desire to repay, Ψ is the value of holding office, and δZ_S is the discounted continuation value of playing the game having never defaulted. We shall subsequently derive Z_S. If, alternatively, the sovereign defaults, the citizens remove her. Her payoff from default is $V + \delta Z_E$, where δZ_E is the discounted value the citizens receive from having a leader who has not previously defaulted. We are assuming here that the leader becomes a regular citizen once removed from power. We might alternatively assume she is removed from the game, which generates very similar results.

Given the relative benefits of repayment and default, the sovereign repays loans provided that $c \leq c_s = (s + \Psi + \delta Z_S - \delta Z_E)/(1+r)$, and defaults otherwise. Given this critical difficulty of repayment c_S, we can now calculate continuation values and interest rates. Z_S is the continuation value for playing the game without prior default:

$$Z_s = (1-q)(\Psi + \delta Z_s) + qV - (1+r)q\int_0^{c_s} cf(c)dc$$
$$+ F(c_s)q(\Psi + s + \delta Z_s) + q(1 - F(c_s))\delta Z_E.$$

With probability $(1 - q)$, no need for a loan will arise. In this circumstance the leader receives the value of officeholding plus the discounted continuation value Z_s, since tomorrow she will be in an identical circumstance as today. With probability q, the need for a loan arises. Once this contingency arises, the nation receives the value of the loan, V. With probability $F(c_s)$ the leader repays the loan, thus retaining office and benefiting from her idiosyncratic desire to repay, s. If she repays then she also receives the discounted continuation value of playing the game given no prior default. The integral part of the expression represents the expected value of repaying the loan. With probability $q(1 - F(c_s))$ the need for a loan arises, but having taken the loan, the cost of repayment is so high that the sovereign defaults. In this case the sovereign's payoff is the discounted continuation value of playing the game for citizens, Z_E, since she is removed from office and returns to private life for all subsequent periods. Given the value c_s, the above expression characterizes the value of playing the game for leaders. We now calculate the continuation value of the game for the average citizen.

The continuation value for the citizens, Z_E, is given by the following expression:

$$Z_E = qV - (1 + r)q\int_0^{c_s} cf(c)dc - qk(1 - F(c_s)) + \delta Z$$

With probability q, the need for a loan arises. When the opportunity for the loan arises, citizens receive the benefits of the loan, V. They also either pay the cost of repayment (the integral part of the expression) or they replace their leader at cost k. The former event occurs with probability $F(c_s)$ and the latter occurs with probability $(1 - F(c_s))$.[3]

As a final step, we characterize when the citizens would depose their leader rather than keep her if she defaults. If the citizens depose their leader, they pay cost k but obtain the discounted continuation value of being able to borrow in the future: $-k + \delta Z_E$. If alternatively the citizens retain a defaulting leader for a single period before deposing her, then their payoff is $0 - \delta k + \delta^2 Z_E$. Provided that $k \le \delta Z_E$, citizens depose leaders who default.[4]

The definitions of Z_S, Z_E, and c_s characterize a subgame perfect equilibrium when the cost of leader removal is low $(k \le \delta Z_E)$. In particular, a leader secures loans whenever the opportunity arises, and repays these loans if and only if she has never previously defaulted and $c \le c_s$; otherwise

---

[3] It is worth noting that for the purposes of calculation we have assumed the leader is succeeded by a leader with the same s value. This is a benign assumption, since leaders practically never default when leader replacement is easy.

[4] We obtain an identical answer if we consider indefinitely retaining the defaulting leader.

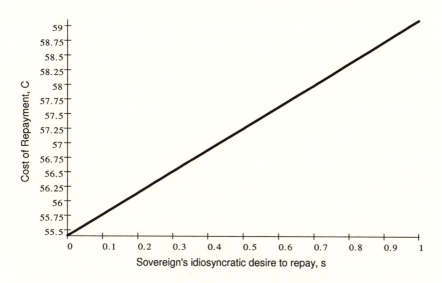

Figure 6.2. The difficulty of repayment (c_s) required before default given the sovereign's idiosyncratic desire to repay loans (s) when leader removal is easy.

the leader defaults. The citizens remove any leader who defaults or who has defaulted in the past. Otherwise they retain their leader. Bankers/creditors lend to sovereigns at the competitive interest rate, $r = (1 - F(c_s))/F(c_s)$, providing the sovereign has never defaulted. Once a leader defaults, creditors refuse her future credit.

The properties of this subgame perfect equilibrium are best seen graphically. Figure 6.2 is the analogous graph to figure 6.1. Specifically, it plots the difficulty of repayment (c_s) required to bring about default given the discount factor $\delta = .9$, the probability of needing a loan $q = .3$, the value of a loan $V = 2$, the cost of leader removal $k = 0$ and the value of office-holding of $\Psi = 5$. Unlike the high-removal-cost case, where we plotted the associated interest rate, figure 6.2 plots the critical repayment cost, c_s, that leads to default since the probability of default and, hence, the interest rates are effectively 0 for all values of s.

Figure 6.3 examines the more interesting comparative static of how the value of officeholding Ψ influences how difficult repayment needs to be to induce default for the case where the leader has no idiosyncratic desire to repay ($s = 0$). By way of reference, under these conditions in the high-removal-cost case the level of repayment difficulty that induced default was $c_H = 2.471$. As figure 6.3 shows, even for relatively modest values of officeholding, the default risk is minimal when leader removal is easy.

When leader replacement is easy, sovereigns repay loans even under very difficult circumstances because it costs them their jobs if they do not

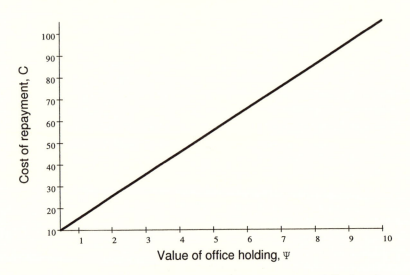

Figure 6.3. How the value of office holding, Ψ, influences the difficulty of repayment sufficient to induce default when leader replacement is easy.

do so. Once a sovereign defaults, then bankers refuse new credit until the leader is deposed, at which point access to credit is resumed. Provided that the cost of removing leaders is sufficiently low, then defaulting on a loan becomes equivalent to losing office. If, as we believe, politicians are primarily driven by officeholding goals, they avoid default in all but the most extreme circumstances. When leader removal is easy, as in large coalition systems, sovereign specific punishments effectively eliminate the risk of sovereign default.

DATA

Empirical studies of creditworthiness take several approaches. Many studies attempt to estimate the probability of default or rescheduling of loans from economic fundamentals (Frank and Cline 1971; Feder 1981; Kutty 1990; McFadden et al. 1986; Savvides 1991). Rather than looking directly at default, other studies examine the determinants of perceived creditworthiness via credit ratings (Lee 1993a, b; Cantor and Packer 1996; Freder and Ross 1982). A third approach utilizes risk premiums charged to the borrower on either bank loans or bonds to estimate market perceptions of default risk (Abdullah 1985; Citron and Nickelsburg 1987; Edwards 1984, 1986; Morgan 1994; Balkan 1992; Feder and Uy 1985; Brewer and Rivoli 1990).

We use the third approach and measure changes in creditworthiness and default risks using sovereign debt bond indices for 70 nations. In large part we use J. P. Morgan Emerging Market Bond Index Global (EMBI Global), although we supplement these with other sources such as J. P. Morgan indices for developed markets and Lehman Brothers bond indices. All the bond data were collected from DATASTREAM on June 16, 2004. Since most political scientists are unfamiliar with these bond indices, we next provide a brief intuitive description of their construction and their use in measuring changes in default risk. J. P. Morgan (1999; see also Erb, Campbell, and Viskanta 1999; Cumby and Pastine 2001) provides a full description of the indices' construction and associated methodology.

The EMBI calculates the average return on holding bonds issued by a sovereign government. Suppose, for example, that the government of nation A wishes to raise funds and issues bonds to do so. A bond is a commitment to repay specific sums at various times in the future. We use an extremely stylized example to explain the logic. Suppose the government states that it will pay $5 returns for each year for thirty years. Investors will then buy and trade these bonds. Suppose initially investors think that the bonds are worth $100. That is, the market price for bonds that pay $150 over thirty years is $100. The basic idea of bond indices is to calculate the value of holding the bond relative to its initial value. As the bonds mature they pay out returns, in our hypothetical example, $5 per year. In terms of constructing the index, it is assumed these payouts are reinvested. The value of holding the bonds also changes as the people's willingness to hold them changes. For instance, suppose having bought the bonds at $100, interest rates in nation A increase. Under this circumstance, investors want to sell their bonds and reinvest the money in the more profitable financial instrument. This causes the price of the bonds to fall. If alternatively interest rates fall, bonds become relatively more profitable and their price rises. The J. P. Morgan indices are composed using a basket of sovereign bond issues, all of which are regularly traded on secondary markets.

In general the bond indices vary in response to three factors: interest rate risk, currency rate risk, and sovereign default risk. The example above dealt briefly with the question of interest rate risk. If the rate of return on other financial instruments changes, then the desirability (and hence price) of holding bonds shifts. Bonds can be denominated in a variety of currencies. If, for example, they are denominated in pesos and the peso falls in value relative to other currencies, investors obtain smaller returns in dollars. As with shifts in interest rates, shifts in currency exchange rates alter the desirably of holding bonds relative to other financial instruments. The EMBI indices look only at U.S. dollar denominated bonds; therefore, currency risk is largely irrelevant, although a large devaluation increases a government's debt burden and hence increases the risk of default.

Thus far our example has assumed the government honors its commitment to pay $5 every year for thirty years. However, the government might suspend repayment or pay less than the full $5. As the risk of such sovereign default increases, then the price of the bond declines. If for instance the market suddenly believes the risk of default is 50 percent, then relative to the initial $100 value of holding bonds, the value shifts to $50 and the bond index falls to from 100 to 50.[5]

The sovereign bond indices reflect the relative value of holding bonds. As the market perceives shifts in the returns on other instruments or sovereign risk, the indices move accordingly. As such, bond indices provide us with a measure of how sovereign default risk changes. If market actors perceive the risk of default as increasing, then they no longer desire holding such bonds and the bond index falls. As the risk of sovereign default diminishes, the bond index rises. As such, proportionate changes in the bond index reflect changes in interest rates and the risk of default. The actual value of the index per se is relatively uninformative except relative to the start of the index (December 31, 1993 = 100 is a common standardization for many of the indices).

We collect bond indices for all available nations. These data provide the closing index value for each trading day. Many of the analyses reported are carried out at the monthly level. The monthly bond index is defined as the closing index value on the last trading day of the month. In principle, bond indices are calculated only for nations with actively traded bonds. For several nations the bond index remains unchanged for many months. This unchanging price might occur because the price was genuinely constant, no trading occurred, or there were reporting errors; unfortunately we cannot ascertain which. The analyses reported exclude observations where the reported index is unchanged for more than ten straight trading days. The inclusion or exclusion of these observations does not significantly alter the results.

Standard and Poor's (Beers and Chambers 2003) provide a list of all known sovereign defaults on both bank debts and bond debts from 1824 to 2003. These data list the years in which nations are in default. While comprehensive, this list has several limitations. The primary problem for our analyses is that the data list only the years in default and not the date that a nation defaulted. This makes it hard to distinguish whether default led to leader change or leader change preceded default. When a nation defaults, peoples' willingness to hold bonds declines, which leads to a drop in the bond index. We use large drops in the bond index as an alternative measure of default. Specifically, we code a shock as a 10 percent decline in the value of the index over a month.

---

[5] Actually the fall in the index is likely to be greater since financial actors tend to be risk averse.

Many of our hypotheses examine changes in sovereign risk that are reflected in proportionate changes in the index. To capture this proportionate change we use a lagged dependent variable structure where our dependent variable is the *Ln(Index)*: the natural logarithm of the index at the end of the month. The variable $Ln(Index_{t-1})$ is the logged value of the index at the end of the preceding month. In this setup the coefficients on other variables can be interpreted as the proportionate change in the index from a unit change in the independent variable.

Our general model is $Ln(Index) = \beta_1 + \beta_2 Ln(Index_{t-1}) + \beta_3 X + \ldots + \varepsilon_t$, where ε_t is a stochastic error and $E[\varepsilon_t^2] = \sigma^2$. Our data have a panel structure of n nations, although the length of time varies drastically by country. In general we report OLS regression analyses. We have replicated these analyses using fixed effects and obtained almost identical results. To examine several hypotheses, we estimate how the variance of the change in the index, σ^2, depends upon institutional variables. Specifically, we assume the stochastic error is normally distributed with mean 0 and variance σ^2. We assume σ depends linearly upon a set of regressors, and we estimate this model using the same maximum likelihood estimation approach we used in chapter 5.

To create a measure of leader turnover we updated the BdM2S2 (2003) compilation of leaders through June 2004. We coded political institutions through June 2004 by extrapolating the most recent Polity IV data. We obtained economic indicators from World Bank Development Indicators (2004) and the International Monetary Fund's International Financial Statistics (2004).

DEBT, REPAYMENT, AND LEADER REPLACEMENT

The model above and more generally the ideas of leader specific punishment developed throughout this book predict relationships between credit, institutions, and leader turnover. We develop these hypotheses and test them.

Default and Leader Survival

Sovereign specific punishments suggest default risk and leader behavior differ drastically as the cost of leader replacement changes. When the cost of leader replacement is high, leaders are relatively immune from the risk of deposition. Leaders in such institutional settings can default with relative impunity. Leaders in small coalition systems can and do default on debt. For instance, the Spanish monarchy defaulted on its debts six times

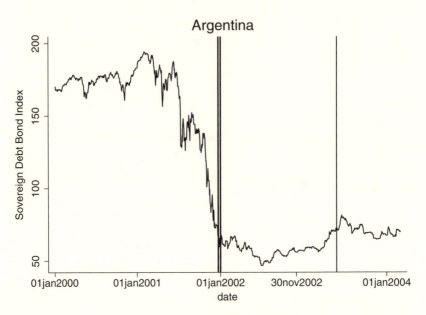

Figure 6.4. Argentina's bond index: Default and its consequences for leader deposition.

from 1557 to 1647. The English king, Edward III, incurred large debts as a result of his involvement in the Hundred Years War against France. Although he promised to repay debts using revenues from a wool tax, declines in the English wool industry led Edward to default on his debts and led to the collapse of the Peruzzi bank in 1343 and the Bardi bank shortly afterward. While the Florentine bankers were ruined, Edward's tenure remained secure. Indeed, in 1346 he achieved probably his most significant victory over the French at the battle of Crécy.

More recently, Nigeria defaulted on bond debts in 2002 and experienced a more than 10 percent decline in its bond index in July of that year. President Obasanjo retained power. Prior to Obasanjo attaining power in 1999, Nigeria had a winning coalition size of $W = 0$ and a democracy score of 0.2. Institutional reforms that followed Obasanjo's coup increased these institutional variables to 0.75 and 0.7 respectively. Despite these institutional improvements, replacing Nigerian leaders remains difficult.

The theory predicts that leaders in large coalition systems who default are removed from power. The case of Argentina at the end of 2001 illustrates this phenomenon. Figure 6.4 graphs Argentina's sovereign debt bond index. As the figure clearly shows, in the latter half of 2001 the bond index collapsed as Argentina defaulted on over $100 billion of sovereign debt, the largest ever default. Between December 21, 2001 and January 2,

2002 there were four changes in political leadership, with Duhalde retaining the presidency until Kirchner won the presidential election (May 25, 2003). The vertical lines represent leader removal (they appear as only two lines because of the closeness of the depositions). During Duhalde's tenure, Argentina continued to default on loans and rescheduled debt. For instance, Argentina defaulted on an $800million loan repayment to the IMF on November 21, 2002.[6]

An overvalued currency contained the seeds of Argentina's debt problems. To combat hyperinflation, between 1991 and 1996 President Menem and his economic minister, Cavallo, set up a currency board that implemented "convertibility," one-to-one parity with the U.S. dollar. Unfortunately, government borrowing, although not outrageous, continued to grow over this period, and with very low domestic savings, Argentina needed to rely on borrowing from overseas. Maintaining this inflow of capital while retaining dollar convertibility placed great strain on the economy. Eventually, currency speculators forced the suspension of dollar parity. In addition to shocking the economy, the collapse of the peso massively increased the effective size of Argentina's U.S. dollar denominated debt. Leaders of large coalition systems lose their jobs if they default. It is not until the deposition of these leaders that Argentina regained some of its creditworthiness.

The Argentinean case suggests that if the cost of leader removal is low, leaders that default are removed. Unfortunately, it is difficult to systematically test this proposition. If, as we assume, officeholding is the primary goal of leaders, then when leader removal is easy, leaders do not default except under extreme economic conditions. Therefore instances of default, such as the Argentinean case, should be rare in large coalition systems. This selection bias makes testing the consequences of default on leader survival extremely difficult. If default costs leaders their jobs, then leaders do not generally default. The set of defaults we observe are cases where either the cost of leader removal is sufficiently high that the leader can survive default or economic conditions are so poor that the leader either cannot pay or is certain to lose her job anyway.

Although selection effect problems make it difficult to statistically test the extent to which leaders are removed from office for defaulting, anecdotal evidence suggests the motivation to replace leaders is often a desire to restore creditworthiness. In the 1840s several U.S. states, including Pennsylvania, Maryland, Mississippi, Indiana, Arkansas, and Michigan, defaulted on loans. George Peabody, a banker who had organized the sale of many of these bonds, helped coordinate political campaigns against many of the defaulters. His express intent was to restore the creditworthiness

---

[6] *Economist*, June 3, 2004. "Becoming a Serious country"; BBC News, "Business: Crisis-Hit Argentina Defaults on Debt" November 21, 2002, bbc.co.uk.

of these states. With elections removing many of those legislators who supported default, the creditworthiness of many of the states was restored (Chernow 1990, chap. 1).

Interest Rates, Default and Political Institutions

Sovereign specific punishments enable leaders in large coalition systems to commit to repay debts under all but the harshest of economic conditions. This commitment to repayment means leaders in such systems can borrow readily at favorable interest rates. In contrast, if the cost of leader removal is high, leaders can default without jeopardizing their hold on power. Although default limits a leader's access to future credit, it does not harm a leader's primary goal of political survival. Since, from a leader's perspective, the punishment associated with default is smaller in small coalition systems than in large coalition systems, hard to replace leaders are more likely to default. Investors need to be compensated for this additional risk, and therefore the interest rate on bonds needs to be higher in small coalition systems.

The superiority of bonds issued by advanced democracies has been documented (Brewer and Rivoli 1990). Unfortunately, bond indices do not readily allow us to distinguish differences in rate of returns from bonds across political systems. Investors who buy bonds issued by small coalition systems assume a greater default risk than investors who buy bonds issued by large coalition systems. Thus, the purchasers of small coalition bonds pay less for them than purchasers of similar bonds from large coalition systems. Unfortunately, bond indices tell us only how the value of holding bonds has changed relative to the arbitrary starting point of the index. Since there is little institutional change in the data, bonds issued by a democracy might always be more desirable than bonds issued by an autocracy, but the process of indexing the bonds normalizes these differences away. The literature has already amassed considerable evidence concerning institutions and interest rates (for instance, Stasavage 2003).

Sovereign specific punishments predict leaders from small coalition systems can default with impunity, at least from domestic political removal. In contrast, large coalition leaders lose their jobs if they default. Tables 6.1, 6.2, and 6.3 test the propensity of leaders to default under different institutional contingencies. The first two tables examine defaults on bond and bank debts denominated in foreign currencies between 1824 and 2003. The tables use the Standard and Poor's annual data on defaults described above (Beers and Chambers 2003, tables 4 and 5). Both tables show that defaults are significantly less likely in large coalition systems than in other systems. For instance, of the 2,110 nation-years where the

TABLE 6.1

Winning Coalition Size and Bond Defaults (default on bonds in foreign currency, 1824–2003)

	Winning Coalition Size				
	W = 0	W = 0.25	W = .5	W = .75	W = 1
No Default	1,791	3.834	2,891	2,520	2,026
	93%	92%	88%	92%	96%
Default	131	320	390	205	84
	7%	8%	12%	8%	4%

Pearson chi2(4) = 119.1 (Pr. = .000).

TABLE 6.2

Winning Coalition Size and Bank Defaults (default on bank debt in foreign currency, 1824–2003)

	Winning Coalition Size				
	W = 0	W = 0.25	W = .5	W = .75	W = 1
No Default	1,805	3,996	3,041	2,482	2,057
	94%	96%	93%	91%	97%
Default	117	158	240	243	53
	6%	4%	7%	9%	3%

Pearson chi2(4) = 136.3 (Pr. = .000)

measure of coalition size takes its largest value ($W = 1$) there are only eighty four instance of default on bonds. That is, default occurs only 3.98 percent of the time for the largest coalition systems. Bond default rates are higher for smaller coalition systems: the rate of default is 6.82 percent if $W = 0$, 7.70 percent if $W = 0.25$, 11.89 percent if $W = 0.5$ and 7.52 percent if $W = 0.75$. The default rates for bank debt reveal a similar pattern.

Table 6.3 examines shocks, that is, collapses of 10 percent or more in the sovereign bond indices over one month. As anticipated by the sovereign specific punishment theory, the largest coalition systems experience fewer shocks than smaller coalition systems. Specifically, 10 percent or larger declines occur in only 0.14 percent of nation-months in the largest coalition systems ($W = 1$), but such declines occur in 0.36 percent of nation-months for smaller coalition systems. These differences are statistically significant.

Table 6.1, 6.2, and 6.3 support the prediction that defaults are less likely in large coalition systems. These results are particularly reassuring, since selection effects in the data are biased against these findings. Nations that are particularly likely to default find it difficult to borrow substantial funds

TABLE 6.3
Winning Coalition Size and 10% Losses on Bond Indices (monthly bond
level data: 10% monthly decline in sovereign debt bond index)

Default	Winning Coalition Size				
	$W = 0$	$W = 0.25$	$W = .5$	$W = .75$	$W = 1$
No shock	3,298	7,562	8,532	11,332	13,590
	99.76%	99.95	99.77%	99.31%	99.86%
Shock	8	4	20	79	19
	.24%	.05%	.23%	.69%	.14%

Pearson chi2(4) = 89.6 (Pr. = .000)

in the first place. The construction of the sovereign debt indices emphasizes
this bias. Bond indices are constructed only for nations with significant secondary markets and actively traded sovereign debt bonds. Such active markets require transparency and market confidence, policies that are promoted
by large, but not small, coalition systems. The existence of a bond index is
itself a significant indicator of coalition size. It is not an accident that no
indices exist for the Congo or the Sudan. The default risk of these nations is
sufficiently high that investors are reluctant to invest or trade in their bonds.
This truncation of institutional variance works against our hypotheses.

Nations with inclusive political institutions borrow at more favorable
interest rates and default less than nations in which leader removal is
difficult. These arguments and results are consistent with many other
findings. Next we examine the novel topic of the dynamics between leadership change and sovereign debt.

Default Risk, Institutions, and Leader Change

In this section we examine the dynamics between leadership turnover and
investors' beliefs that leaders will repay sovereign debt, as measured by
sovereign debt bond indices. We derive predictions from leader specific
punishment strategies in the context of sovereign debt and test these
hypotheses. These tests are critical in terms of theory building because
rival theoretical explanations do not predict relations concerning leader
change. For clarity of presentation, we gradually build our empirical analyses step-by-step before concluding with a fully specified model.

LEADER CHANGE, POLICY VOLATILITY, AND DEBT

The institutional context in which leaders govern shapes the impact of
leader change on sovereign debt indices. If the cost of leader removal

is low, as in large coalition systems, then leaders do not default except under extreme circumstances because they are removed from office for defaulting. In such large coalition systems, the sovereign's idiosyncratic willingness to repay debt and economic conditions have relatively little impact on default risk and interest rates. In large W systems, the threat of losing office through default ensures that all political leaders, regardless of their personal convictions, want to repay loans. Leaders in such systems do their utmost to pay. Regardless of who is U.S. president or British prime minister, it is the institutionally induced constraint against default that keeps the default risk small.

In contrast, if leader removal is hard, as in small coalition systems, then leaders' idiosyncrasies and economic condition have a large influence on the prevailing default risk and interest rate. When leaders are not easily removed, it is the personal convictions of leaders regarding the desirability of repayment and financial conditions that shape the default risk. As figure 6.1 demonstrated, interest rates and default risks vary greatly with the idiosyncrasies of the incumbent leader.

Institutions shape the borrowing patterns of nations. Not only should the interest rates that large coalition systems pay be low, they are consistently low. In contrast, in small winning coalition systems, not only must sovereigns pay higher interest rates, but the rates they must pay vary drastically with perceptions of the leaders' idiosyncrasies and the nation's financial situation.

Leader turnover has little impact on default risk in large coalition systems. Both the predecessor and the successor leader face the same institutionally induced constraint against default. In small coalition systems leadership change alters the default risk since the willingness to repay debts is shaped by the idiosyncrasies of individual leaders. Leader change in small coalition systems affects sovereign debts. Tables 6.4 and 6.5 examine this effect. Models 6.1 through 6.6 examine monthly sovereign debt bond indices. The dependent variable is the logarithm of the bond index at the end of the month *(LnIndex)*. The models include the lagged dependent variable $(LnIndex_{t-1})$. As one would expect, last month's index is the best predictor of the index this month. A convenient interpretation of the coefficient estimates on the other regressors is the proportionate change in the index for a unit change in a regressor.

Model 6.1, which has 7,098 nation-month observations, contains three regressors in addition to the lagged dependent variable. W is BdM2S2's measure of winning coalition size (on a 0 to 1 scale). *LeaderChange* is a dummy variable (0/1) indicating whether or not there is any leader turnover during the month. *W*LeaderChange* is the interaction of the leader change variable and coalition size variable.

The statistically significant negative coefficient estimate off −.050 on the *LeaderChange* variable indicates that in the smallest coalition systems

TABLE 6.4
The Impact of Institutions and Leader Change on Bond Indices

	Ln(Index)			
	Model 6.1	Model 6.2	Model 6.3	Model 6.4
Ln(Index)t−1	.996**	.996**	.996**	.995**
	(.001)	(.001)	(.003)	(.003)
W	.0014	.0001	−.001	.003
	(.003)	(.004)	(.006)	(.006)
LeaderChange	−.050**	−.063	−.006	−.046*
	(.018)	(.047)	(.029)	(.025)
W* LeaderChange	.046*	.061	−.012	.042
	(.021)	(.048)	(.038)	(.032)
GrowthGDP			.0002*	.0006
			(.0001)	(.0004)
W* GrowthGDP				−.0005
				(.0005)
ΔExchangeRate			−.0016**	−.008
			(.0001)	(.001)
W* ΔExchangeRate				.009**
				(.001)
Debt/GDP			.0002	
			(.002)	
Debt/Exports			.00000	
			(.00007)	
Exports/GDP			.019	
			(.085)	
Inflation			.020**	−.001
			(.009)	(.112)
W*Inflation				.026
				(.149)
Constant	.029	.029	.027	.029
	(.007)	(.006)	(.016)	(.013)
σ equation				
W		−.091**		
		(.003)		
LeaderChange		.164**		
		(.034)		
W* LeaderChange		−.168**		
		(.035)		
Constant		.127**		
		(.003)		
Observations	7,098	7,098	2,545	3,383

** Statistically Significant at the 1% level in a one tailed test.
* Statistically Significant at the 5% level in a one tailed test.

($W=0$) leadership turnover reduces the sovereign debt index by about 5 percent. However, leadership turnover in large coalition systems has no appreciable effect on bond indices. For the largest coalition systems ($W=1$) the impact of leadership change depends upon the sum of the coefficients on the *LeaderChange* variable and the interaction variable *W*LeaderChange*. Hence the estimated net effect of leader change in large coalition systems is $-.004$, which is statistically indistinguishable from 0. While this joint hypothesis that the sum of the coefficients on the variables *LeaderChange* and *W*LeaderChange* is 0 cannot reject the null hypothesis, the joint hypothesis test that both these coefficients are simultaneously 0 is strongly rejected. Throughout the analyses reported this is a consistent pattern: leader change has no significant impact on bond indices in large coalition systems but significantly reduces the bond index in small coalition systems.

In large coalition systems, all leaders face the same institutional constraint against defaulting. The default rate is consistently low for all leaders in large coalition systems. In small coalition systems, the default rate is partly determined by the sovereign's idiosyncratic desires to repay debts. Incoming leaders are relatively unknown and, therefore, there is considerable uncertainty about the default risk in small coalition systems. Since financial actors are notoriously risk averse, this uncertainty reduces the attractiveness of sovereign bonds following leader change in small coalition systems and leads to a drop in the value of the index. This effect is clearly seen in model 6.1.

Leader change affects the volatility of bond indices. Model 6.2 explicitly models the variance of the error term, σ^2, as a function of independent variables. The theory predicts greater variance in sovereign debt bond values in small coalition systems. Further, leader change in small coalition systems increases the variance in bond valuations. Model 6.2 models the standard deviation of the error term, σ, as a linear function of *W*, *LeaderChange*, and *W*LeaderChange*.

The coefficient estimates on the *LeaderChange* and *W*LeaderChange* variable in the standard β equation tell a similar story with regard to the level of bond indices to that observed in model 6.1, although the coefficients on these variables are no longer statistically significant. Leader change reduces the value of sovereign debt bonds in small, but not in large, coalition systems. Institutions and leader change strongly influence the variance in bond indices. In the σ equation, the significant negative coefficient on the *W* variable indicates that bond indices in large coalition systems are less variable that those in small coalition systems. This is consistent with expectations. In large *W* systems leaders face a relatively constant institutionally induced constraint against default. In contrast, default risks in small coalition systems depend upon the more variable factors of leaders' idiosyncrasies and economic conditions.

Leader change in large coalition systems is not anticipated to significantly increase the variance in bond valuations, since both predecessor and successor leaders face the same institutional constraint against default. The analysis supports this prediction. In the σ equation, the coefficient estimates on *LeaderChange* and *W*LeaderChange* are -0.063 and 0.061, respectively. Therefore, in large coalition systems the net impact of leader turnover is a statistically insignificant -0.002. In contrast, in the smallest winning coalition systems ($W = 0$), leadership change significantly increases the variance of sovereign debt bonds. Since the σ equation deals with a second-order statistic, the substantive impact of leader change is best seen by calculating the estimated variance under a variety of contingencies. If no leader change occurs, the variance in the stochastic error, σ^2, in the largest coalition system ($W = 1$) is about 0.0012. In contrast, in the smallest coalition system ($W = 0$) σ^2 is about 0.016, more than ten times greater than that for large coalitions. Leader change does not significantly increase variance in large coalition systems. Yet, in the smallest coalition systems ($W = 0$) leader turnover increases the estimated σ^2 to 0.085, more than sixty five times larger than the estimated σ^2 for a large coalition system. Leader turnover significantly affects sovereign debt bonds in small coalition systems but has no appreciable effects in large coalition systems.

Thus far our analyses have been devoid of controls for economic conditions. Model 6.3 includes standard economic control variables. The variable *GrowthGDP* is the annual rate of economic growth. $\Delta ExchangeRate$ measures monthly percentage changes in the exchange rate. These data are taken from the IMF's IFS, and exchange rates are measured as the number of units of local currency needed to purchase one SDR, which is effectively an IMF basket of currencies. In this setting, a currency devaluation is represented as an increase in the exchange rate, so positive values of $\Delta ExchangeRate$ indicate devaluation. The variable Inflation is the quarterly inflation rate based on the IFS quarterly consumer price index. The variables *Debt/GDP*, *Debt/Exports*, and *Exports/GDP* are foreign debt as a proportion of GDP, the ratio of foreign debt to exports, and exports as a proportion of GDP. The variables were created using annual data on foreign debt, GDP, and exports. The GDP and export figures are from IMF's IFS. The data on foreign debt are primarily from the IMF. Where these data were unavailable, we supplement them with WBDI data.

Model 6.3 indicates, as we would expect, that economic growth, inflation, and an appreciating currency increase sovereign debt bond indices. The coefficients on the variables Debt/GDP, Debt/Exports, and Exports/GDP are all insignificant. At a first glance these latter results are somewhat surprising. Increasing debt is likely to increase the default risk, while exports, the ability to earn foreign currency, improve a nation's ability to service its debt. However, while debt size is a fundamental determinant of default risk, it is relatively invariant. The accumulation or paying off of debt takes time, so a nation's indebtedness does not change dramatically from one month to the next. If a nation is mired in debt, then its bonds are relatively cheap and are likely to remain cheap over successive months. Although the nominal size of a nation's foreign debt changes only slowly, currency shifts can radically alter the effective size of debt repayment. As we discussed above in the case of Argentina in 2001, the collapse of a nation's currency can greatly magnify the size of debt repayments. The highly significant negative coefficient on the $\Delta ExchangeRate$ variable reflects this.

In the presence of these control variables the *LeaderChange* variable no longer has a significant impact on sovereign debt bonds. However, model 6.3 is misspecified and problematic in several ways.[7] The inclusion of economic controls greatly reduces the number of observations. Model 6.3 contains only 2,545 nation-month observations compared with the over 7,000 observations in models 6.1 and 6.2. The missing economic data are disproportionately from small coalition systems. The theory predicts leader change affects bond indices only in these systems. The loss of observations means that very few instances of leader change in small coalition systems are left in the data. In particular, when the full set of economic controls is used, as in model 6.3, then there are only seven cases of leader change in small coalition systems ($W \leq 0.5$) in the data. The most problematic data are the debt data. Since model 6.3 suggests these relatively invariant variables do not significantly influence proportionate changes in bond indices, although they certainly influence the absolute level of bonds, we exclude debt variables from subsequent analyses.

The theory suggests that while small coalition leaders are relatively sensitive to economic and financial consideration in their decisions to repay debt, in large coalition systems the default decision is shaped by institutionally induced constraints, so leaders are less sensitive to economic fundamentals. Therefore, sovereign debt indices in small coalition systems should be more sensitive to economic factors than are bonds issued by large coalition systems. This suggests model 6.3 is misspecified. Model 6.4 includes not only the control variables *GrowthGDP*, $\Delta ExchangeRate$, and *Inflation*, but it also includes the interactions of these variables with coalition size. In the smallest coalition systems ($W = 0$) the effect of economic factors is given by the coefficient on the economic variables alone.

---

[7] In addition to the factors discussed we need to be concerned about the stability of the system. The coefficient estimate on the lagged dependent variable is .9958 with a standard error of .0030. The 95 percent confidence interval on this variable includes values greater than one suggesting a potentially unstable time series.

In large coalition systems ($W = 1$), the sum of the coefficients on an economic variable and the interaction of that variable with W determines the effect of the economic factor.

Model 6.4, based on 3,383 nation-month observations, supports the prediction that bond indices in small coalition system are more sensitive to leader turnover and economic conditions than bond indices in large coalition systems. Consistent with the pattern that we observed in model 6.1, the negative estimate for the LeaderChange coefficient of -0.046 indicates that leader change in small coalition systems ($W = 0$) reduces the value of sovereign debt bonds in such systems by about 4.5 percent. In large coalition systems, the estimated impact of leader change is given by the sum of the coefficient estimates on *LeaderChange* and its interaction with W. This estimate is indistinguishable from 0.

The estimated coefficient on the variables *GrowthGDP* and *W*Growth GDP* are 0.00058 and -0.00052. Although neither of these coefficient estimates is individually statistically significant, the joint hypothesis test that both coefficients are simultaneously zero is statistically significant at the 6 percent level. The sum of the two coefficient estimates is indistinguishable from zero. This implies that economic growth rates affect sovereign bond indices in small, but not in large, coalition systems. The effect of changes in exchange rates exhibits a similar pattern. The coefficient estimate on the variable $\Delta ExchangeRate$ is a highly significant -0.0083, indicating that currency devaluation reduces the value of sovereign debt bonds in small coalition systems. The positive coefficient estimate on $W^*\Delta ExchangeRate$ negates this effect in large coalition systems. Consistent with theoretical prediction, economic conditions have a bigger role in shaping the value of sovereign debt indices in small coalition systems.

LEADER CHANGE AND THE RESTORATION OF CREDITWORTHINESS

Sovereign specific punishment strategies imply that leader change helps restore creditworthiness. We now test this hypothesis. To do so we need a measure of whether prior defaults have occurred during a leader's time in office. Unfortunately, Standard and Poor's measure of default provides only the calendar year of a default, making it difficult to assign the default to a specific leader. Since defaults are typically associated with a radical drop in the value of sovereign bonds, we utilize shocks, using our measure of a 10 percent decline within a month in the bond index, as the basis for coding default. The variable *Prior10%Drop* measures whether the incumbent leader in a state has ever experienced a drop of 10 percent or more in the sovereign debt bond index in any previous month during their term in office. The dummy variable *Prior10%Drop*LeaderChange*

TABLE 6.5
Restoration of Cooperation: The Impact of Institutions, Leader
Change, and Prior Default on Bond Indices

	Ln(Index)	
	Model 6.5	Model 6.6
Ln(Index)t−1	.995**	.995**
	(.001)	(.002)
W	.002	.007
	(.003)	(.008)
LeaderChange	−.191**	−.287**
	(.027)	(.081)
W*LeaderChange	.185**	.285**
	(.030)	(.082)
Prior10%Drop*LeaderChange	.231**	.294**
	(.038)	(.107)
W*Prior10%Drop*LeaderChange	−.213**	−.263**
	(.045)	(.108)
GrowthGDP		.0006
		(.0006)
W*GrowthGDP		−.0005
		(.0008)
ΔExchangeRate		.006**
		(.001)
W*ΔExchangeRate		−.010**
		(.002)
Inflation		.001
		(.183)
W*Inflation		.028
		(.243)
Constant	.031	.025
	(.007)	(.011)
σ equation		
W		−.095**
		(.005)
LeaderChange		.199**
		(.038)
W*LeaderChange		−.224**
		(.038)
Constant		.132
		(.004)
Observations	7,098	3,383

** Statistically Significant at the 1% level in a one tailed test.
 * Statistically Significant at the 5% level in a one tailed test.

interacts prior defaults, measured as a 10 percent decline in the index, with leader change. This variable is coded as 1 in those months where leadership turnover occurs and the departing leader had experienced a default in a previous month. Under all other circumstances, *Prior10%Drop* LeaderChange* is coded as 0.

Model 6.5 tests the impact of leader change, prior default, and institutions on bond indices using 7,098 nation-month observations. All four of the coefficient estimates associated with leader change variables are highly statistically significant. Rather than discuss each of the coefficient estimates separately, we use table 6.6 to estimate the bond index at the end of the month relative to an index base of 100 for the previous month. In the absence of leader change, the bond indices are expected to rise to 100.88 in small coalition systems and 101.03 in large coalition systems. The difference between these figures is not statistically significant. If leader change occurs in large coalition systems, then the predicted bond index is either 100.38 or 102.22, depending upon whether prior default had occurred. Neither of these estimates is statistically different from the predicted index without leadership change. However, leadership change in small coalition systems significantly affects the predicted level of bond indices.

Leadership turnover in small coalition systems affects bond indices. When the departing leader has not experienced a prior instance of default, as measured by the 10 percent decline in bond index criteria, leader turnover leads to an expected bond index of 83.319. As we saw in models 6.1, 6.2, and 6.3, the increased uncertainty surrounding the new leader, who is not institutionally constrained to avoid default, lowers investors' willingness to hold sovereign bonds.

The predicted index of 104.97 in the bottom left cell of table 6.6 corresponds to the instances of leader change in small coalition systems where the departing leader had previously defaulted. Although the incoming leader is relatively unknown, and so there is considerable uncertainty about her idiosyncratic desires to repay debt, this uncertainty is offset by the removal of a leader who had lost her integrity. Consistent with the predictions of sovereign specific punishments, leader replacement helps restore creditworthiness, as measured by sovereign debt indices.

Model 6.5 is a particularly difficult test. As with the problems we discussed in chapter 5 regarding our measure of trade collapse, the 10 percent decline in the index is a noisy measure of default. Some defaults might occur without inducing a large decline in the index, particularly if the defaults were widely anticipated. On the other hand, not all large declines in indices are associated with defaults. This latter measurement error is particularly pertinent in large coalition systems, where defaults are expected to be rare events. Although the theory anticipates that leader turnover will help restore creditworthiness in large coalition systems, the instance of default

TABLE 6.6

Impact of Leader Change and Prior Default on Bond Indices (estimates based on model 6.5 with the previous month's index = 100, prior default measured as 10% monthly decline in sovereign debt bond index during the leader's tenure)

	Coalition Size, W	
	W = 0	W = 1
No Leader Change, No Prior Default	100.88	101.03
Leader Change, No Prior Default	83.32	100.38
Leader Change, Prior Default	104.97	102.22

should be rare, given the institutional constraint that easy-to-remove leaders who default are deposed. In large coalitions there are few 10 percent shocks in bond indices, and many of those that do occur may not be the result of default. For these selection and measurement reasons, the impact of leader change following a previous shock is not expected to alter bond prices significantly in large coalition systems.

The tests are additionally tricky because bond indices are only constructed for relatively stable bonds that are actively traded. Nations in the sample are disproportionately large coalition systems, and given this bias, it is likely that BdM2S2's measures of coalition size systematically underestimate true coalition size. These problems of sample selection and measurement error suggest that the true effect of leadership change on creditworthiness in small coalition systems is even greater than that estimated here.

Model 6.6 puts together all the pieces of the puzzle in a single model. In particular, model 6.6 examines the impact of leader turnover under different institutional circumstances controlling for prior default. The model also controls for economic factors under different institutional contingencies. Finally, model 6.6 explicitly models variance as a function of institutional arrangements and leader turnover.

Based on 3,383 nation-month observations, the analysis in model 6.6 largely supports the earlier analyses of separate parts of the problem. In large coalition systems, leader change has no significant impact on the price of sovereign bonds, as anticipated. Additionally, compared to small coalition systems, the impact of economic factors on the movement of bond indices is much smaller. Indeed, the only economic variable that significantly affects the price of sovereign debt in large coalitions is changes in the exchange rate, with devaluations improving bond prices.

Leader change in small coalition systems significantly impacts bond prices. In the absence of prior default, model 6.6 estimates that leader change in the smallest coalition systems ($W = 0$) reduces bond indices by about 25 percent. In contrast, the estimates indicate that bond prices do not suffer this decline if leader change follows a prior default. Consistent with earlier results, economic variables have a greater impact on bond prices in small coalition systems than in large coalition systems.

The estimates in model 6.6 also support the hypotheses relating to the volatility of bond indices. As in model 6.2, the σ equation models the standard deviation of the stochastic error term as a linear function of independent variables. Large coalition systems have significantly smaller variances in bond indices than do small coalition systems. Further leader change greatly increases sovereign debt price variance in the small coalition systems, but not in large coalition systems.

CONCLUSIONS

Leader change and institutions strongly influence sovereign debt bond indices in ways consistent with the predictions of leader specific punishment theory. To our knowledge, no other study has examined the impact of leadership turnover on sovereign debt. The results here provide compelling evidence that leaders matter, at least in some institutional contexts. Despite the statistical significance of many of the analyses, these results must be treated with some degree of caution. Sovereign debt indices have only been collected for a limited set of states and for limited time periods. Unfortunately, the bias in the data collection has been toward developed democracies. As predicted by the theory and supported by the empirical evidence, leader change in such systems has minimal impact on the creditworthiness of nations. The evidence presented here must be treated as preliminary, because there are so few instances of leader change in small coalition systems within the sample. Yet, the strength of the results based on even this limited sample suggests future studies on the effect of leader change on sovereign debt will prove extremely enlightening.

CHAPTER 7

Conflictual Interactions

THUS FAR WE HAVE OFTEN illustrated the concept of leader specific punishments with examples of international sanctions and conflictual relations. In this chapter we systematically examine the consequences of LSP in conflictual circumstances through a model of crisis bargaining and an examination of the relationships between the termination of economic sanctions and leader change. LSP offers a powerful policy prescription to improve the quality of a nation's foreign policy. We explore the logic of these claims and the feasibility of using explicitly leader specific punishments. In particular, leader specific threats within crisis bargaining situations increase the likelihood of the other side capitulating.

INTERNATIONAL CRISES

We consider a simple crisis scenario in which two nations, *A* and *B*, are in dispute. Nation *A* contemplates the use of force to extract what it wants from nation *B*. If nation *A* does use force, then nation *B* must decide whether to resist—starting a war—or capitulate, letting *A* obtain the concession it seeks. Strategic considerations dominate such a crisis. The more likely nation *B* is to resist, the less likely it becomes that nation *A* wants to press its demands. Thus, from nation *B*'s perspective, success within a crisis requires convincing *A* that, if attacked, it will resist.

Unfortunately, communicating an intention to resist is difficult because of the incentive to bluff. Unless there is a mechanism that, in some way, makes it costly for nation *B* to make statements it does not intend to follow through on, then simple declarations of intent can not act as a deterrent. A reputation for honesty provides a means through which *B* can make it costly to make false statements, and so is a mechanism through which *B* can credibly reveal its intentions to *A*. However, such a mechanism requires nations to value the maintenance of an honest reputation sufficiently to offset the immediate gains from lying. If a leader's retention of office is tied to this reputation, as happens with LSP and easily replaced leaders, then simple statements can serve as credible declarations of intentions. If the leader of nation *B* stakes her personal reputation on a pledge to resist, then the citizens have an incentive to remove her if she does not

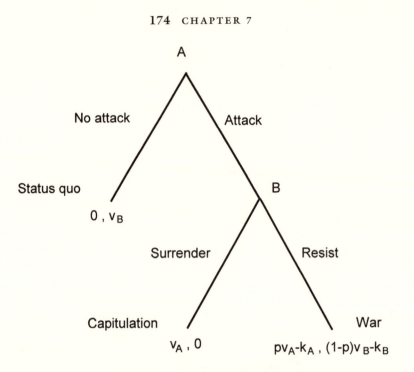

Figure 7.1. International crisis (from Guisinger and Smith 2002).

follow through on her commitment. Since leader B's primary motivation is to stay in office, she does not want to break her word. If the citizens can easily replace leader B, then leader specific punishments allow leaders to effectively tie their hands and communicate their intentions.

Guisinger and Smith (2002) formalize these arguments in a model of international crises. Drawing heavily on their work, we discuss their model and examine the impact of leader specific punishments on the ability of nations to communicate during international crises. We are very grateful to Alexandra Guisinger for assisting us with this material. Since the formal arguments and mathematical proofs are published in the *Journal of Conflict Resolution*, we focus here on the intuition behind the results.

Figure 7.1 shows a generic international crisis. Nation A seeks a concession from nation B. Retaining the status quo is worth v_B to nation B and obtaining the concession is worth v_A for nation A. As with all the proceeding arguments, we create differences in behavior through institutional differences rather than generating results by asserting different preferences for different actors within the state. If A does not challenge, then the outcome is the status quo and players receive payoffs of $(0, v_B)$. If, alternatively, A attacks and B capitulates, the payoffs are $(v_A, 0)$. If B resists A's attack, the crisis results in a war. We assume nation A wins with probability p and

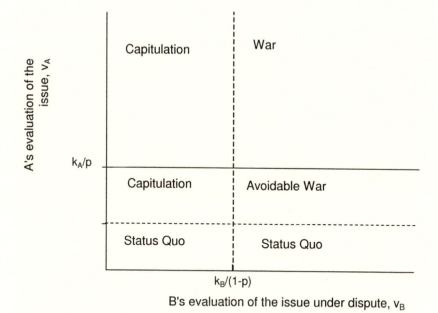

Figure 7.2. Outcomes of international crises (from Guisinger and Smith 2002).

both nations pay cost k for fighting. The expected payoffs for the war outcome are thus $(pv_A - k, (1-p)v_B - k)$.

We assume that while each nation knows its own valuation of the concession, it is uncertain of the value the other side places on the concession. Specifically, we assume that v_A is distributed with distribution $F_A(x) = Pr(v_A < x)$ and that A knows the value of v_A but B knows only the distribution from which it is drawn. Similarly we assume the distribution of B's type, v_B, is distributed $F_B(x) = Pr(v_B < x)$ and only B knows the actual value of v_B. We now analyze behavior within a single period crisis.

If attacked, then nation B would only resist if $(1-p)v_B - k \geq 0$. Hence from nation A's perspective, the probability that B will resist if attacked is $\beta = Pr(v_B \geq k/(1-p)) = 1 - F_B(k/(1-p))$. If A attacks, its expected payoff is $\beta(pv_A - k) + (1-\beta)v_A$. Nation A attacks only when this value is greater than 0, the payoff from the status quo, which occurs with probability $\alpha = Pr(v_A >= k\beta/(1-\beta+p\beta)) = 1 - F_A(k\beta/(1-\beta+p\beta))$. Figure 7.2 show the outcome of the game as a function of the types of each player. The shaded areas in the upper right portion of figure 7.2 represent parameters (values of v_A and v_B) that result in war. Figure 7.2 divides this area into two separate areas, labeled war and avoidable war. When $v_B > k/(1-p)$ and $v_A > k/p$, the upper shaded war area of figure 7.2, B resists any attack and A attacks even if certain that nation B will resist. To a large extent, war is unavoidable in this region. In contrast, if $v_B > k/(1-p)$ and $k/p > v_A > k\beta/(1-\beta+p\beta)$, then A chooses to attack B but has ex post regret about doing so. Nation A attacks B because it is uncertain whether B will fight back. For these parameter values, if A was certain of B's resolve, A would prefer the status quo. Yet A's uncertainty as to B's intentions leads A to attack. Under these parameters, if B can convince A that it is willing to resist, then A is much less likely to attack, to be precise, $F_A(k/p) - F_A(k\beta/(1-\beta+p\beta))$ less likely to attack.

Unfortunately for nation B, convincing A that it is willing to resist is a difficult task. Suppose, for example, that nation B simply told nation A that it was willing to resist. If A believed this claim, it would be much less likely to attack. This increase in the likelihood of the status quo improves nation B's welfare whether it is willing to resist or not. Therefore, if A were to believe them, all types of nation B, be they willing to resist or not, would state a willingness to resist. Unfortunately, this creates a paradox, since if all types send the message whether or not it is true, then the signal is uninformative and no-one should believe the message. This is an inherent problem of cheap talk signaling; when players have conflictual preferences and the physical cost of sending messages is low, then messages are uninformative (Crawford and Sobel 1982; Farrell and Gibbons 1989; Austen-Smith 1992). Unless it is costly to send a message or costly for B if it fails to follow through on its commitment, the message cannot deter A (Fearon 1997; Morrow 1989; Smith 1995).

Reputation offers a mechanism through which messages can be made costly. Specifically, if nation B claims it will resist, but subsequently does not do so, then in the future other nations should ignore all of B's foreign policy messages. This effectively makes reneging on a message costly because by doing so, nations give up the opportunity to send meaningful messages in the future. Sartori (2002, 2005) examines such reputational mechanisms. An alternative mechanism through which messages can be made costly is audience costs. Audience costs are a domestic political cost that leaders pay if caught bluffing (Fearon 1994). Unfortunately, most simple accounts of audience costs simply assert the existence of such costs, although it is often actually counter to the citizens' interests to impose costs on the leader. Leader specific punishment considers reputational arguments at the level of the individual leader, rather than the nation as a whole.

We made a distinction between reputation and integrity in chapter 2. Many theories of reputation explain behavior as attempts by one side of a dispute to influence the beliefs of the other side about some innate attribute, such as strength or willingness to fight. In contrast, throughout this book we treat reputation as integrity—that is, not being observed to "lie".

We show a reduced form of Guisinger and Smith's arguments. We consider an infinitely repeated version of the game shown in figure 7.1.

In each period the types of the players, v_A and v_B, are drawn from the distributions $F_A(x)$ and $F_B(x)$, and the nations play the crisis game. While the attacker might vary each period and the parameters of the model differ greatly,[1] the inherent nature of the problem remains the same so that without significant loss of generality, the model can be conceived as repeated interactions between A and B. Our objective is to show how a reputational mechanism, in which a nation's message is believed only if it has never been caught cheating in the past, enables effective communication; and to show how making this reputational argument leader specific increases the credibility of the signal.

If a leader claims she will resist an attack but then fails to do so, we say she loses her integrity. In future periods no nation will believe her statements. Yet, prior to such a loss of integrity, suppose other nations believe B's claims about whether it will resist or not. Thus, if leader B has an honest reputation, she can influence the beliefs of nation A. Suppose the value of an honest reputation is Z. We now derive when leader B declares an intention to resist and the conditions under which she honors such a commitment. As we shall see, these factors vary according to whether leader B is easy or difficult to replace.

Suppose a leader declares she will "resist" but fails to do so. By failing to resist, leader B loses her integrity ands is therefore deprived of the opportunity to communicate in future interactions. In contrast, by fighting, she preserves her reputation. The expected values of the former and latter options are 0 and $v_B(1-p) - k + Z$, respectively, where Z recall, is the value of maintaining an honest reputation. B resists if and only if $v_B \geq (k-Z)/(1-p)$. The effect of the reputational cost is to lower the value of the type that will honor its commitment to resist. In this context, a declaration of "resist" ties a leader B's hands (Fearon 1997).

Next we consider the signaling incentives. If B sends the message that it will resist, then much of the time it deters A. Knowing that B will resist if attacked, A only attacks if $pv_A - k \geq 0$. In this setting the probability that A will attack following a declaration to resist is $\alpha = 1 - F_A(k/p)$. In contrast, if B says it will not resist, then A knows that B will not resist, and therefore A always attacks.

We characterize an equilibrium in which B's claims are always credible. If B declares it will resist (and subsequently does so if attacked), then its payoff is $(1 - \alpha)(v_B + Z) + \alpha(v_B(1 - p) - k + Z)$. In this setting, the second terms corresponds to A attacking and B fighting back (which preserves reputation). In contrast, if B declares it will not resist, then its payoff is

---

[1] Extending the model to random selection of opponent in each period and varying parameters would require integrating over all possible future crises when calculating continuation values.

$0 + Z$, as B forgoes the value of the concession but retains an honest reputation. Given these payoffs, B sends the message "resist" if $v_B \geq k\alpha/(1 - p\alpha)$, where $\alpha = 1 - F_A(k/p)$; otherwise B declares it will not resist and A always attacks. Thus far we have assumed the value for an honest reputation is exogenously given as Z. We could now calculate the value of Z by integrating this equilibrium behavior over all future crises and solving for Z, α and β. However, for the purposes of this exposition, we leave the value of integrity as exogenous. Instead we focus on the credibility of B's claim.

In the current characterization, B declares "resist" if $v_B \geq k\alpha/(1 - p\alpha)$ but actually only resists if $v_B \geq (k - Z)/(1 - p)$. Such behavior can only be a credible equilibrium if $(k\alpha)/(1 - p\alpha) \geq (k - Z)/(1 - p)$, which depends upon the extent to which A is deterred. If this condition is not met, then signaling becomes less informative because nation B starts declaring an intention to resist that is not always credible. Once this occurs, A is deterred less often and, as a consequence, the value of an honest reputation declines. Although it is possible for equilibria to exist in which messages are not fully credible, the lack of a fully credible commitment to resist undermines B's ability to communicate.[2]

Credible signaling requires that B is actually prepared to resist if it said it would. To some extent B can "tie its hands" because it jeopardizes its integrity—reputation for honesty. Once the claim has been made, B will actually resist in circumstances when it would not have done so absent the initial claim. However, the whole system of credible communication within crises is dependent upon the credibility that B resists which depends upon the value of an honest reputation. Leader specific punishments enhance the value of maintaining an honest reputation, at least for leaders who are easily removed.

Following the logic developed throughout this book, if a reputation is attached to a leader, then once a leader is caught cheating, the citizens want to remove her to restore their nation's integrity. Leaders who are easily removed lose their jobs if they do not follow through on their claims to resist. Thus, leaders resist to save their jobs (worth Ψ) rather than to preserve their ability to communicate in future crises (worth Z). In terms of the math developed above, B's payoff for resisting is $v_B(1 - p) - k + \Psi + Z$, where Ψ is the net present value of officeholding. If

---

[2] There is an equilibria where B's threat to resist is only partially credible. That is, B declares "resist" if $v_B \geq \alpha Z/(1 - \alpha)$ but only resists if $v_B \geq (k - Z)/(1 - p)$. The claim is not always credible, as types $\alpha Z/(1 - \alpha) < v_B < (k - Z)/(1 - p)$ signal "resist" but do not do so. Therefore the appropriate value for α is solved as follows. Having declared "resist," B actually resists with probability $\beta = Pr(v_B \geq (k - Z)/(1 - p) \mid v_B \geq \alpha Z/(1 - \alpha)) = (1 - F_B((k - Z)/(1 - p)))/(1 - F_B(\alpha Z/(1 - \alpha)))$, and α solves $\alpha = 1 - F_A(k(\beta/(1 - \beta + p\beta)))$. The key difference here is that since B's claim to resist is not fully credible, it has a smaller deterrent impact on nation A. This in turn reduces the value of an honest reputation.

B does not resist, then she is replaced, the expected value of which is $0 + Z$ (note that B receives the value of an honest reputation either way). Provided that Ψ is sufficiently large and a leader is easily removed, B's claims to resist are always credible. The ability of easily removed leaders to tie their hands means that they can effectively communicate their intentions and so can often deter aggressors.

We have only examined crises in the context of Guisinger and Smith's model. However, the arguments readily generalize. For instance, the chicken game is a common conceptualization of international crisis (Schelling 1963; Zagare and Kilgour 2000). In the classic exposition of the game, two players drive cars toward each other. The loser is the player that "chickens" and swerves off the road, while the winner is the one who drives straight. Of course, if neither player swerves, then they are both even worse off. There are three equilibria to this game: one in which A swerves and B goes straight, another in which B swerves and A goes straight, and a third mixed strategy equilibrium in which both players randomize and all outcomes occur with positive probability. Obviously player A prefers the outcome of the second equilibrium, in which she prevails. Leader specific punishments enable a large coalition leader to commit to drive straight and thus win the crisis. If leader A is easily replaced and she explicitly links her reputation with a commitment to drive straight, then nation B is likely to back down. A public commitment to drive straight effectively enables player A to "throw the steering wheel out the window."

Once a leader has staked her domestic political survival on standing firm, her claims are credible even if the international stakes are huge. Allison and Zelikow's (1999) account of the 1962 Cuban missile crisis is a good case in point. In the early 1960s U.S.-Cuban relations were extremely poor and Cuba became increasingly reliant upon the Soviet Union for its defense. Fidel Castro's Cuban government had good reason to be suspicion of U.S. intentions. President Kennedy gave the go-ahead for the Bay of Pigs invasion in 1961, a failed military invasion of Cuba by Cuban nations who had been trained and supported by the United States (primarily under the Eisenhower administration). Although in the end President Kennedy refused to authorize the direct use of the U.S. military in support of the invasion, Cuba might realistically perceive that its security was threatened by the United States. One consequence of this tension was a buildup of the Soviet military stationed in Cuba. The Kennedy administration saw Cuba as its Achilles' heel, in large part due to Kennedy's indecision during the Bay of Pigs. To resolve ambiguities in the administration's Cuban position, in the summer of 1962, having received assurances that the Soviets had no intention of placing nuclear weapons in Cuba, Kennedy publicly declared his acceptance of Soviet defenses in Cuba, but explicitly stating that he could not tolerate "offensive" (i.e., nuclear) weapons in Cuba.

In October 1962 surveillance photographs from U2 spy planes revealed that the Soviets were assembling nuclear missiles in Cuba. Thus started the Cuban missile crisis—the most heated superpower confrontation of the Cold War. Kennedy stated that he thought the chance of the crisis escalating to nuclear war was one in three. Yet despite these huge stakes, Allison and Zelikow (1999, chap. 6) describe how Kennedy felt that it was impossible to back down. If Kennedy backed down, his administration would no longer be able to credibly communicate its position in future crisis and would have been handicapped domestically. Kennedy believed that if he did not take actions to remove the Soviet missiles from Cuba, "I think I would have been impeached" (Allison and Zelikow 1999, p. 340). Having publicly stated a clear position, backing down would have discredited Kennedy and resulted in the collapse of political support for his administration and his dismissal from office. Although in this case, Kennedy had been inadvertently drawn into declaring his position, once declared, either he stood firm or lost his job.

The Cuban missile crisis emphasizes the differences in policy making between large and small winning coalition systems. Although Kennedy assembled a committee, ExCom, which met in secret to formulate a policy response, policy was carried out in public. Rather than secret communications with the Soviets, Kennedy announced his policy to the American people in a television broadcast. In contrast, to this day relatively little is known about the formulation of Soviet policy. Democratic leaders can effectively communicate their position and commit to a strategy through public announcement; autocratic leaders cannot. A result of this is that the smoke-filled backroom deals prevalent in accounts of eighteenth- and nineteenth-century European diplomatic history have been replaced by the press conference, at least in democratic nations.

Although we do not report analyses here, there is systematic evidence to support this trend toward policy in the public domain. On the basis that publicly announced policies are easier to report on than other less public forms of intergovernment communication, newspapers should be more likely to report stories about democratic foreign nations than autocratic ones. This is indeed the case, at least with respect to reporting in the *New York Times*. As a crude measure of policy openness we counted the number of stories reported in each year about each nation in the world from 1946 to 2003.[3]

---

[3] As a practical matter we relied on electronic search methods using ProQuest historical newspapers and the help of Sean Brandt. We excluded certain nations, such as Georgia, since it was often impractical to determine from the title whether stories related to the state or the nation. Other problematic nations included Chad and Jordan (as common names) and Turkey during the month of November.

Fixed effects regression models using the logarithm of the number of stories as the dependent variable show that, controlling for wealth (as logarithm of per capita income), size (as logarithm of population), distance from the United States (as logarithm of capital to capital distance and contiguity), and controls for year (and year squared) with fixed effects of either region-year or nation, the *New York Times* writes around 40 percent more stories about a nation with a large coalition system than one with less inclusive political institutions.

The ability to credibly communicate a policy position can be of great value. Much has been made of Russia's inability to credibly communicate its intention to support Serbia prior to the initiation of the First World War. In 1909 Russia declared itself the protector of the Serbs. This declaration came despite the concerns of the Russian foreign minister, Izvolsky: "To strain our relations with Austria (and hence with Germany too) and to risk a war on account of Bosnia and the Herzegovina would be madness" (quoted in Mercer 1996, pp. 114–15). In part as a planned ruse by Izvolsky that the tsar subsequently refused to endorse, however, the Russians declared themselves to be the protectors of the Serbs, and yet did nothing when the Austrians invaded Bosnia. Having failed to live up to this promise, Russia's foreign policy statements were discounted. As the German undersecretary of state for foreign affairs, Alfred Zimmermann, commented, "[B]luffing constitutes one of the favorite weapons of Russian policy, and while the Russian likes to threaten with the sword, yet he does not willingly draw it for the sake of others at the critical moment" (quoted in Huth 1988, p. 186). Having been caught lying and their reputation damaged, the Russians could not reliably communicate their intentions in 1914.

Lord Grey in a 1914 speech to the British House of Commons reiterated concerns about integrity when he argued Britain must honor its obligations to defend Belgium: "If in a crisis like this, we run away from these obligations of honour and interest as regards the Belgian Treaty, I doubt whether, whatever material force we might have at the end, it would be of very much value in face of the respect that we should have lost" (quoted in Robbins 1994, 179).

In a letter to Lord Camden in 1813, the British diplomat Lord Malmesbury also emphasized the value of maintaining an honest reputation. "[It] is scarcely necessary to say that no occasion, no provocation, no anxiety to rebut an unjust accusation, no ideal—however tempting—of promoting the object you have in view—can need, much less justify, a falsehood. Success obtained by one is a precarious and baseless success. Detection would ruin, not only your own reputation for ever, but deeply wound the honour of your Court" (quoted in Nicolson [1939] 1964, p. 59).

The British and Russia cases above show the value of maintaining integrity by the lengths the British went to maintain their reputation and the disastrous consequences that resulted from the loss of Russian integrity. Yet while diplomatic historians often describe integrity as a national trait, even in times when monarchy was the dominant form of government, there is evidence that leaders perceive reputations to reside with individual leaders rather than nations, as the following examples show. In 1898, negotiations with the Spanish throne over Cuban independence were brought to a standstill by the publication of a private letter from the Spanish minister involved in negotiations, Dupuy de Lome, to the Spanish military leader in Cuba. Although Dupuy's depiction of the American president McKinley as "weak" and a "would-be politician" was easily compensated for with Dupuy's forced resignation, recovering from the portions of the letter that showed that Spain was bluffing in terms of both its political and trade negotiations was less straightforward. Despite the previous U.S. preference for a negotiated settlement, without a change in the throne itself, the U.S. administration was increasingly wary of Spanish claims, and talks faltered (Offner 1992). Similarly, Madison, preceding the War of 1812, awaited news of King George III's failing health. King George had duped Madison in the past and this made it very hard for Madison to negotiate with the king in good faith. Madison hoped that with the king's health deteriorating, the regent would be placed on the throne, which would have enabled him to negotiate the Ordinances of Council without resorting to war (Stagg 1983).

Nations can most effectively resolve crises when they can credibly communicate. Maintaining a reputation for integrity plays a vital role in allowing nations to communicate. Integrity belongs to a leader. The ease with which citizens can replace their leader to restore integrity dictates the extent to which leaders can credibly commit. China's communist government frequently saber rattles over Taiwan without being taken particularly seriously (see, for instance, *The Economist,* August 21, 1999). While a major shakeup of the Chinese government might encourage Taiwan to take new threats seriously, the absence of any significant domestic political consequences for tarnishing national integrity means China's claims should not be taken as seriously as those made by an easily deposed large coalition leader. This makes Chinese policy hard to discern, which increases the likelihood of conflict that might otherwise be avoided. In contrast, ultimatums by the democratically elected leaders are taken much more seriously.

ECONOMIC SANCTIONS

Economic sanctions are often targeted against specific individual leaders. Throughout this book we have drawn attention to instances in which leader turnover ended sanctions. Western sanctions against Iraq ended following the deposition of Saddam Hussein. Similarly, the shift in Yugoslavia's status from a pariah state subject to harsh economic sanctions to a recipient of Western reconstruction aid followed the deposition of its president, Slobodan Milosevic.

These cases are not simply isolated examples but rather part of a systematic pattern. Using Hufbauer, Schott, and Elliot's (1990) data, McGillivray and Stam (2004) find evidence consistent with leader specific punishments concerning the termination of sanctions. Here we derive the implications of leader change for the termination of sanctions and discuss McGillivray and Stam's empirical support for these arguments. In particular they show that leadership change in nondemocratic states has a large impact on the probability of sanctions ending. This effect is present in both target and sender states. Leader turnover in large coalition democratic states has a much smaller impact on the probably of sanctions ending.

Sanctions, by cutting off customary economic relationships—such as trade, investment, and aid—impose costs on the target state. The ability to impose these costs provides the sender nation with leverage to extract concessions from the target state. Speaking at the 1919 Versailles treaty conference that followed the end of the First World War, U.S. President Woodrow Wilson stated that "[T]he one who chooses this economic, peaceful, quiet, lethal remedy will not have to resort to force. It is not such a painful remedy. It doesn't take a single human life outside the country exposed to boycott, but instead subjects that country to a pressure that, in my view, no modern nation can withstand." A casual observation of sanctions episodes in the twentieth century suggests Wilson's predictions were badly wrong. Although the success of sanctions is a highly controversial topic, it is clear that sanctions fail to obtain policy concessions in many cases. Hufbauer, Schott, and Elliot (1990), for instance, suggest that 34 percent of 115 sanctions episodes were at least partially successful. Many scholars think this 34 percent figure greatly exaggerates sanctions' success (Drezner 1999; Dashti-Gibson, Davis, and Radcliff 1997; Hufbauer, Schott, and Elliot 1990; Hass and O'Sullivan 2000; Hass 1998; Martin 1992; Kaempfer and Lowenberg 1988; Pape 1997; Tsebelis 1990).

While the success of sanctions dominates much of the academic debate, we believe this focus is profoundly misplaced, as the value of sanctions as a foreign policy instrument cannot be adequately assessed by observing sanctions episodes. Sanctions arise when the sender's threats to use them are insufficient to coerce concessions from the target and when the sender is still prepared to use sanctions despite their lack of effectiveness. The sender's threat to apply sanctions, the target's decision to comply, and the sender's decision to impose sanctions are linked in a strategic manner that suggests that the mere application of sanctions represents their failure. An understanding of the strategic circumstances that lead to sanctions episodes is essential for explaining the relationship between leader turnover and sanctions. Therefore we start our analysis of sanctions by examining the strategic interactions that lead to sanctions. We then explain the impact of leader turnover and the moderating influence of political institutions.

Sanctions as Strategic Choices

Economic sanctions are the suspension of customary economic relations between states. Typical actions by a sender nation might include suspending foreign aid, imposing a ban on investment and halting imports and exports with the target nation. Sanctions disrupt economic flows and so impose economic costs on both the sender and the target. Senders try to ensure that the sanctions inflict more pain on the target than on themselves. Yet, it is important to remember that high economic costs do not necessarily translate into high political costs. Economic sanctions can provide a convenient cover to protect a favored industry and, as experiences in Iraq reveal, the smuggling opportunities created by economic sanctions provide leaders with valuable benefits with which to reward political supporters.[4]

A typical sanctions episode begins when a potential sender nation threatens a target nation with sanctions if it does not grant some concession, such as a change in policy. Some sanctions are explicitly leader specific punishments rather than an attempt to extract policy concessions. In this context, the concession sought can be thought of as regime change. Sanctions against Saddam Hussein's Iraq are a good case in point. Across three U.S. administrations, it is unclear, what, if any, concessions by Hussein would have induced the United States to lift sanctions.

> President Bush [senior] said today that the United States would oppose the lifting of the worldwide ban against trading with Iraq until President Saddam Hussein is forced out of power in Baghdad. ("Bush Links End of Trading Ban to Hussein Exit," *New York Times*, May 21 1991.)

> We do not agree with the nations who argue that if Iraq complies with its obligations concerning weapons of mass destruction, sanctions should be lifted. (Madeleine Albright, U.S. Secretary of State)

> Sanctions will be there until the end of time, or as long as he [Saddam] lasts. (U.S. President Clinton). (*New York Times*, November 23, 1997)

[4] http://usinfo.state.gov/regional/nea/iraq/iraq99d.htm.

Once sanctions are threatened, the target decides whether or not to concede to the demands. If the target refuses, then the sender must decide whether or not to actually impose the sanction. The strategic implications involved in sanctioning mean that instances of sanctions occurring are unusual events.

If we assume sanctions impose costs on both the sender and the target, as is generally taken as the starting point for analyses, then sanctions should not generally occur (Kaempfer and Lowenberg 1988; Smith 1996a). Suppose the sender can credibly impose high costs on the target. If these costs are higher than the value of the concessions sought, then the target concedes. In such a case, sanctions succeed. However, observation of such instances is unusual. Since the target anticipates conceding, it can avoid the sanctions completely (and any domestic cost from being seen to back down to foreign pressure) by granting concessions prior to the actual applications of sanctions. When sanctions are likely to succeed, we should rarely observe them.

If the sender seeks concessions that are worth more to the target than the cost of the threatened sanctions, or if the ability of sender to impose the sanctions is in doubt, then the target refuses to make concessions when threatened. Such sanctions are likely to fail. Under these circumstances the sender has little incentive to sanction, or to threaten to do so, in the first place.

This simple analysis suggests actual instances of sanctions are something of an aberration. If sanctions will succeed, their mere threat is enough to obtain concessions, which removes the necessity for the actual sanctions themselves. If sanctions are costly to the sender and likely to fail, then the sender has no interest in sending them. Where, then, do the actual cases of sanctions we observe come from? Sanctions occur when the cost of sanctions is insufficient to obtain the desired concessions and when the sender still wants to sanction despite the lack of efficacy.

Actual instances of sanctions represent a very biased sample of all the possible instances where sanctions might have been used. Strategic considerations mean we can learn little about the efficacy of sanctions from observing historical instances of sanctions. The sanctions that actually occur are selected to be cases that are likely to fail. Simply because sanctions are typically seen to fail does not mean that they are not a successful foreign policy tool. Instead, when they work, their actual application is not necessary. These selection arguments suggest sanctions should be relatively infrequent and generally be instances where the target will not concede but where the sender wants to sanction anyway.

Although this simple analysis suggests successful sanctions do not occur as part of equilibrium behavior, more sophisticated analyses suggest they can. Sanctions episodes are often modeled as a war-of-attrition or timing model (Maynard Smith 1974). In such models in each period each nation must decide whether to continue or quit. If the sender quits, the target gets to enjoy its preferred policy; if the target quits, the sender enjoys the policy concessions; and if neither nation quits, both suffer the cost of sanctions. In our simple analysis above we considered only cases where one nation always quits in each period, with the target quitting in every period in the first case and the sender always quitting in the second. War-of-attrition models also predict equilibria in which sanctions occur with positive probability where each nation hopes to prevail by out-waiting the other. Yet, the existence of such equilibria requires that each nation is indifferent between quitting and continuing in every period. As we derive in a footnote, the conditions under which such equilibria exist are quite restrictive. Incomplete information does not necessarily make sanctions any more likely either. As Smith (1996a) shows, the occurrence of war-of-attrition type equilibria in an incomplete information model of sanctions requires very strict assumptions about the distribution of preferences.[5]

Strategic considerations shape the occurrence of sanctions. Based on these arguments, we believe sanctions are most likely to occur when the sanctions are insufficient to elicit concessions and when senders still want to send them anyway. Such selection arguments suggest a sample bias problem in examining the success of sanctions based upon actual instances of sanctions (Achen 1986; Smith 1996b). Testing sanctions theories using data looking only at actual instances of sanctions is highly problematic. Meaningful scientific progress is better made by examining a different set of theoretical predictions. Selection effects suggest that it is impossible to

---

[5] We briefly develop a war-of-attrition model using an infinitely repeated game with a common discount factor, δ. In each period, the sender and target nations decide whether to continue or quit. If the sender quits, sanctions end (forever) and in the current and every future period the target enjoys the value of its preferred policy, which is worth V_T. If the sender continues and the target quits, then the target makes (permanent) policy concessions, which give the sender per period payoffs of V_S. If both the sender and target continue, then sanctions occur that impose per-period costs of K_S and K_T. Thus, if sanctions occur, the sender's per-period payoff is $-K_S$ and the target's per-period payoff is $V_T - K_T$. Once either side quits, sanctions end and any policy concessions become permanent.

There are stationary pure strategy equilibria. (1) If $K_T > V_T$ and $K_S > 0$, then there are two equilibria in which either the target or the sender quits in every period and the other nation never quits. (2) If $K_T < V_T$ and $K_S > 0$, then the target never quits and the sender always quits. In neither of these cases do sanctions actually occur. (3) If $K_T < V_T$ and $K_S < 0$ then neither the target nor the sender ever quits. In these cases sanctions occur but never work.

We now examine a stationary equilibrium in which nations randomize their decisions to quit. If $V_T/(1-\delta) > K_T > V_T$, then there exists an equilibrium in which during each period the target continues with probability $\sigma_T = V_S/(V_S + K_S(1-\delta))$ and the sender continues with probability $\sigma_S = (V_T - K_T(1-\delta))/\delta V_T$. These continuation probabilities ensure that both the sender and the target are indifferent between continuing and quitting in every period. Outside of the stated sanctions costs for the target, war-of-attrition type equilibria do not exist.

test the efficacy of sanction by looking only at cases of sanctions. Morgan, Krustev and Bapat (2006) are collecting Threat and Implementation of Economic Sanctions (TIES) data, which is composed of 888 events from 1971 to 2000. These data include not just instances of sanctions, but also events where sanctions were threatened but not implemented.

Leader Turnover and the Termination of Sanctions

The set of actual sanctions episodes is a highly biased sample from all the possible instances where nations might have used sanctions to settle their disagreements. From this starting point we examine the likely implications of leader change under different institutional contexts. We compare our theoretical predictions with McGillivray and Stam's (2004) prior empirical tests.

Sanctions occur when either the target of sanctions would prefer to endure the cost of economic sanctions rather than make concessions or when the target leader undertook actions that incurred leader specific punishments. The types of issues and policies likely to lead to such situations vary by domestic political institutions. As we have argued throughout this book, leaders from large coalition systems are reluctant to take actions that incur the ire of other nations. That is to say they cannot afford to take reckless actions that lead to the initiation of leader specific punishments. Further, leaders in large coalition systems pursue public-goods-oriented policies. That is to say, relative to small coalition leaders, their policies focus on enriching the vast majority of the people rather than implementing policies that reward small, particularistic interests. Large coalition leaders do not generally take actions that make them the target of sanctions, but should they do so, it is likely that the issue in dispute is public goods in nature and of value to a large proportion of the selectorate.

If the target of economic sanctions is a large coalition system, then leader turnover is unlikely to end sanctions. The predecessor would most likely only have maintained policies that led to sanctions if they were in the public interest. Since any successor's policies also focus on the public interest, it is relatively unlikely that the successor will back down and make concessions either. Large coalition leaders risk incurring sanctions only when the policies under dispute provide public goods benefits.

In contrast, leader turnover in small coalition targets often results in the end of sanctions. The reasons are twofold. First, small coalition leaders can afford to incur the ire of foreign states without jeopardizing their tenure in office. Such leaders can find themselves the target of leader specific punishments. Small coalition leaders, unlike their large coalition counterparts, can take actions that cause them to become the target of leader specific punishments.

Second, leaders in small coalition systems best survive in office by implementing policies that focus on private goods that greatly reward their small number of supporters. Although such policies might lead to sanctions, the leader's supporters are happy to tolerate the sanctions since they benefit from the policies. Leader change in small coalition systems often results in coalition realignment such that different interests are represented. Since these new supporters have different particularistic interests than their predecessors, new leaders enact substantial shifts in policy provisions. Such policy changes are particularly appealing to new leaders if the previous policy led to sanctions. By making concessions on policies that their realigned coalition is likely to care relatively little about anyway, a new leader can end sanctions.

Consistent with these predictions, McGillivray and Stam (2004) find that regime type moderates the impact of leader turnover in target states. In nondemocratic systems leader change makes sanctions about five times more likely to end than would be the case absent leader change. However, in democratic systems, leader change has no appreciable impact on the likelihood of sanctions ending.[6]

Next we consider the impact of leader change in the sender state. Again, the impact of leader change on the likelihood of sanctions ending is greatest in small coalition systems, and once more the logic of the argument stems from the policy focus induced under different political regimes. The desire for political survival forces leaders in large coalition systems to concentrate on policies that effectively generate public goods. As a result of this focus, leadership turnover does little to shift the desire to sanction. If sanctions were of sufficient interest to a large proportion of the selectorate that a leader chose to sanction, then subsequent democratic leaders are also likely to pursue these policies. Large coalition leaders are likely to perpetuate the sanctions policies of their predecessors, and so sanctions persist.

In contrast, in small coalition systems leadership change produces a radical shift in the policy objectives of leaders. Leaders in such systems are best able to survive by pandering to the particularistic interests of their supporters.

---

[6] Using their TIES data, which includes both threats to use sanctions and actual instances of sanctions, Kustev and Morgan (2007) find less support for these arguments. This is perhaps a result of the average magnitude of the 888 events in the TIES data being much smaller than those in Hufbauer, Schott and Elliot's data (1990). Our initial exploration of the TIES data suggests that while leader change is a relatively poor predictor of sanctions ending, the probability of sanctions ending while the leader who was in office at the time of the initiation of the sanctions differ from the likelihood of sanctions ending under subsequent leaders.

Since coalition realignment accompanies leader turnover, the policy objectives of the new leader often differ substantially from those of her predecessor, which means that often the new leader has little interest in continuing sanctions.

Political institutions moderate the impact of leadership turnover in sender nations. In large coalition systems the public goods focus means that sanctions are typically enacted in pursuit of some public goods benefit. Since the policy focus of any successor leader remains the provision of public goods, leader turnover has relatively little impact on the desire to sanction. In small coalition systems, leader change often results in the end of sanctions because public policy shifts to represent the different particularistic interests privileged before and after the leader change.[7]

McGillivray and Stam's (2004) empirical tests support these predictions. They estimate that for the least democratic systems, leader change in the sender state increases the likelihood of sanctions ending by about twentyfold relative to the case of no leader change. However, there is no significant impact on the likelihood of sanctions ending as a result of leadership change in the most democratic of states.

The leader specific punishment theory predicts a pattern between the end of sanctions and the turnover of leaders that is consistent with empirical evidence. In addition to addressing this specific question, we believe investigating the relationship between leader change and the termination of sanctions provides an important step toward understanding sanctions in general. Much of the sanctions literature has focused on their effectiveness in obtaining concessions. Unfortunately, the selection effects created by the strategic application of sanctions mean that assessments of success cannot provide systematic evidence with which to test sanctions theories. With our ability to falsify theoretical predictions on the basis of success being so badly impaired, it is difficult to distinguish between competing explanations. While understanding the success of sanctions might be the eventual goal of many scholars, this is better achieved by rigorously testing those theoretical predictions that are more amenable to empirical testing. Expanding the range of questions asked about sanctions is a better way to assess which theories provide the best explanation of sanctions than continually readdressing the issue of success.

---

[7] If sanctions are explicitly leader specific punishments, such as a demand for regime change, then we anticipate similar predictions. If an incoming leader does not maintain sanctions then she is likely to loose her ability to either communicate or threaten sanctions in the future. Since this reduces the value of retaining her as leader, easily replaced large coalition leaders maintain sanctions. In contrast, small coalition leaders do not jeopardize their term in office if they loose their integrity from failing to maintain sanctions (See McGillivray and Smith 2006 for a formalization of these arguments).

CHAPTER 8

Positive Political Theory and Policy

BUILDING TRUST AND COOPERATION

LEADER SPECIFIC PUNISHMENT allows for improvements in the level of trust and cooperation between nations, at least in institutional settings where leader replacement is relatively easy. Of course, leader specific punishments are not the only way to ensure trust, but we argue it is one of the best. In a Russian Television interview, President G. W. Bush discussed his relationship of trust with Russian President Putin.

> I'll never forget the first question I was asked after meeting Putin in Slovenia. "Do you trust Vladimir Putin?" I said, "Yes." I was asked why and I said: "I have looked him in the eye and seen his soul."[1]

This might seem reassuring for U.S.-Russian relations. Unfortunately, Bush's ability to divine the honesty of world leaders by looking them in the eyes is a highly specialized skill. Admittedly the authors have not met President Putin face-to-face, and we know relatively little about him. However, we suspected that he might turn out to be a nasty piece of work. Our initial instincts about Putin were biased by our prior beliefs that this former Soviet KGB officer would turn out to be an uncooperative leader—not because Putin is ex-KGB, but because of the institutional structure of leader replacement in Russia. Putin has turned out to be less than trustworthy. The Bush administration has subsequently changed its stance and rebuked Putin.[2] Perhaps President Bush's instincts were wrong. Or perhaps the political pressures induced by Russia's increasingly small coalition system forced an otherwise honest man to behave disingenuously.

Leader specific punishments enable political leaders from large coalitions systems to commit to honest and trustworthy relationships. In chapter 6's model of sovereign borrowing, we compared relying on a leader's idiosyncratic desire to repay versus the desire to commit to repay induced in large coalition leaders by LSP. While, as Stasavage (2003) showed in the case of seventeenth- and eighteenth-century Britain, leaders with a

---

[1] "Excerpts: Bush on Russian TV," BBC.co.uk, May 31, 2003.
[2] "Administration Rebukes Putin on His Policies," *New York Times*, June 1, 2007, p. A1.

strong desire (or soul) for repayment are more trustworthy, the ability of democratic leaders to mortgage their political tenure provides a far more powerful commitment to repayment.

Directing punishments against individual leaders rather than the nations they represents provides automatic opportunities for the restoration of good relations and, when leaders are easily replaced, it also allows for much deeper cooperation. Leader specific punishments also enhance the ability of democratically accountable leaders to signal their intentions during crises and commit themselves to a course of action.

The driving force of the theory is its combination of different levels of analyses. Relations are between states, but the policies are chosen by individual leaders whose grip on power depends upon domestic political institutions. It is the interplay between these three levels that produces the novel dynamics between interstate relations and leader change uncovered in this book. The theory assumes common goals for the members of each nation and office-seeking motivations for leaders. Although such an approach avoids stumbling into the tautology of explaining patterns of behavior by claiming actors take the actions they prefer so that when actors pick different things in different circumstances it is simply because they want to, it has limitations.

In some situations there can be great heterogeneity about the desirability of cooperation. As we saw from Stasavage's (2003) analysis of Tory and Whig borrowing following the Glorious Revolution, some groups are naturally better cooperators than others. The dynamics of leader specific punishments in the face of such diversity of domestic preferences needs to be examined, particularly when preferences are intense. In chapter 1 we quoted Israeli Prime Minister Sharon's hope in 2002 that new Palestinian leadership would allow the peace process to resume. While the Israeli government is far from blameless, a major stumbling block to finding a peaceful settlement has been the inability of the Palestinian leadership to abide by agreements and to negotiate in good faith.

Leader specific punishment theory suggests that the death of the Palestinian leader Yasser Arafat in 2004 and his Fatah party's loss in the Palestinian parliamentary elections in 2006 would rejuvenate Israeli-Palestinian relations and offer the opportunity for meaningful negotiations. Unfortunately this has not happened, and is unlikely to. Fatah's parliamentary successor was Hamas, a political organization that seeks the destruction of the State of Israel. Cooperation and negotiations between Israel and Hamas are extremely unlikely because there is little common ground. Although leadership change can reinvigorate sour relations, preferences matter too. While the dynamics of leader specific punishments in heterogeneous populations deserve further examination, we leave this for future research.

POSITIVE POLITICAL THEORY OR POLICY ADVICE?

Throughout our exposition of leader specific punishment theory we have walked a fine line between a positive political theory that explains how the world works and a policy prescription as to how it could be made to work better. It is time to distinguish between these aspects of the argument.

The theoretical model shows logically how the targeting of punishments against individual leaders rather than the nations they represent affects the dynamics of interstate relations. In particular, such punishment strategies endogenously generate opportunities to restore good relations and, when leaders are easy to replace, avoid many instances of poor relations in the first place. Anecdotally we have offered examples of the use of leader specific strategies. We have also shown experimental and empirical evidence that is consistent with the implications of leader specific punishments. These tests indicate a strong relationship between interstate relations and leader change and show how political institutions moderate this relation, as predicted by LSP. Of course logically we cannot confirm that LSP is the correct explanation for these observations, but they help reassure us as to the usefulness of the theory. This is the positive political theory aspect of the project: we assumed some primitives, logically derived the implications of these assumptions, and tested whether the predictions were falsified. There is evidence consistent with the use of leader specific punishments.

Leader specific punishment theory also provides policy prescriptions by showing how to improve the quality of a nation's foreign policy. It is important to draw the distinction between policy advice and extant evidence of the use of LSP. The positive political theory aspects of this book suggest that to some extent foreign policies are already conditioned against leaders. However, we certainly do not wish to imply that every single aspect of a nation's foreign policy is explicitly leader specific. This is clearly not the case. What we wish to argue, however, is that if national leaders incorporated more explicit leader specific components into their foreign policies, then they could (on average) improve the welfare of their citizens. The value of LSP as a policy prescription follows from the logical arguments that show the welfare advantages of LSP, not from any empirical evidence for LSP. Indeed, if we had found no evidence for the existing use of LSP, then the marginal value of including explicit leader specific features in foreign policy would be even greater. The value of LSP as a policy recommendation is logically distinct from evidence consistent with the extant use of LSP.

We address how leader specific punishments could improve the quality of foreign policies in conflictual and cooperative settings by discussing two specific examples, crises and the design of international agreements. Since the (ex ante) welfare improvement of these policies follows directly from the theory, we focus primarily on feasibility and implementation issues. These issues are important because while improving the quality of foreign policies through LSP increases the expected welfare of the citizens, leaders are primarily concerned with their welfare and not that of their citizens. Improving the depth of cooperation between nations might make the people better off, but leaders have little interest in such improvements if it jeopardizes their survival in office.

More Persuasive Threats in Crises

Targeting foreign policy statements against specific leaders leverages policy. This enables leaders to provide, on average, better outcomes for their citizens. The superiority of leader specific threats is twofold. First, leader specific threats explicitly provide for the normalization of relations, such that if a leader, for example, threatens sanctions, she does not make a commitment to do so forever. She commits herself for only as long as the opposing leader remains in office. Second, leader specific threats discourage leaders in opposing states from taking actions that are liable to initiate the application of the punishments because the leader specific nature of the punishments weakens their position domestically (Marinov 2005). Targeting specific leaders improves the efficacy of foreign policy.

The leader specific nature of the threatened punishments means that punishments are not indefinite. Relations between states are restored upon the replacement of political leaders. Although in exceptional cases, such as Fidel Castro in Cuba, this can result in tarnished relations for decades, the average autocratic leader lasts only 5.69 years in office (defined by $W < 0.75$, BdM2S2 2003, p. 294). As we have argued throughout this book, the prospects of restoring relations encourage citizens to depose leaders who incur the ire of other nations. Of course, in small coalition systems the increase in the deposition risk is only minimal. But compared to making threats without including a leadership component, this, admittedly small, increase in deposition risk improves the prospects that a leader will comply.

With regard to dealing with large coalition systems, leader specific threats provide even greater leverage. The desire of the citizens to restore relations greatly increases a democrat's risk of deposition. For this reason, we rarely observe the application of leader specific punishments against leaders from large coalition systems. Unless the concessions being demanded are public goods highly valued by the citizens, the threat of a leader specific punishment is typically sufficient to induce compliance. For example, U.S. President Eisenhower's threat to sell pounds sterling and collapse British currency and endanger the Conservative government was sufficient to induce Prime Minister Anthony Eden to withdraw from the Suez crisis in 1956.

Compared to directing foreign policies against nations, targeting specific leaders improves the prospects of obtaining compliance from foreign nations. Even when the policy fails to gain concessions, the policy prevents acrimonious relations dragging on indefinitely by providing explicit conditions for the restoration of good relations. The targeting of specific leaders leverages foreign policy, making it a more powerful tool. Critics of our policy prescription might argue that creating a more powerful tool simply encourages leaders to take on more difficult problems and might point to examples of failed leader specific threats. While it is true that the superior efficacy of leader specific threats encourages leaders to actively engage in trying to influence events in more situations, this critique incorrectly conflates poor ex post outcome with bad ex ante decision making.

Suppose the leader of nation A faces ten foreign policy crises per year and suppose that without a leader specific component to her policies, she would attempt to influence the outcomes in four of these crises. Although not all of these four crises will be successfully resolved, on average the leader believes she can obtain a more desirable outcome by becoming involved. Now suppose leader A targets specific leaders when formulating her policies. This leverages the power of her foreign policy. In the four cases in which she was already intervening, leader specific threats increase the prospects of her obtaining a favorable resolution for her nation. With respect to these four cases, the use of LSP appears unambiguously good. The worry for critics, particularly dovish critics, is that enhancing the power of foreign policy encourages leader A to engage in some of the other six crises and that these will not always resolve well. This is certainly true. Giving leaders better tools enables them to tackle more difficult jobs. However, the key is that the leader still does not want to engage in an additional crisis unless she thinks the expected resolution of the crisis is improved by doing so. It is always easy to look to ex post failures to indict a policy that must be formulated ex ante.

Targeting foreign policy against a specific leader rather than the nation she represents leverages the persuasive power of foreign policy. Even if the policy fails to obtain the desired outcomes, LSP provides contingencies for the normalization of relations. We have argued for the advancement of targeting specific leaders in the context of crises (Smith 2000). We now turn to the value of leader specific contingencies in the design of international institutions.

Building Leader Specific Punishments into International Agreements and Institutions

Through our examination of the stochastic prisoners' dilemma and the continuous choice prisoners' dilemma games we have shown that leader specific punishments enable nations in which leader removal is easy to attain higher levels of cooperation than other nations. The intuitions developed from these models suggest that international agreements and international institutions can be made that deepen cooperation between nations, at least in those nations with accountable leaders. We have offered evidence that to some extent nations already implicitly practice leader specific policies. Yet to date international institutions do not explicitly invoke LSP in their design. We consider some features of extant international institutions and examine how leader specific punishments might be integrated into such institutional designs. We also consider the political incentives of leaders to implement such agreements.

We have shown, at least theoretically, that LSP allows for deeper, more reliable cooperation between nations with easily replaceable political leaders. If international agreements incorporated explicit LSP, then compliance with these agreements could be enhanced. Some critics would argue that such modifications to international agreements would be worthless and generate unnecessary complications. Constructivist scholars, such as Chayes and Chayes (1995), Hathaway (2002, 2004), and Raustiala and Slaughter (2002) point to the fact that compliance with international agreements is already very high and so there is little point adding contingencies that further enhance compliance. They argue that people inherently want to follow rules and that over time compliance with the rules increases the legitimacy of international institutions, which feeds back to further enhance compliance.[3]

Counter to these arguments, Downs, Rocke, and Barsoom (1996; see also Gilligan 2004; Simmons 1998) argue that it is not just that nations comply with their obligations that is important, but also what these obligations are. To illuminate this debate is it worth returning to the continuous choice PD game developed in chapter 2. If nations institute a full cooperative agreement, that is to say one that induced P_A, $P_B = 0$, then (absent an extremely high discount factor and long punishments), the nations do not abide by the agreement: there is no compliance and no cooperation. However, if an agreement states that the nations should cooperate at the Nash equilibrium levels ($P_A = P_B = 100$), then nations can always abide by this agreement for the simple reason that the agreement simply states that nations should do what they were doing anyway: there is full compliance, but still no cooperation. With leaders under domestic pressure to be seen to secure agreements, and the complexity and legal ease of agreements making it virtually impossible for the average voter to interpret, we should perhaps worry about

---

[3] Young (1979) defines compliance as "said to occur when the actual behavior of a given subject conforms to prescribed behavior, and noncompliance or violation occurs when actual behavior departs significantly from prescribed behavior."

the depth of some of agreements. As Downs and his colleagues point out, observing compliance with an agreement without taking into consideration the content of the agreement tells us little about cooperation.

Leader specific punishment theory shows that through leader specific contingencies, leaders who are easily removed can commit to much deeper levels of cooperation than their autocratic counterparts and still maintain compliance. Yet, in the noisy world of international agreements, for leaders to tie their political careers to the vagaries of international institutions is a lot to ask. It is therefore beholden upon us to pause and examine some of the real world features of international institutions that make them attractive to political leaders and consider how LSP might be integrated into these agreements.

The World Trade Organization (WTO) helps negotiate and implement international trade agreements. Unlike many other international institutions, the WTO specifies explicitly a mechanism for detecting noncompliance and punishments in the event of noncompliance. Treaties and agreements vary greatly in their provisions for detection and punishment. The WTO specifies both how to detect cheating and what is to be done in the event of cheating. In contrast, arms control agreements typically provide huge provisions for the detection of cheating but rarely specify what should be done in the event of detection. Other agreements specify neither a detection mechanism nor a punishment mechanism. The Kyoto agreement on global warming was little more than a statement that its signatories would like to reduce greenhouse gas emissions. The agreement failed to specify how a nation's emissions should be monitored or what should be done if a nation did not cut emissions.

Once the WTO member nations agree to a trade agreement, the WTO's dispute resolution mechanism provides a means to enforce the agreement. During the postwar period, international trade agreements have managed to substantially eliminate tariffs. Unfortunately, the decline in tariffs has potentially led to the substitution of other, less transparent forms of protection, such as subsidies, quotas, and regulatory policies. It is increasingly difficult to distinguish between a regulatory policy that is designed to protect public health and one that is designed to discriminate against foreign goods. In the continuous choice PD game, a nation's actions were observed as $Q = P + \varepsilon$. Although a nation chooses action P, this cannot be directly observed and the judgment as to whether the nation cheated has to be made of the basis of the observation Q. There is substantial risk that a nation's good intentions are falsely interpreted or that a nation utilizes this slack to protect domestically important constituents.

The WTO's dispute resolution mechanism aids cooperation by clarifying what constitutes a breach of the agreement. The shift toward nontransparent forms of protectionism creates great ambiguities in interpreting whether or not a nation's actions constitute a breach of the rules. If nations could unilaterally decide whether another nation's actions constitute cheating then the whole system would degenerate into accusation and counteraccusation. It is common for both sides in a trade dispute to accuse the other of illegal trade practices. For example in the civilian airplane business, the United States accuses the European Union of illegally subsidizing airbus, while the European Union claims Boeing receives subsidies and preferential treatment within the United States (Disputes DS316, DS317) The WTO's Web site, which is particularly informative, provides a full description of the dispute resolution mechanism rules and numerous illustrative cases (www.wto.org).

Under the WTO, when nation A believes nation B's policies constitute a breach of WTO rules, nation A can appeal the case to the WTO. Although the details are complex with numerous stages and appeals, the inherent process is that the dispute resolution mechanism creates a panel that considers evidence from both parties and then rules as to whether or not nation B has indeed broken the rules. If so, then the panel recommends remedial actions and, in the event that B fails to comply with these remedies, authorizes a level of retaliatory tariffs.

For instance, in March 2002 U.S. President Bush imposed a 30 percent tariff on imported steel. His actions, designed to help constituents in key electoral states, such as Ohio and Pennsylvania, angered many nations who referred the case to the WTO.[4] The WTO ruled that the tariff violated trade laws and authorized retaliatory tariffs worth up to $2.2 billion. The EU and other complainants announced that the products they intended to apply these sanctions against were made in the electorally important states Bush was trying to help. Following the United States failure to reverse the ruling via the appeals procedure, Bush repealed the tariff.[5]

The dispute resolution mechanism adjudicates as to whether or not a nation has cheated. However, unlike the simple continuous choice PD game, the WTO does not call for immediate punishment, but rather provides leaders with an opportunity to "apologize" before the application of punishments or sanctions. This ability to take remedial action before being punished is an important real world feature that helps preserve

---

[4] The European Union filed complaint DS 248 on March 7, 2002. This dispute was subsequently joined by Japan (WT/DS249), Korea (WT/DS251), China (WT/DS252), Switzerland (WT/DS253), Norway (WT/DS254), New Zealand (WT/DS258), and Brazil (WT/DS259). The WTO panel concluded on July 11, 2003 that the United States' actions violated WTO agreements. On August 11, 2003 the United States appealed the case to the Appellate Body, which upheld the origin ruling on November 10, 2003. On December 4, 2003, the United States announced it had withdrawn the tariff.

[5] "Europe Praises Bush steel Repeal," BBC News, Dec 5, 2003, http://news.bbc.co .uk/1/hi/business/3293387.stm.

cooperation by allowing leaders to temporarily "opt out" (Rosendorff and Milner 2001). The opportunity to apologize makes leaders much more willing to enter agreements and abide by them. Rosendorff (2004) and Rosendorff and Milner (2001) argue that domestic politics often creates intense incentives for leaders to want to temporarily violate agreements. The ability to default and apologize helps create and maintain robust cooperation. It maintains cooperation because a one-time defection does not lead to long-term punishment and it creates cooperation because leaders are more willing to sign up for agreements when a decision adjudicated against them still gives them an opportunity to redress the problem.

In McGillivray and Smith 2006 we explicitly modeled compliance and apology, by asking whether nation A can compel nation B to abide by the terms of an agreement through the threat of sanctions. In a noisy environment, nation B sets a policy that provides concessions to nation A. Nation A noisily observes this policy, and if nation B is judged to have violated the agreed threshold, then nation B is given one period to apologize (by making additional concessions to A). If nation B fails to apologize, then nation A can sanction nation B. In this model we assumed sanctions hurt both sides, which creates credibility issues. In the context of trade, nations often want to impose retaliatory tariffs and it is a "legalized" way of providing protection. However, if it is costly for nation A to punish B, then B might legitimately dismiss A's threats to punish it as lacking credibility.

Leader specific punishments enhance effectiveness and credibility. Suppose we consider nation A's reputation (integrity) for punishing. If A fails to punish B when B fails to apologize appropriately, then we might say A loses her integrity. In all future interactions, neither nation B nor any other nation will believe A's threats to sanction are credible and will therefore have no reason to comply with the concessions that A seeks. To maintain its integrity, nation A has an incentive to apply sanctions, or other punishments, even when it suspects that the sanctions will do no good in terms of eliciting cooperation.

These incentives are magnified if reputations are leader specific. If the leader of nation A fails to punish B, then the citizens can restore their nation's integrity by removing her. This link between punishing nonapologetic defaulters or risk being removed from office allows easily replaced leaders to credibly commit to sanction.

Leaders who can credibly commit to sanction (as a leader specific reputation allows easily replaced leaders to do) can effectively compel other nations to comply with agreements. Once nation A can credibly commit to punish nation B, nation B is more likely to comply by following agreements and apologize when it is judged not to have done so. By making sanctions, or other punishments, leader specific, easily replaced leaders can more credibly commit to punish defaulters. The leader specific nature of punishments also increases the incentives of easily replaced leaders to abide by the terms of agreements or to apologize if they don't.

Leader specific punishments can enhance the depth and reliability of cooperation between nations with easily replaced leaders. However, being able to design more cooperative international institutions or agreements is worth naught if leaders won't agree to them. Leaders do not want to enter international agreements that threaten to jeopardize their political survival down the line. As we have explored above, "opt-out" clauses, such as those in the WTO that temporarily allow leaders to break the rules and then take remedial actions, remove the immediate link between being judged to have cheated and being removed from office. This clearly makes the idea of explicit leader specific punishments more palatable for leaders. However, leaders might still be reluctant to explicitly put their tenure in office on the line simply to enforce an increased level of international cooperation.

The ability to commit to deeper cooperation improves the quality of international cooperation, and therefore the welfare of citizens in the cooperating nations. However, leaders are motivated by the desire to re-tain office; improving societal welfare is always secondary to this primary goal. Leaders are thus naturally reluctant to trade security in office for improved welfare for their citizens. Yet opposition leaders are not. By of-fering to make explicit leader specific commitments, opposition politicians improve the quality of the public policy they can offer the electorate. This makes them more electable. To counter this threat from the opposition, political leaders might themselves find it attractive to contemplate adding leader specific features to international institutions.

Despite the potential improvements in international cooperation, few self-interested leaders will pursue the inclusion of leader specific clauses for international institutions. While leaders would likely claim that such contingencies violate national sovereignty, the truth is that it is not in their interest. It is in the interest of the average voter, however, and so is a potentially attractive strategy for opposition parties to pursue. Of course, once in power these opposition parties would like to forget any such prom-ises, but calls for such contingencies from opposition parties increase the relative attractiveness of LSP from the perspective of the incumbent. Any move toward the explicit use of LSP in international agreements is unlikely to be a government initiative, unless in response to opposition pressure.

CONCLUSIONS

Leader specific punishment theory bridges the divide between different perspectives on international relations. Rather than argue interstate rela-tions are derived from unitary actor states, domestic political systems, or individual leaders, the theory's predictive power is obtained from examining the interactions across these three levels of analysis. Individual leaders and the institutional context in which they serve shape the dynamics of the relations between states.

In addition to accounting for existing empirical findings, such as the superiority of cooperation between democratic states, leader specific punishment theory predicts previously unexplored dynamics between the turnover of leaders and interstate relations. These hypothesized relations led us to examine new empirical puzzles. No doubt our arguments are too simplistic to account for all the intricacies of interstate relations. However, we hope that at a minimum our theory can be usefully wrong, and that by proposing an additional set of questions and demonstrating a new set of empirical regularities, we can help advance the understanding of interstate relations.

Bibliography

Abdullah, F. A. 1985. "Development of an Advanced Warning Indicator of External Debt Servicing Vulnerability." *Journal of International Business Studies* 16:135–41.

Achen, Christopher H. 1986. *The Statistical Analysis of Quasi-experiments*. Berkeley and Los Angeles: University of California Press.

Ahn, T. Kyeong, E. Ostrom, and J. Walker. 1998. "Trust and Reciprocity: Experimental Evidence from PD Games." Indiana University, Discussion Paper.

Andreoni, J., and J. H. Miller. 1993. "Rational Cooperation in the Finitely Repeated Prisoner's Dilemma: Experimental Evidence." *Economic Journal* 103:570–85.

Andreoni, J., and H. Varian. 1999. "Pre-Play Contracting in the Prisoner's Dilemma." *Proceedings of the National Academy of Sciences* 96:10933–38.

Allison, Graham, and Philip Zelikow. 1999. *Essence of Decision: Explaining the Cuban Missile Crisis* 2nd ed. New york: Addison Wesley Longman.

Alt, James, Randall Calvert, and Brian Humes. 1988. "Reputation and Hegemonic Stability: A Game Theoretic Analysis." *American Political Science Review* 82:446–65.

Atkeson, A. 1991. "International Lending with Moral Hazard and Risk of Repudiation." *Econometrica* 59:1069–90.

Austen-Smith, D. 1992. Strategic Models of Talk in Political Decision Making. *International Political Science Review* 13 (1): 45–58.

Axelrod, R. 1970. *Conflict of Interest*. Chicago: Markham.

———. 1984. *The Evolution of Cooperation*. New York: Basic Books.

———. 1986. "An Evolutionary Approach to Norms." *American Political Science Review* 80:1095–111.

Axelrod, Robert, and Robert O. Keohane. 1986. "Achieving Cooperation under Anarchy: Strategies and Institutions." In Kenneth A. Oye, ed., *Cooperation under Anarchy*. Princeton: Princeton University Press, pp. 226–54.

Azar, Edward E. 1982. *The Codebook of the Conflict and Peace Data Bank (COPDAB)*. College Park, MD: Center for International Development, University of Maryland.

Baldelli, Pia G. Celozzi. 1998. *Power Politics, Diplomacy, and the Avoidance of Hostilities between England and the United States in the Wake of the Civil War*. Lewiston, NY: Edwin Mellen.

Baldwin, David A., ed. 1993. *Neorealism and Neoliberalism: The Contemporary Debate*. New York: Columbia University Press.

Balkan, E. M. 1992. "Political Instability, Country Risk and Probability of Default." *Applied Economics* 24:999–1008.

Banks, Arthur. 2001. Cross-National Time Series Data Archive. CD-ROM.

Bates, R. 1996. "Institutions as Investments." Harvard Institute for International Development, Discussion Paper No. 527.

Bates, Robert H. 2001. *Prosperity and Violence: The Political Economy of Development*. New York: W. W. Norton and Co.

Beck, Nathaniel, and Jonathan Katz. 2001. Throwing Out the Baby with the Bath Water: A Comment on Green, Kim, and Yoon. *International Organization* 55 (2): 487–95.

Beers, David T., and John Chambers. 2003. "Sovereign Defaults: Heading Lower into 2004." *Standard and Poor's: Sovereigns*, Sept. 18, 2003.

Bendor, Jonathan. 1987. "In Good Times and Bad: Reciprocity in an Uncertain world." *American Journal of Political Science* 31:531–38.

———. 1993. "Uncertainty and the Evolution of Cooperation." *Journal of Conflict Resolution* 37:709–34.

Bendor, Jonathan, R. Kramer, and S. Stout. 1991. When in Doubt . . . : Cooperation in a Noisy Prisoner's Dilemma. *Journal of Conflict Resolution* 35: 691–719.

Benoit, Kenneth. 1996. "Democracies Really Are More Pacific (in General)." *Journal of Conflict Resolution* 40 (Dec.): 636–57.

Bienen, Henry, and Nicolas van de Walle. 1992. "A Proportional Hazard Model of Leadership Duration." *Journal of Politics* 54 (Aug. 3): 685–717.

Bixenstine, E., C. Levitt, and K. Wilson. 1966. "Collaboration among Six Persons in a Prisoner's Dilemma Game." *Journal of Conflict Resolution*: 10488–96.

Bliss, H., and B. Russett. 1998. "Democratic Trading Partners: The Liberal Connection." *Journal of Politics* 60:1126–47.

Bonacich, P. 1970. "Putting the Dilemma Back into Prisoner's Dilemma." *Journal of Conflict Resolution* 14:379–87.

Bornstein, G., I. Erev, and H. Goren. 1994. "The Effect of Repeated Play in the PG and IPD Team Games." *Journal of Conflict Resolution* 38 (4): 690–707.

Brecher, Michael, and Jonathan Wilkenfeld. 1997. *A Study of Crisis*. Ann Arbor: University of Michigan Press.

Bremmer, Stuart. 1992. "Dangerous Dyads: Conditions Affecting the Likelihood of Interstate War, 1816–1965. *Journal of Conflict Resolution* 26 (June): 309–41.

Brewer, T. L., and P. Rivoli. 1990. "Politics and Perceived Country Creditworthiness in International Banking." *Journal of Money, Credit and Banking* 3: 357–69.

Browne, Eric C., John P. Frendreis, and Dennis W. Gleiber. 1986. "The Process of Cabinet Dissolution: An Exponential Model of Duration and Stability in Western Democracies." *American Journal of Political Science* 30 (Aug. 3): 628–50.

Bueno de Mesquita, Bruce, and David Lalman. 1992. *War and Reason: Domestic and International Imperatives*. New Haven, CT: Yale University Press.

Bueno de Mesquita, Bruce, James D. Morrow, Randolph Siverson, and Alastair Smith. 1999. "An Institutional Explanation of the Democratic Peace." *American Political Science Review* 93:769–1044.

———. 2001. "Political Survival and International Conflict." In *War in the Changing World*, edited by Zeev Maoz and Azar Gat. Ann Arbor: University of Michigan Press, pp. 183–206.

———. 2002. "Political Institutions, Policy Choice and the Survival of Leaders" *British Journal of Political Science* 32(4):559–90.

———. 2004. "Testing Novel Implications from the Selectorate Theory of War." *World Politics* 56:363–88.

Bueno de Mesquita, Bruce, and Randolph Siverson. 1995. "War and the Survival of Political Leaders: A Comparative Study of Regime Types and Political Accountability." *American Political Science Review* 89 (December): 841–55.

Bueno de Mesquita, Bruce, Randolph Siverson, and Gary Woller. 1992. "War and the Fate of Regimes: A Comparative Analysis." *American Political Science Review* 86 (3): 638–46.

Bueno de Mesquita, Bruce, Alastair Smith, Randolph M. Siverson and James D. Morrow. 2003. *"The Logic of Political Survival."* Cambridge: MIT Press.

Bulow, J., and K. Rogoff. 1989. "Sovereign Debt: Is to Forgive to Forget?" *American Economic Review* 79:43–50.

Busch, Marc, and Eric R. Reinhardt. 1993. "Nice Strategies in a World of Relative Gains: The Problem of Cooperation under Anarchy." *Journal of Conflict Resolution* 37 (3) (Sept. 1993): 427–45.

Cantor, R., and F. Packer. 1996. "Determinants and Impact of Sovereign Credit Ratings." *FRBNY Economic Policy Review* (October 1996).

Carr, E. H. [1946] 1962. *The Twenty Years' Crisis.* London: St. Martin's.

Chayes, Abram, and Antonia Handler Chayes. 1995. *The New Sovereignty: Compliance with International Regulatory Agreements.* Cambridge: Harvard University Press.

Chernow, Ron. 1990. *The House of Morgan: An American Banking Dynasty and the Rise of Modern Finance.* New York: Grove Press.

Chiozza, Giacomo, and Hein E. Goemans. 2003. "Peace through Insecurity: Tenure and International Conflict." *Journal of Conflict Resolution* 4 (4) (Aug. 2003): 443–67.

———. 2004. "International Conflict and the Tenure of Leaders: Is War Still Ex Post Inefficient?" *American Journal of Political Science* 48 (3): 604–19.

Citron J., and G. Nickelsburg. 1987. "Country Risk and Political Instability." *Journal of Development Economics* 25:385–92.

Cole, H. L., and P. J. Kehoe. 1994. "Reputation Spillover across Relationships with Enduring and Transient Benefits: Reviving Reputation Models of Debt." Federal Reserve Bank of Minneapolis. Research Department Staff Report 137/JV.

Cooper, R., D. V. Dejong, R. Forsythe, and T. W. Ross. 1992. "Communication in Coordination Games." *Quarterly Journal of Economics* 107:739–71.

———. 1994. "Alternative Institutions for Evaluating Coordination Problems: Experimental Evidence on Forward Induction and Pre-Play Communication." In *Problems of Coordination in Economic Activity,* edited by J. W. Friedman. Dordrecht: Kluwer.

———. 1996. "Cooperation without Reputation: Experimental Evidence from Prisoner's Dilemma Games." *Games and Economic Behavior* 12 (2): 187–218.

Coser, Lewis, A. 1956. *The Functions of Social Conflict.* New York: Free Press.

Crawford, Vincent, and Joel Sobel. 1982. "Strategic Information Transmission." *Econometrica* 50:1431–51.

Cumby, R. E., and T. Pastine. 2001. "Emerging Market Debt: Measuring Credit Quality and Examining Relative Pricing." *Journal of International Money and Finance.* 20:591–609.

Dashti-Gibson J., P. Davis, and B. Radcliff. 1997. "On the Determinants of Success of Economic Sanctions: An Empirical Analysis." *American Journal of Political Science* 41:608–18.

Davis, D. D., and C. A. Holt, eds. 1993. *Experimental Economics* Princeton: Princeton University Press.

Deardorff, Alan V. 1995. "Determinants of Bilateral Trade: Does Gravity Work in a Neoclassical World?" Working Paper 5377. Cambridge, MA: National Bureau of Economic Research.

De Cecco, Marcello. 1975. *Money and Empire: The International Gold Standard, 1890–1914.* Totowa, NJ: Rowman and Littlefield.

De Long, J. B., and A. Shleifer. 1993. "Princes and Merchants: European City Growth before the Industrial Revolution." NBER Working Paper no. 4274.

Diermeier, Daniel, and Randy T. Stevenson. 1999. "Cabinet Survival and Competing Risks." *American Journal of Political Science* 43 (4) (Oct.): 1051–68.

Dixit, A., and J. Londregan. 2000. "Political Power and the Credibility of Government Debt." *Journal of Economic Theory* 94:80–105.

Dixon, William. 1994. "Democracy and the Peaceful Settlement of International Conflict." *American Political Science Review* 88 (1):14–32.

Dolbear Jr., F. T., L. Lave, G. Bowman, A. Lieberman, E. Prescott, F. Reuter, and R. Sherman. 1968. "Collusion in the Prisoner's Dilemma: Number of Strategies." *Journal of Conflict Resolution* 13:252–61.

Downs, George W., and David M. Rocke. 1990. *Tacit Bargaining, Arms Races, and Arms Control.* Ann Arbor: University of Michigan Press.

———. 1995. *Optimal Imperfection? Domestic Uncertainty and Institutions in International Relations.* Princeton: Princeton University Press.

Downs, George W., David M. Rocke, and Peter N. Barsoom. 1996. "Is the Good News about Compliance Good News about Cooperation?" *International Organization* 50:379–406.

Drezner, Daniel. 1999. *The Sanctions Paradox.* Cambridge: Cambridge University Press.

Eaton, J., and L. Taylor. 1985. "Developing Country Finance and Debt." *Journal of Development Economics* 22:209–65.

Eaton, J., and M. Gersovitz. 1981. "Debt with Potential Repudiation: Theoretical and Empirical Analysis." *Review of Economic Studies* 48:289–309.

Edwards, S. 1984. "LDC's Foreign Borrowing and Default Risk: An Empirical Investigation, 1976–1980." *American Economic Review* 74:352–68.

———. 1986. "The Pricing of Bonds and Bank Loans in International Markets: An Empirical Analysis of Developing Countries' Foreign Borrowing." *European Economic Review* 30:565–89.

Eichengreen. B. 1991. "Historical Research on International Lending and Debt." *Journal of Economic Perspectives* 5:149–69.

Elster, Jon. 2000. *Ulysses Unbound.* New York. Cambridge University Press.

Erb, C. B., H. R Campbell, and T. E. Viskanta. 1999. "Understanding Emerging Market Bonds." Draft, Oct. 1991.

Eyerman, Joe, and Robert A. Hart, Jr. 1996. "An Empirical Test of the Audience Cost Proposition." *Journal of Conflict Resolution* 40:597–616.

Farrell, Joseph, and Robert Gibbons. 1989. "Cheap Talk Can Matter in Bargaining." *Journal of Economic Theory* 48:221–37.

Farrell, Joseph, and Eric Maskin. 1989. "Renegotiation in Repeated Games." *Games and Economic Behavior* 1 (4): 327–60.

Fearon, James D. 1994. "Domestic Political audiences and the Escalation of International Disputes." *American Political Science Review* 88:577–92.

———. 1997. "Signaling Foreign Policy Interests: Tying Hands versus Sinking Costs." *Journal of Conflict Resolution* 41:68–90.

Fearon, James D., and David Laitin. 1996. "Explaining Interethnic Cooperation." *American Political Science Review* 90 (4): 715–35.

Feder, G. 1981. "Economic Growth, Foreign Loans and Debt Servicing Capacity of Developing Countries." *Journal of Development Studies* 16:651–69.

Feder, G., and L. Uy. 1985. "The Determinants of International Creditworthiness and Their Implications." *Journal of Policy Modeling* 7:133–56.

Feis, Herbert. 1930. *Europe, the World's Banker*. New Haven, CT: Yale University Press.

Firmin-Sellers, K. 1994. "The Politics of Property Rights." *American Political Science Review* 89:867–88.

Fisk, Robert. 2002. "The Mantra that Means This Time It's Serious." *Independent*, September 13, 2002, http://news.independent.co.uk.

Flores, Alejandro Quiroz. 2005. "Coalition Dynamics, Interstate War, and the Political Survival of Foreign Ministers." Working Paper, Department of Politics, New York University.

Ford, A. G. 1962. *The Gold Standard, 1880–1914*. Oxford: Clarendon Press.

Frank, C. R., and W. R. Cline. 1971. "Measurement of Debt Servicing Capacity of Developing Countries." *Journal of Financial and Quantitative Analysis* 16:651–69.

Frankel, Jeffrey A., and David Romer. 1999. "Does Trade Cause Growth?" *American Economic Review* 89 (3): 379–99.

Freder, G., and K. Ross. 1982. "Risk Assessments and Risk Premiums in the Eurodollar Market." *Journal of Finance* 37:679–92.

Fudenberg, Drew, and Eric Maskin. 1986. "The Folk Theorem in Repeated Games with Discounting and with Incomplete Information." *Econometrica* 54 (3): 533–54.

Gaubatz, Kurt Taylor. 1991. "Election Cycles and War." *Journal of Conflict Resolution* 35 (2): 212–44.

———. 1996. "Democratic States and Commitment in International Relations." *International Organization* 50:109–39.

Gelpi, Christopher, and Joseph Grieco. 2000. "Democracy, Crisis Escalation, and the Survival of Political Leaders, 1918–1992." Manuscript, Duke University.

Gilligan, Michael J. 2004. "Is There a Broader-Deeper Tradeoff in Multilateral International Agreements?" *International Organization* 58 (3) (Summer): 459–84.

Gleditsch, Kristian S. 2002. "Expanded Trade and GDP Data." *Journal of Conflict Resolution* 46 (5): 712–24.

Glick, R., and H. J Kharas. 1986. "The Costs and Benefits of Foreign Borrowing: A Survey of Multi-Period Models." *Journal of Development Studies* 22: 279–99.

Goemans, Hein E. 2000a. *War and Punishment*. Princeton: Princeton University Press.

———. 2000b. "Fighting for Survival: The Fate of Leaders and the Duration of War." *Journal of Conflict Resolution* 44:555–80.

Goldstein, Joshua S. 1991. "Reciprocity in Superpower Relations: An Empirical Analysis." *International Studies Quarterly* 35:195–209.

———. 2001. *War and Gender: How Gender Shapes the War System and Vice Versa*. Cambridge: Cambridge University Press.

Gourevitch, Peter A. 1996. "Squaring the Circle: The Domestic Sources of International Cooperation." *International Organization* 50 (2) (Summer 1996): 349–73.

Gowa, Joanne. 1986. "Anarchy, Egoism and Third Images. The Evolution of Cooperation and International Relations." *International Organization* 40 (1): 167–86.

———. 1994. *Allies, Adversaries, and International Trade*. Princeton: Princeton University Press.

Green, Donald P., Soo Yeon Kim, and David H. Yoon. 2001. "Dirty Pool." *International Organization* 55(2): 441–68.

Green, E., and R. Porter. 1984. "Non-cooperative Collusion under Imperfect Price Information." *Econometrica* 52: 87–100.

Grofman, Bernard, and Peter van Roozendaal. 1994. "Towards a Theoretical Explanation of Premature Cabinet Termination." *European Journal of Political Research* 26:155–70.

Grossman, H., and J. V. Huyck. 1988. "Sovereign Debt as a Contingent Claim: Excusable Default, Repudiation, and Reputation." *American Economic Review* 78:1088–97.

Guisinger, Alexandra, and Alastair Smith. 2002. "Honest Threats: The Interaction of Reputation and Political Institutions in International Crises." *Journal of Conflict Resolution* 46:175–200.

Gunaratne, Shelton A. 2003. "Proto-Indo-European Expansion, Rise of English, and the International Language Order: A Humanocentric Analysis." *International Journal of the Sociology of Language* 164 (1):1–32.

Hardin, R. 1971. "Collective Action as an Agreeable n-Prisoner's Dilemma." *Behavioral Science* 16 (5): 472–81.

Hass, R. N., ed. 1998. *Economic Sanctions and American Diplomacy*. Washington, DC: Brookings Institution Press.

Hass, R. N., and M. L. O'Sullivan, eds. 2000. *Honey and Vinegar*. Washington, DC: Brookings Istitution Press.

Hathaway, Oona. 2002. "Do Human Rights Treaties Make a Difference?" *Yale Law Journal* 111 (8): 1935–2042.

———. 2004. "Between Power and Principle: A Political Theory of International Law." Mimeo, Yale University Law School.

Helpman, Elhanan, and Paul Krugman. 1985. *Market Structure and Foreign Trade: Increasing Returns, Imperfect Competition, and the International Economy*. Cambridge: MIT Press.

Hermann, Margaret G., Thomas Preston, Baghat Korany, and Timothy M. Shaw. 2001. "Who Leads Matters: The Effects of Powerful Individuals." *International Studies Review* 3 (2): 83–131.

Herrmann, Richard, Philip Tetlock, and Matthew Diascro. 2001. "How Americans Think about Trade: Reconciling Conflicts among Money, Power, and Principles." *International Studies Quarterly* 45 (2): 191–218.

Horowitz, Michael, Rose McDermott, and Allan C. Stam. 2005. "Leader Age, Regime Type, and Violent International Relations." *Journal of Conflict Resolution*, 49 (5) (October): 661–85.

Hufbauer, G. C., J. J. Schott, and K. E. Elliot. 1990. *Economic Sanctions Reconsidered*. Washington, DC: Institution for International Economics.

Huth, Paul. 1988. *Extended Deterrence and the Prevention of War*. New Haven, CT: Yale University Press.

International Monetary Fund. 2004. *International Financial Statistics*. CD-ROM. Washington, DC.

Jacobson, Harold K., William Reisinger, and Todd Matthews. 1986. "National Entanglements in International Organizations." *American Political Science Review* 80 (March): 141–59.

Johnston, Louis D., and Samuel H. Williamson. 2002. "What Was GDP Then? A Source Note for US GDP, 1789–2002." http://www.eh.net/hmit/gdp/GDPsource.htm.

Jones, Benjamin F., and Benjamin A. Olken. 2004. Do Leaders Matter? National Leadership and Growth since World War II. Working paper, Northwestern University.

J. P. Morgan Securities Inc. Emerging Market Research. 1999. "Methodology Brief: Introducing the J.P. Morgan Emerging Market Bonds Index Global (EMBI Global)." New York, August.

Kaempfer, W., and A. D. Lowenberg. 1988. The Theory of International Economic Sanctions: A Public Choice Approach. *American Economic Review* 4:786–93.

Keohane, Robert O., and Joseph S. Nye, eds. 1977. *Power and Interdependence: World Politics in Transition*. Boston, MA: Little, Brown.

Keohane, R. O. 1984. *After Hegemony*. Princeton: Princeton University Press.

Keohane, Robert. 1986. "Reciprocity in International Relations." *International Organization*. 40 (1): 1–27.

Kindleberger, Charles P. 1981. "Dominance and Leadership in the International Economy." *International Studies Quarterly* 25 (3): 242–54.

King, Gary. 2001. "Proper Nouns and Methodological Propriety: Pooling Dyads in International Relations Data." *International Organization* 55 (2): 497–507.

Krasner, Stephen D., ed. 1983. *International Regimes*. Ithaca, NY: Cornell University Press.

Krustev, Valentin L., and T. Clifton Morgan. 2007. "Domestic Political Institutions, Leaders, and the Duration of Economic Sanctions." Department of Political Science, MS-24, Rice University.

Kutty, G. 1990. "Logistic Regression and Probability of Default of Developing Countries' Debt." *Applied Economics* 21:1649–60.

Lake, David A. 1992. "Powerful Pacifists: Democratic States and War." *American Political Science Review* 86 (Mar.): 24–37.

Lave, Lester B. 1962. "An Empirical Approach to the Prisoner's Dilemma." *Quarterly Journal of Economics* 76:424–36.

———. 1965. "Factors Affecting Cooperation in the Prisoner's Dilemma." *Behavioral Science* 10:26–38.

Ledyard, J. O. 1993. "Public Goods: A Survey of Experimental Research". In *Experimental Foundations of Political Science*, edited by D. R. Kinder and T. R. Palfrey. Ann Arbor: University of Michigan Press.

Lee, S. H. 1993a. "Are the Credit Ratings Assigned by Bankers Based on the Willingness of LDC Borrowers to Repay?" *Journal of Development Economics* 40:349–59.

———. 1993b. "Relative Importance of Political Instability and Economic Variables on Perceived Country Creditworthiness." *Journal of International Business Studies* 4:801–12.

Leeds, Brett Ashley. 1999. "Domestic Political Institutions, Credible Commitments and International Cooperation." *American Journal of Political Science* 43:979–1002.

Levy, B., and P. Spiller. 1996. *Regulation, Institutions and Commitment: Comparative Studies of Telecommunications*. Cambridge: Cambridge University Press.

Levy, Jack S. 1988. "Domestic Politics and War." *Journal of Interdisciplinary History* 18:653–73.

———. 1989. "The Diversionary Theory of War: A Critique." In *Handbook of War Studies*, edited by M. I. Midlarsky. New York: Unwin-Hyman.

Lewis-Beck, Michael. 1986. "Comparative Economic Voting: Britain, France, Germany, Italy." *American Journal of Political Science* 30 (2): 315–46.

Lichbach, M. I. 1996. *The Cooperator's Dilemma*. Ann Arbor: University of Michigan Press.

Lindert, Peter H. 1969. *Key Currencies and Gold, 1900–1913*. Princeton Studies in International Finance no. 24. Princeton: Princeton University Press.

Mansfield, Edward D., and Jack Snyder. 1995. "Democratization and War." *Foreign Affairs* 74 (May/June): 79–97.

Mansfield, Edward D., Helen V. Milner, and B. Peter Rosendorff. 2000. "Free to Trade: Democracies, Autocracies, and International Trade." *American Political Science Review* 94 (June): 305–21.

———. 2002. "Why Democracies Cooperate More: Electoral Control and International Trade Agreements." *International Organization* 56 (3): 477–513.

Mansfield, Edward. D., and Jon C. Pevehouse. 2000. "Trade Blocs, Trade Blows, and International Conflict." *International Organization* 54 (4): 775–808.

———. 2006. Democratization and International Organizations. *International Organization* 60:137–67.

Mansfield, Edward, and Brian Pollins. 2001. "The Study of Interdependence and Conflict: Recent Advances, Open Questions, and New Directions for Future Research." *Journal of Conflict Resolution* 45:834–59.

Maoz, Zeev, and Nazrin Abdolali. 1989. "Regime Types and International Conflict, 1816–1976." *Journal of Conflict Resolution* 33 (2): 3–36.

Maoz, Zeev, and Bruce M. Russett. 1993. "Normative and Structural Causes of the Democratic Peace." *American Political Science Review* 87:624–38.

Marinov, Nikolay. 2005. "Do Economic Sanctions Destabilize Country Leaders?" *American Journal of Political Science* 49 (3): 564–76.

Marshall, Monty G., Keith Jaggers, and Ted Robert Gurr. 2002. "Polity IV Project Political Regime Characteristics and Transitions, 1800–2000." Available at http://www.cidcm.umd.edu/inscr/polity.

Martin, L. 1992. *Coercive Cooperation: Explaining Multilateral Economic Sanctions.* Princeton: Princeton University Press.

Martin, Lisa L. 1993. "Credibility, Costs and Institutions: Cooperation on Economic Sanctions." *World Politics* 45:406–32.

Maynard Smith, J. 1974. Theory of Games and the Evolution of Animal Contests. *Journal of Theoretical Biology* 47:209–21.

McFadden, D., R. Eckaus, G. Feder, V. Hajivassiliou, and S. O'Connell. 1986. "Is There Life after Debt?" In *International Debt and the Developing Countries.* Washington, DC: World Bank, pp. 179–212.

McGillivray, Fiona. 1997. "Party Discipline as a Determinant of the Endogenous Formation of Tariffs." *American Journal of Political Science* 41:584–607.

———. 1998. "How Voters Shape the Institutional Framework of International Agreements." In *Strategic Politicians, Institutions, and Foreign Policy,* edited by Randolph M. Siverson. Ann Arbor: University of Michigan Press, pp. 79–96.

McGillivray, Fiona, and Alastair Smith. 2000. "Trust and Cooperation through Agent-Specific Punishments." *International Organization* 54 (4) (Autumn 2000): 809–24.

———. 2004. "The Impact of Leadership Turnover on Relations between States." *International Organization* 58 (Summer): 567–600.

———. 2005. "The Impact of Leadership Turnover and Domestic Institutions on International Cooperation." *Journal of Conflict Resolution* 49 (5) (Oct. 2005): 639–60.

———. 2006. "Credibility in Compliance and Punishment: Leader Specific Punishments and Credibility." *Journal of Politics* 68 (2) (May): 248–58.

McGillivray, Fiona and Allan C. Stam. 2004. "Political Institutions, Coercive Diplomacy, and the Duration of Economic Sanctions." *Journal of Conflict Resolution* 48 (2) (April): 154–72.

Mercer, Jonathan. 1996. *Reputation and International Politics.* Ithaca, NY: Cornell University Press.

Meredith, Martin. 2005. *The State of Africa: A History of Fifty Years of Independence.* London: Simon and Schuster.

Milgrom, Paul R., Douglas C. North, and Barry Weingast. 1990. "The Role of Institutions in the Revival of Trade: The Medieval Law Merchant, Private Judges, and the Champagne Fairs." *Economics and Politics* 2 (March): 1–23.

Milner, Helen 1992. International Theories of Cooperation among Nations: Strengths and Weaknesses. *World Politics* 44 (3):466–94.

———. 1997. *Interests, Institutions, and Information: Domestic Politics and International Relations.* Princeton: Princeton University Press.

Milner, Helen, and Peter Rosendorff. 1997. "Democratic Politics and International Trade Negotiations." *Journal of Conflict Resolution* 41:117–46.

Moreno, D., and J. Wooders. 1998. "Experimental Study of Communication and Coordination in Noncooperative Games." *Games and Economic Behavior* 24:47–76.

Morgan, J. B. 1994. "A New Look at Debt Rescheduling Indicators and Models." *Journal of International Business Studies* 17:37–54.

Morgan, T. Clifton, and Sally Howard Campbell. 1991. "Domestic Structure, Decisional Constraints, and War: So Why Kant Democracies Fight?" *Journal of Conflict Resolution* 35 (2): 187–211.

Morgan, T. Clifton, Valentin Krustev, and Navin A. Bapat. 2006. Threat and Imposition of Sanctions (TIES) Data Users's Manual Case Level Data. Available at http://www.personal.psu.edu/faculty/n/a/nab12/sanctionspage.htm. (accessed February 16, 2007).

Morrison, Philip, and Phylis Morrison. 2001. *Enriching the Earth: Fritz Haber, Carl Bosch, and the Transformation of World Food Production.* Cambridge: MIT Press.

Morrow, James D. 1989. Capabilities, Uncertainty and Resolve. *American Journal of Political Science* 33:941–72.

———. 1994. "Modeling the Forms of International Cooperation: Distribution versus Information." *International Organzation* 48 (3) (Summer):387–423.

Morrow, J. D., R. Siverson, and T. Taberes. 1998. "The Political Determinants of International Trade: The Major Powers, 1907–1990." *American Political Science Review* 92:649–62.

Mousseau, Michael. 1998. "Democracy and Compromise in Militarized Interstate Conflicts, 1816–1992." *Journal of Conflict Resolution* 42 (2): 210–30.

New York Times. 1999. "Neighbors Rally to Jordan, Easing Financial Fears," February 19, 1999, A3.

Nicolson, Harold (Sir). [1939] 1964. *Diplomacy.* Reprint Oxford: Oxford University Press.

North, D. 1981. *Structure and Change in Economic History.* New York: W. W. Norton.

———. 1990. *Institutions, Institutional Change and Economic Performance.* New York: Cambridge University Press.

North, D., and B. Weingast. 1989. "Constitutions and Commitment: The Evolution of Institutions Governing Public Choice in Seventeenth-Century England." *Journal of Economic History* 49:803–32.

Ochs, J. 1995. "Coordination Problems." In *The Handbook of Experimental Economics;* edited by J. H. Kagel and A. E. Roth. Princeton: Princeton University Press.

Offerman. T., J. Sonnemans, and A. Schram. 1996. "Value Orientations, Expectations and Voluntary Contributions in Public Goods." *Economic Journal* 106:817–45.

Offner, John L. 1992. *An Unwanted War: The Diplomacy of the United States and Spain over Cuba, 1895–1898.* Chapel Hill: University of North Carolina Press.

Olson, Mancur. 1965. *The Logic of Collective Action.* Cambridge,: Harvard University Press.

———. 1993. "Dictatorship, Democracy and Development." *American Political Science Review* 87:567–76.

———. 2000. *Power and Prosperity.* New York: Basic Books.

Olson, Mancur, and Richard Zeckhauser 1966. "An Economic Theory of Alliances." *Review of Economics and Statistics* 48:(3):266–79.

Oneal, John R. 2003. "Empirical Support for the Liberal Peace." In *Economic Interdependence and International Conflict: New Perspectives on an Enduring Debate*, edited by Edward D. Mansfield and Brian M. Pollins. Ann Arbor: University of Michigan Press.

Oneal, John R., and Bruce Russett. 1997. "The Classical Liberals Were Right: Democracy, Interdependence, and Conflict, 1950–1985." *International Studies Quarterly* 41 (June): 267–93.

———. 1999a. "Assessing the Liberal Peace with Alternative Specifications: Trade Still Reduces Conflict." *Journal of Peace Research* 36:423–42.

———. 1999b. "The Kantian Peace: The Pacific Benefits of Democracy, Interdependence, and International Organizations, 1885–1992." *World Politics* 52:1–37.

———. 2000. "Why 'An Identified Systemic Analysis of the Democracy-Peace Nexus' Does Not Persuade." *Peace and Defense Economics* 11:1–17.

———. 2001. "Clear and Clean: The Fixed Effects of Democracy and Economic Interdependence." *International Organization* 55:469–86.

Oneal, John R., Bruce Russett, and Michael L. Berbaum. 2003. "Causes of Peace: Democracy, Interdependence, and International Organizations, 1885–1992." *International Studies Quarterly* 47 (3): 371–93.

Oye, Kenneth A., ed. 1986. *Cooperation under Anarchy*. Princeton: Princeton University Press.

Pahre, Robert. 1994. "Multilateral Cooperation in an Iterated Prisoners' Dilemma." *Journal of Conflict Resolution* 38 (2) (June 1994): 326–52.

Palfrey, T. R., ed. 1991. *Laboratory Research in Political Economy*. Ann Arbor: University of Michigan Press.

Palfrey, T. R., and H. Rosenthal. 1985. "Voter Participation and Strategic Uncertainty." *American Political Science Review* 79:62–78.

———. 1994. "Repeated Play, Cooperation and Coordination: An Experimental Study." *Review of Economic Studies* 61:545–65.

Pape, R. 1997. "Why Economic Sanctions Do Not Work." *International Security* 2:90–136.

Partell, Peter J., and Glenn Palmer. 1999. "Audience Costs and Interstate Crises: An Empirical Assessment of Fearon's Model of Dispute Outcomes." *International Studies Quarterly* 43 (2): 389–406.

Polachek, S. 1997. "Why Do Democracies Cooperate More and Fight Less? The Relationship between Trade and International Cooperation." *Review of International Economics* 5:295–309.

Pollins, B. 1989. Conflict, Cooperation, and Commerce: The Effect of International Political Interactions on Bilateral Trade Flows. *American Journal of Political Science* 33:737–61.

Porter R. 1983. "Optimal Cartel Trigger-Price Strategies." *Journal of Economic Theory* 29:313–38.

Post, Jerrold M., ed. 2003. *The Psychological Assessment of Individual Leaders: With Profiles of Saddam Hussein and Bill Clinton*. Ann Arbor: University of Michigan Press.

Powell, G. Bingham, and Guy D. Whitten. 1993. "A Cross-National Analysis of Retrospective Voting: Integrating Economic and Political Variables." *American Journal of Political Science* 37:391–414.

Przeworski, A., and F. Limongi. 1993. "Political Regimes and Economic Growth." *Journal of Economic Perspectives* 7:51–69.

Przeworski, Adam, Michael E. Alvarez, Jose Antonio Cheibub, and Fernando Limongi. 2000. *Democracy and Development*. New York: Cambridge University Press.

Rapoport, A. 1988. "Experiments with N-Person Social Traps I: Prisoner's Dilemma, Weak Prisoner's Dilemma, Volunteer's Dilemma, and Largest Number." *Journal of Conflict Resolution* 32:457–72.

Rapoport, A., and A. M. Chammah. 1965. *Prisoner's Dilemma: A Study in Conflict and Cooperation*. Ann Arbor: University of Michigan Press.

Raustiala, Kal, and Anne-Marie Slaughter. 2002. "International Law, International Relations and Compliance." In *The Handbook of International Relations*. Thousand Oaks, CA: Sage Publications, 538–58.

Ray, James Lee. 1995. *Democracies in International Conflict*. Columbia: University of South Carolina Press.

Raymond, Gregory A. 1994. "Democracies, Disputes, and Third-Party Intermediaries." *Journal of Conflict Resolution* 38 (March): 24–42.

Reiter, Dan, and Allan C. Stam III. 1998a. "Democracy and Battlefield Military Effectiveness." *Journal of Conflict Resolution* 42 (June): 259–77.

———. 1998b. "Democracy, War Initiation and Victory." *American Political Science Review* 92 (June): 377–89.

———. 2002. *Democracies at War*. Princeton: Princeton University Press.

Remmer, Karen. 1998. "Does Democracy Promote Interstate Cooperation?" *International Studies Quarterly* 42:25–52.

Reuveny, R. 2000. "The Trade and Conflict Debate: A Survey of Theory, Evidence and Future Research." *Economics, Peace Science and Public Policy* 6: 23–49.

———. 2001. Bilateral Import, Export, and Conflict/Cooperation Simultaneity. *International Studies Quarterly* 45:131–58.

Reuveny, R., and H. Kang. 1996. "International Trade, Political Conflict/Cooperation, and Granger Causality." *American Journal of Political Science* 40: 943–70.

———. 1998. "Bilateral Trade and Political Conflict/Cooperation: Do Goods Matter?" *Journal of Peace Research* 35:581–602.

Robbins, Keith. 1994. *Politicians, Diplomacy, and War in Modern British History*. London: Hambledon.

Root, H. 1989. "Tying the King's Hands: Credible Commitments and Royal Fiscal Policy during the Old Regime." *Rationality and Society* 1:240–58.

Rosato, Sebastian. 2003. "The Flawed Logic of Democratic Peace Theory." *American Political Science Review* 97 (4): 585–602.

Rosen, Stephen P. 2005.*War and Human Nature: The DNA of Strategy*. Princeton: Princeton University Press.

Rosendorff, B. Peter. 2004. "Stability and Rigidity: Politics and Design of the WTO's Dispute Settlement Procedure." Working paper, May 2004.

Rosendorff, B. Peter, and Helen V. Milner. 2001. "The Optimal Design of International Trade Institutions: Uncertainty and Escape." *International Organization* 55 (4): 829–57.

Ruggie, John Gerald. 1993. *Multilateralism Matters: The Theory and Praxis of an Institutional Form*. New York: Columbia University Press.

Russett, Bruce. 1993. *Grasping the Democratic Peace*. Princeton: Princeton University Press.

Russett, Bruce and John R. Oneal. 1999. "The Kantian Peace: The Pacific Benefits of Democracy, Interdependence, and International Organizations." *World Politics* 52 (1): 1–37.

———. 2001. *Triangulating Peace: Democracy, Interdependence, and International Organizations*. New York: W. W. Norton, 2001.

Russett, Bruce, John Oneal, and David R. Davis. 1998. "The Third Leg of the Kantian Tripod: International Organizations and Militarized Disputes, 1950–1985." *International Organization* 52 (Summer): 441–67.

Russet, Bruce, Harvey Starr, and David Kinsella. 2005. *World Politics: The Menu for Choice. 8th ed*. Belmont, CA: Wadsworth Publishing

Sarkees, Meredith Reid. 2000. "The Correlates of War Data on War: An Update to 1997." *Conflict Management and Peace Science* 18 (1): 123–44.

Sartori, Anne. 2002 "The Might of the Pen: A Reputational Theory of Communication in International Disputes." *International Organization* 56 (1) (Winter): 123–51.

———. 2005. *Deterrence by Diplomacy*. Princeton: Princeton University Press.

Savvides, Andreas. 1991. "LDC Creditworthiness and Foreign Capital Inflows; 1980–1986." *Journal of Development Economics* 34:309–27.

Schelling, Thomas C. 1963. *The Strategy of Conflict*. Cambridge, MA: Harvard University Press.

———. 2001. "Looking for Audience Costs." *Journal of Conflict Resolution* 45 (1): 32–60.

Schultz, Kenneth A. 1998. "Domestic Opposition and Signaling in International Crises." *American Political Science Review* 92:829–44.

———. 1999. "Do Democratic Institutions Constrain or Inform? Contrasting Two Institutional Perspectives on Democracy and War." *International Organization* 53:233–66.

———. 2002. *Democracy and Coercive Diplomacy*. Cambridge: Cambridge University Press.

Schultz, Kenneth A., and Barry Weingast. 1998. "Limited Governments, Powerful States." In *Strategic Politicians, Institutions and Foreign Policy*, edited by R. M. Siverson. Ann Arbor: University of Michigan Press.

Senese, Paul D. 1997. "Between Dispute and War: The Effect of Joint Democracy on Interstate Conflict Escalation." *Journal of Politics* 59 (February): 1–27.

Shanks, Cheryl, Harold K. Jacobson, and Jeffrey H. Kaplan. 1996. "Inertia and Change in the Constellation of International Governmental Organizations." *International Organization* 50 (Autumn): 593–627.

Shepsle, K, 1991. " Discretion, Institutions, and the Problem of Government Commitment." In *Social Theory for a Changing Society;* edited by Pierre Bourdieu and J. Coleman. Boulder, CO: Westview; 245–60.

Signorino, Curtis S. 1996. Simulating International Cooperation under Uncertainty. *Journal of Conflict Resolution* 40 (1): 152–206.

Simmons, Beth. 1998. "Compliance with International Agreements." *Annual Review of Political Science* 1:75–93.

Simmons, Beth, and Lisa Martin. 1998. "Theories and Empirical Studies of International Institutions." *International Organization* 52 (4): 729–57.

Singer, J. David, and Melvin Small. 1972. The *Wages of War, 1816–1965: A Statistical Handbook.* New York: John Wiley.

Siverson, Randolph M. 1995. "Democracies and War Participation: In Defense of the Institutional Constraints Argument." *European Journal of International Relations* 1 (December): 481–90.

Small, Melvin, and J. David Singer. 1982. *Resort to Arms: International and Civil Wars, 1816–1980.* Beverly Hills, CA: Sage Publications.

Smith, Alastair. 1995. "Alliance Formation and War." *International Studies Quarterly* 39 (4): 405–425.

———. 1996a. "The Success and Use of Sanctions." *International Interactions* 21 (2): 229–245.

———. 1996b. "To Intervene or Not to Intervene: A Biased Decision." *Journal of Conflict Resolution* 40 (1): 16–40.

———. 1998. "International Crises and Domestic Politics." *American Political Science Review* 92 (3): 623–38.

———. 2000. "Personalizing Crises." In *Essays in Public Policy No. 106.* Stanford, CA: Hoover Institution on War, Revolutions and Peace, Stanford University.

———. 2004. *Election Timing.* Cambridge: Cambridge University Press.

Stasavage, David. 2003. *Public Debt and the Birth of the Democratic State: France and Great Britain, 1688–1789.* New York: Cambridge University Press.

Stagg, J.C.A. 1983. *Mr. Madison's War: Politics, Diplomacy, and Warfare in the Early American Republic, 1783–1830.* Princeton: Princeton University Press.

"Taiwan's High-Stakes game." 1999. *Economist,* August 21.

Throup, David, and Charles Hornsby. 1998. *Multi-Party Politics in Kenya.* Athens: Ohio State University Press.

Tomz, M. 1999. "Do Creditors Ignore History?" Mimeo, Harvard University.

———. 2001. "How Do Reputations Form? New and Seasoned Borrowers in International Capital Markets." Mimeo, Stanford University.

Tsebelis, George. 1990. Are Sanctions Effective? A Game Theoretic Analysis. *Journal of Conflict Resolution* 34:2–28.

———. 2002. *Veto Players: How Political Institutions Work.* Princeton: Princeton University Press.

Tullock, G. 1999. "Non-Prisoner's Dilemma." *Journal of Economic Behavior and Organization* 39:455–58.

Velde, F., and D. Weir. 1992. "The Financial Market and Government Debt Policy in France, 1746–1793." *Journal of Economic History* 52:1–28.

Verdier, Daniel. 1998. "Democratic Convergence and Free Trade?" *International Studies Quarterly* 42:1–24.

Wall, Howard. 1999. "Using the Gravity Model to Estimate the Costs of Protection." *Federal Reserve Bank of St. Louis Review* (January/February): 33–41.

Wallerstein, Immanuel. 1980. *The Modern World System II: Mercantilism and the Consolidation of the European World-Economy, 1600–1750.* New York: Academic Press.

Ward, Michael D., and Kristian S. Gleditsch. 1998. "Democratizating for Peace." *American Political Science Review* 92 (March): 51–62.

Warren, W. L. 1997. *King John*. New Haven: Yale University Press.

Warwick, Paul V. 1995. *Government Survival in Parliamentary Democracies.* Cambridge: Cambridge University Press

Weart, Spencer R. 1998. *Never at War: Why Democracies Will Not Fight One Another.* New Haven: Yale University Press.

Weingast, B. 1995. "The Economic Role of Political Institutions: Market-Preserving Federalism and Economic Development." *Journal of Law, Economics and Organization* 11:1–31.

———. 1997a. "The Political Foundations of Limited Government: Parliament and Sovereign Debt in Seventeenth- and Eighteenth-Century England." In *Frontiers of the New Institutional Economics;* edited by John Drobak and John Nye. London: Harcourt Brace; 213–46.

———. 1997b. "The Political Foundations of Democracy and the Rule of Law." *American Political Science Review* 91:245–63.

World Bank. 2004. *World Bank Development Indicators.* CD-ROM. Washington, DC.

Wu, Jianzhong, and Robert Axelrod. 1995. "How to Cope with Noise in the Iterated Prisoner's Dilemma." *Journal of Conflict Resolution* 39:183–87.

Young, Oran. 1979. *Compliance and Public Authority.* Baltimore: Johns Hopkins University Press.

Zagare, Frank C., and D. Marc Kilgour. 2000. *Perfect Deterrence.* Cambridge: Cambridge University Press.